AN ARCHAEOLOGY OF THE POLITICAL

COLUMBIA STUDIES IN POLITICAL THOUGHT /
POLITICAL HISTORY

COLUMBIA STUDIES IN POLITICAL THOUGHT /
POLITICAL HISTORY

Dick Howard, General Editor

Columbia Studies in Political Thought / Political History is a series dedicated to exploring the possibilities for democratic initiative and the revitalization of politics in the wake of the exhaustion of twentieth-century ideological "isms." By taking a historical approach to the politics of ideas about power, governance, and the just society, this series seeks to foster and illuminate new political spaces for human action and choice.

Pierre Rosanvallon, *Democracy Past and Future*, edited by Samuel Moyn (2006)

Claude Lefort, *Complications: Communism and the Dilemmas of Democracy*, translated by Julian Bourg (2007)

Benjamin R. Barber, *The Truth of Power: Intellectual Affairs in the Clinton White House* (2008)

Andrew Arato, *Constitution Making Under Occupation: The Politics of Imposed Revolution in Iraq* (2009)

Dick Howard, *The Primacy of the Political: A History of Political Thought from the Greeks to the French and American Revolution* (2010)

Paul W. Kahn, *Political Theology: Four New Chapters on the Concept of Sovereignty* (2011)

Stephen Eric Bronner, *Socialism Unbound: Principles, Practices, and Prospects* (2011)

David William Bates, *States of War: Enlightenment Origins of the Political* (2012)

Warren Breckman, *Adventures of the Symbolic: Post-Marxism and Radical Democracy* (2013)

Martin Breaugh, *The Plebeian Experience: A Discontinuous History of Political Freedom*, translated by Lazer Lederhendler (2013)

Dieter Grimm, *Sovereignty: The Origin and Future of a Political and Legal Concept*, translated by Belinda Cooper (2015)

Frank Palmeri, *State of Nature, Stages of Society: Enlightenment Conjectural History and Modern Social Discourse* (2016)

AN ARCHAEOLOGY OF THE POLITICAL

REGIMES OF POWER
from the
SEVENTEENTH CENTURY
TO THE PRESENT

———

ELÍAS JOSÉ PALTI

Columbia University Press
New York

Columbia University Press
Publishers Since 1893
New York   Chichester, West Sussex
cup.columbia.edu
Copyright © 2017 Columbia University Press
Paperback edition, 2020
All rights reserved

Library of Congress Cataloging-in-Publication Data
Names: Palti, Elías José, author.
Title: An archeology of the political: regimes of power from the seventeenth century to the present / Elías José Palti.
Description: New York: Columbia University Press, [2016] | Series: Columbia studies in political thought/political history | Includes bibliographical references and index.
Identifiers: LCCN 2016034387| ISBN 9780231179928 (cloth) | ISBN 9780231179935 (pbk.) | ISBN 9780231542470 (e-book)
Subjects: LCSH: Power (Social sciences)—Philosophy—History. | Political science—Philosophy—History. | Sovereignty.
Classification: LCC JC330 .P284 2016 | DDC 320.01—dc23
LC record available at https://lccn.loc.gov/2016034387

Cover design: Rebecca Lown
Cover image: El Greco, *El entierro del señor de Orgaz* (Wikipedia Commons)

He has consulted the Torah,

has created other worlds,

and has consulted with the letters of the alphabet

which of them should be the agent of creation.

Midrash (Tehillim, 90, 391), quoted in Giorgio Agamben,
The Kingdom and the Glory

CONTENTS

Series Editor's Foreword
Dick Howard   ix

Acknowledgments   xv

Introduction: A Conceptual History of the Political—
the Archaeological Project   xvii

1 THE THEOLOGICAL GENESIS OF THE POLITICAL
1

2 THE TRAGIC SCENE: THE SYMBOLIC NATURE OF POWER AND THE PROBLEM OF EXPRESSION
32

3 THE DISCOURSE OF EMANCIPATION AND THE EMERGENCE OF DEMOCRACY AS A PROBLEM: THE LATIN AMERICAN CASE
66

4 THE REBIRTH OF THE TRAGIC SCENE AND
THE EMERGENCE OF THE POLITICAL AS
A CONCEPTUAL PROBLEM
110

Conclusion: The End of a Long Cycle—
the Second Disenchantment of the World
167

Notes *181*

Bibliography *221*

Index *233*

SERIES EDITOR'S FOREWORD

DICK HOWARD

Elías Palti insists that his archaeology of the political is a "conceptual history," the goals and methods of which differ from what is commonly, if loosely, called the history of ideas. He underlines two differences between these approaches. For the conceptual historian, the definition of "the political" is not given at the outset; it is, itself, constantly redefined, transformed, and contested on the basis of its own internal logic. As a result, reconstruction of an essential nature of "the political" is not the *telos* of Palti's far-reaching investigation (as it would be in an empirical history of ideas) but rather its *arche* (its ever-mutable, irreducible origin). In an apparent paradox, the mutations of the concept of the political are not so much temporal as they are spatial; they define a framework within which the active configuration of the political can take place. This configuration is not "political" in the everyday means/ends sense of the term; when it becomes explicit, it is often manifested in the aesthetic sphere. Some of Elías Palti's richest pages treat the work of painters (El Greco's *The Burial of the Count of Orgaz*), playwrights (Lope de Vega's *Punishment Without Revenge*), and musicians (particularly modern serial music).

This aesthetic dimension of Palti's archaeological tableau is the result of his interpretation of the proper emergence of "the political" in the age of the baroque, which spans roughly the two centuries, from 1550 to 1750. Palti refers to the baroque as a period marked by the effects of what he calls the "first disenchantment." He is alluding, of course, to the effects of the Reformation, which broke open the unitary Catholic representation of a world in which the divine is fully present. This rupture is usually studied from the perspective of Protestantism and its contribution to the creation of modern individualism. Palti's turn to the baroque does more than just right the balance.

For Palti, the overarching project of the baroque is to restore symbolically the broken unity and harmony between the immanent and the transcendent worlds, even while it recognizes that the two realms remain immutably different, distinct, and autonomous. This challenge opened the conceptual space for the discovery of the properly political during the "age of representation." There ensues what a (Protestant) Hegelian might refer to as a "unity-in-difference," the unstable logic of which defines the unstable and changing parameters of the political as it appears, sometimes as the pole of unity, sometimes as that of difference.[1] The unitary variant of the political takes the form of absolutism; its differential appearance (for example, in Shakespeare) represents the emergence of a type of individualism. The baroque complicates this picture, insofar as what is represented at either pole is always enfolded in a symbolic representation (a painting, church architecture, or a staged narrative), the force of which comes from its ability to unify the transcendent and the immanent, and whose further unfolding begins to define the parameters of the political as it emerges in the age of the baroque. The baroque world is not what it seems to be; it is both more and less, greater than and inferior to, and aware of its own ambiguity.

Palti's stress on the baroque origins of the political distinguishes his account from interpretations that situate its emergence two centuries later, as an essential part of the Enlightenment. That vision, which apparently seeks to harmonize peacefully, and eventually unify, the poles of state and individual, has been the target of the withering, antiliberal criticism of Carl Schmitt and his appropriators on the left as well as on the right. A different interpretation of the place of the Enlightenment in the genealogy of the political is suggested by David William Bates's *States of War*.[2] Bates sets up a sort of dialectical interdependence between the modern individual and the sovereign state, neither of which is possible, or viable, without the support of the other.

Palti's conceptual history takes a different tack, because baroque absolutism, exemplified by Counter-Reformation Hapsburg Spain, could not conceive of a terrestrial absolute sovereignty (even though it knew full well that the divine lies outside the folds of the present). For the same reason, the baroque vision of the political role of the modern individual could never have the kind of potential democratic implications that enlightened absolutism is said to have possessed. As a result of this double self-limitation of the baroque, Palti's conceptual history has to leave the age of representation; the concepts with which it defined the political had reached their limit.

Palti's account advances into the "age of history," by means of a detour to the Spanish dominions of Latin America. For the Anglo-American reader, this third major chapter of the book is the most innovative; it is also the most provocative illustration of the distinction between the baroque and the enlightened absolute sovereign. As in England's North American colonies, so too in Spain's Latin American possessions did the question of the power and the legitimation of the state to tax its inhabitants came to the fore. The old problem of representation reappeared in a new guise. For a moment, it appears in Palti's account that the North and South implicitly recognized a shared challenge. As they struggled with the question of legitimate state action and the rights of the individual, they created the conceptual space in which the idea of the "people" emerged. But, in the case of the United States, repeated iterations of the question of legitimacy gave rise to the creation of a republican democracy, whereas in the South American case, the temptation was to reify the people by creating what I have called elsewhere a democratic republic.[3]

Palti's account of the conceptual challenges opened in the age of history is more narrative than his earlier analyses, but his focus remains conceptual rather than conventional. At the culmination of his presentation, he describes the notion of "antipolitics" and refers to my own use of this concept. The emergence of this problematic is said to mark the passage from the age of history to what Palti calls the "age of forms." In more conventional narrative terms, the conceptual problems that fall under this heading are those of the twentieth century, many of which are still with us today.

At this new conceptual moment, what had previously stood "outside" of the political (first the divine, then such grand unities as the people, the nation, history, or the revolution) came to appear as illusory, mythical, even potentially perverse (as in varieties of totalitarianism). The attempt to unfold the irresoluble enfolding of immanence and transcendence, which had been the conceptual framework of the age of history, itself came to an end. This is the moment that Palti calls the "second disenchantment of the world."

As with its baroque predecessor, however, this sobering experience of the impossibility of realizing that which is both most desired and most necessary does not put an end to the quest for a real unity, even though it is known to be impossible; the impossibility itself seasons the taste for more. An illustration of the irresoluble challenge as it appeared early in the century is furnished by Hans Kelsen's attempt to formulate a purely normative and formal theory of law, which proves unable to explain the origin of the very norms that it continues to try to purify, only to culminate in their reification. The conceptual countermove in this dilemma is, of course, furnished by Carl Schmitt's existential decisionism, which claims to produce a form that is itself originary, and thus is self-contradictory. It seems that the upshot of the age of forms is that it negates itself in the figure of a necessary quest for an unreachable justice, which is all the more desired simply because it is known to be impossible. The reader recognizes here the influence of such near-contemporaries as Jacques Derrida and a host of French postmodernists.

Palti begins his concluding reflections by referring to Alain Badiou's *The Century*, which makes the tendentious claim that the only conceptual option today is a "voluntaristic historicism." This admitted oxymoron echoes more Hegelian-Marxism than the subtle account of the political baroque traced at the outset of *The Archaeology of the Political*. Palti, who frequently invokes the work of Claude Lefort, seems to be aware of the difficulty when he notes that this political claim is itself a "collusion of opposite terms." The "collusion" results from the fact that both concepts spring from the same "totalitarian" matrix, and its result is the "collapse of the political." This claim will no doubt be the theme of a future publication by the author. Palti anticipates the direction that will be taken in his account of contemporary political challenges by asking, "What kind of political practice might take place beyond the field of the political?" Though it is logically consistent, this question, coming at the end of a wide-ranging tableau, is nonetheless surprising. Although Palti has thoroughly read Claude Lefort, his book could be profitably read in conjunction with *Complications: Communism and the Dilemmas of Democracy*, included in this series.

ACKNOWLEDGMENTS

This book is the result of a period of reflection, research, and writing over many years. Throughout this time, I received help and encouragement from a large number of friends, associates and institutions. It is impossible to adequately thank all to whom I am indebted. I would, though, like to express particular gratitude to colleagues at the Center for Intellectual History at the National University of Quilmes, and at the School of Philosophy and Letters at the University of Buenos Aires, where I worked for nearly two decades. Each of these individuals was a source of intellectual and creative stimulation. This book (and I) have been nourished as well as by conversations with students, professors, and old friends at a number of universities in Latin America, Europe, and the United States where I was a visiting professor. The Master's of Conceptual History, directed by Claudio Ingerflom-Nun at the National University of San Martín, and the research projects *Iberconceptos*, directed by Javier Fernández Sebastián, and *Posthegemonía*, directed by Alberto Moreiras and José Luis Villacañas, have provided excellent venues for presenting my ideas and exploring and elaborating on some of the issues I was working on. I am also grateful to their members for allowing me to do this.

I'd also like to extend my appreciation to the editors at Columbia University Press, who supported and encouraged this book from its earliest days. I especially want to thank Amy Allen and Wendy Lochner, who recommended my manuscript for publication, as well as Alexander Davis, Christine Dunbar, and the editor of the Columbia Studies in Political Thought/Political History series, Dick Howard. I am very glad that the present book is appearing in this prestigious series and I want to thank Dick Howard for it. María Pía Lara was an adviser during both the writing and the editing process of the book and also smoothed my way with introductions to the editors and the publisher at Columbia University Press. She and Federico Finchelstein were the two main supporters of this project from the very beginning, and I am most grateful to both of them. I thank Lucas Margarit for his insights and assistance with the bibliography, and Kitty Ross for her important help in revising the manuscript.

Finally, I must mention ANPCyT and CONICET, of Argentina, and the Guggenheim Foundation for their financial aid during various stages of the research process. Their support has been essential for the completion of this project.

I wish to dedicate this book to my beloved parents, Dolores Larrea and Salomón Palti, and my brother, Osvaldo Palti, who have been the beautiful companions of my entire life, and my wondrous son, Andrés, whose charm and humor fills each day with light and indescribable joy.

Buenos Aires, January 2016

INTRODUCTION

A Conceptual History of the Political—the Archaeological Project

In the past twenty years, there have been an enormous number of studies referring to "the political." The term was originally coined by Carl Schmitt in *The Concept of the Political* (1932), where he identified it with what he named "sovereignty." In his definition, the sovereign is "the one who decides in the state of exception."[1] In the end, "the political" refers to a plane prior to the legal, that which escapes all norms and, indeed, fetters them. In other words, it is the original instituting act of every political-institutional order.

Schmittean theory was vilified for a long time because of the irrationalist (and ultimately totalitarian) consequences that it entails. Nevertheless, in the past few decades his texts have become the basis for a crucial reformulation of philosophical and theoretical debate. Thanks to precursor works by authors such as Claude Lefort, they have emerged as a key for understanding modern democracy. As a result, the focus of political-philosophical reflection has recently been reoriented to penetrate that dimension of reality known as "the political," which is now clearly differentiated from "politics." Whereas politics represents just one instance of social totality, the political refers to the way diverse instances are disaggregated and mutually articulated. This also has methodological derivations. To understand this dimension would require an approach that is both historical and conceptual, one that does not simply describe processes and phenomena but is also able to disclose the political and conceptual problems at stake in each case.

This type of approach underlies a wide range of perspectives. Authors as diverse as Reinhart Koselleck, Jacques Rancière, Alain Badiou, Carlo Galli, Giorgio Agamben, Roberto Espósito, Ernesto Laclau, and Slavoj Žižek—to cite only some of the more notable names—have dedicated themselves to the task of elaborating on the concept of the political, pointing out the plurality of aspects it encompasses.

This book follows this line, while, at the same time, it engages in a critical debate with the key authors who have brought about this change in contemporary political theory. It takes on many of their conceptual tools and disputes others. Nevertheless, there is a point on which this work sets itself apart from all the rest: the historical perspective it brings to this debate.

In previous books on the subject, the presence of the realm of the political is simply taken for granted. It appears as a given, an eternal essence.[2] Covering a wide chronological range, beginning in the seventeenth century and reaching the present, this book shows that the realm of the political is not a natural, transhistorical entity. This is true not only in the sense that, as a category, it only became a subject of discourse relatively recently (as we have seen, it cannot be traced further back than the beginning of the twentieth century, when Carl Schmitt devised the term). But also, and more importantly, it did not always exist as an empirical reality. Here we find the fundamental hypothesis that presides over our analysis: The opening up of the horizon of *the political* is the result of a crucial inflection that was produced in the West in the seventeenth century as a consequence of a series of changes in the regimes of exercise of power brought about by the affirmation of absolute monarchies. It is at this point that the series of dualisms articulating the horizon of the political emerged, giving rise to the play of immanence and transcendence hitherto unknown.

Of paramount importance in this work is explaining how such an inflection was produced: how the horizon of the political could emerge out of the very theological universe it came to dislocate, and how that new terrain, within which all the subsequent political debates took place, became established. As we will see, if we lose sight of the nature of the crucial transformation produced at that moment, we will not be able to fully comprehend the ultimate meaning of those debates.

In addition, this book intends to show that the dimension of the political is a historical entity in the sense not only that it has an origin that can be traced but also that it has undergone a number of crucial reformulations in the course of the four centuries of its existence. From the seventeenth century to the present, the political became successively redefined, accompanying changes in the regimes of the exercise of power. These latter actually indicate the different ways in which the series of dualisms that articulate that field become structured, the different logics of functioning of the play of immanence and transcendence, or, more precisely stated, the different modes of production of the transcendence effect (the justice effect) out of immanence.

The present book thus seeks to provide a more accurate picture of modern political-intellectual history—one more attentive to the discontinuities in its trajectory—than the picture offered in the current texts on political history and political philosophy. Ultimately, it will help us to understand why we cannot transpose ideas from one conceptual context to another, why to do so inevitably entails inflicting violence on the logic that articulates the symbolic webs from which political concepts take their meaning. This was, I think, the aim of Michel Foucault's project of an archaeology of knowledge, although, as we will see, I object to some aspects of it and ask for precision in others.

In addition to the two systems of knowledge that Foucault analyzed in his classical work *Les mots et les choses*—the "age of representation," which corresponds to the classical period (the seventeenth and eighteenth centuries), and the "age of history," which corresponds to the modern period (the nineteenth century)—I will identify a third specific regime of knowledge, "the age of forms." This emerged in the twentieth century as a result of the breakdown of the evolutionary-teleological assumptions inherent in the age of history—a conceptual shift that passed unnoticed in Foucault's archaeological reconstruction. Each period in this archaeology of knowledge corresponds, in turn, to a particular regime of exercise of power whose emergence entailed the reconfiguration of the horizon of the political. It would be articulated (and rearticulated) according to different types of logic: a "logic of folding," for the age of representation;

a "logic of undifferentiation/identification," for the age of history; and a "logic of leap," for the age of forms.

These changes are what we will explore in the following pages. This is thus a kind of archaeological endeavor in the sense that its goal is to recover and retrace the different political-conceptual niches in which the regimes of exercise of power were displayed, the series of successive transformations they underwent, as well as the different historical-conceptual constellations to which they gave rise. Overall, the present book describes the long cycle of the emergence, transformation, and final dissolution of the political.

Making this archaeological reconstruction has actually required the inscription of the development of political thinking within a broader historical-intellectual perspective and an approach to various kinds of discourses coming from different cultural records—the history of the arts, literature, science, and so on—in addition to the history of political thinking. It thus intends to provide the basic framework for understanding the terms in which the discourse on the political was established in each historical moment and the basic coordinates whereby political languages were articulated, defining the particular modes of conceiving and practicing political power. Ultimately, by hewing to a historical-conceptual perspective throughout, this book intends to provide a map of the different conceptual frameworks on which the different forms of political discourse must be placed and, as a result, to prevent the anachronistic projections that are common in the traditional approaches to the history of political philosophy.

Yet, for this it is necessary to transcend the level of ideas or thinking and place our focus on a conceptual dimension embedded in political practices themselves, which is an intrinsic dimension of them and without which, these practices cannot exist, a phenomenological realm previous to the distinction between the symbolic and the material, in which the two are fused and, therefore, cannot be detached from each other. It is at penetrating that realm that the project of an archaeology of the political is aimed.

AN ARCHAEOLOGY OF THE POLITICAL

1

THE THEOLOGICAL GENESIS OF THE POLITICAL

> *In a historical moment that witnesses a radical crisis of classical conceptuality, both ontological and political, the harmony between the transcendent and eternal principle and the immanent order of the cosmos is broken, and the problem of "government" of the world and of its legitimation becomes the political problem that is in every sense decisive.*
>
> —GIORGIO AGAMBEN, *THE KINGDOM AND THE GLORY*

In his seminal article "Meaning and Understanding in the History of Ideas" (1969), Quentin Skinner defines what he calls the "mythology of doctrines," by which he means turning doctrines into entities whose development over time historians should trace, as the authors and their ideas would matter only insofar as they contributed to the elaboration of that doctrine.[1] One of the examples he gives is Marsilius of Padua, who is generally known as the thinker who anticipated the modern doctrine of the division of powers. In fact, the entire thinking of the late Middle Ages and the early modern periods is approached from the perspective of the extent to which the authors of the time anticipated our own ideas of democracy, representation, sovereignty, and so on.[2] This is the characteristic procedure of the history of ideas.[3] The focus on "ideas" thus leads, almost by definition, to missing the underlying changes in political and social languages, which can be observed only if we recreate an entire conceptual field and penetrate its underlying cosmology or worldview, that is, the set of assumptions upon which that vocabulary was erected.[4]

In *Le problem de l'incroyance au XVIe siécle: La religion de Rabelais* (1942), Lucien Febvre had shown the anachronism implicit in seeing the criticism of religious ideas in the sixteenth century as the forerunner of the secular ideas of the present. As he stated:

> It is absurd and puerile, therefore, to think that the unbelief of men of the sixteenth century, insofar as it was a reality, was in any way comparable to our own. It is absurd and it is anachronistic. And it is utter madness to make Rabelais the first name in a linear series at the tail end of which we put the "freethinkers" of the twentieth century (supposing, moreover, that they are a single bloc and do not differ profoundly from each other in turn of mind, scientific experience, and particularly arguments).[5]

The men of the sixteenth century, he asserted, lacked the conceptual *outillage* and experience that would have allowed them to conceive of the idea of a regular order of nature, of a universe that followed its own immanent laws and did not require the intervention of a supernatural force that presided over it and guaranteed its preservation. According to Reinhart Koselleck, it was only much later, in the hundred years from 1750 to 1850 (which he calls *Sattelzeit*), that a radical conceptual shift took place. At that point, all social and political concepts became redefined, gaining a new meaning. Yet Koselleck's view remains problematic, as it raises a new question: How could this conceptual shift have happened?[6]

Though the kind of conceptual history he elaborated made a fundamental contribution toward understanding the depth of the historical-conceptual rupture occurring during the period he analyzes, his focus on that period led him to postulate that there had been only a single conceptual break in Western intellectual history. As a result, all that had gone before the *Sattelzeit* is grouped together under the label of "traditional," and all that came after it, under that of "modern." In this way, his *Begriffsgeschichte* overlooks the series of profound and radical conceptual changes that occurred both before and after the *Sattelzeit*, providing a rather flat picture of both the premodern and the modern periods.

Even more importantly, it also precludes the correct understanding of the very conceptual break he analyzed, that is, what really changed at that moment (the *Sattelzeit*) and how the kind of rupture it brought about was possible. As we will see, any attempt to explain the conceptual shift that gave birth to our modern worldview entails the dislocation of the homogeneous picture of the preceding period, the image of premodern thinking as if it were a single, uniform whole.

At this point, we must go back to Febvre. He warns us against the anachronism that confuses the sixteenth century's ideas with our own. Yet the fact that these ideas had a religious character and were inserted within a theological framework does not mean that the kind of conceptual shift produced was not significant for the comprehension of the emergence of a modern, secular worldview. Febvre's intention was not to deny the radicalism of sixteenth-century thinking but to underline its religious premises.[7] Thus we find the fundamental paradox that Febvre brings to the fore and the hermeneutical challenge it poses to historians: How could a radically new secular worldview emerge out of the very theological universe that was, in fact, the only type of thought available at the time?[8]

Now, though Febvre raises the question, he does not provide an answer to it, and seventy years later his interrogation remains open.[9] In this chapter, we will approach the issue from a particular point of view: explaining the changes that occurred in the regimes of exercise of power between 1550 and 1650, accompanying the affirmation of absolute monarchies. More precisely, it intends to trace the crucial shift at the very heart of theological thinking that allowed for the emergence of a wholly new phenomenon in the West: the horizon of politics. To put it another way: How was it that theology became *political theology*?[10]

Unlike the traditional practice in the history of ideas, our search here is not for the presumed precursors of modern democracy. To put it in Febvre's words, this study do not seek to trace a linear series (like that of "civic humanism") at the tail end of which we find ourselves.[11] All of the thinkers we will study here were deeply imbued with the absolutist ideal and a theological matrix of political thought. Yet, precisely because of it (and herein lies the paradox), in the midst of their controversies they will reveal to us how the foundation on which modern democracy would eventually be erected became established.[12]

4　THE THEOLOGICAL GENESIS OF THE POLITICAL

THE TWISTS IN THE ANCIENT THEORY OF THE FORMS OF GOVERNMENT

Using the terminology employed by Koselleck, we can identify the period from 1550 to 1650, the baroque period, as an initial *Sattelzeit*. I will call it *Schwellenzeit*, to distinguish it from the period studied by Koselleck, which took place two centuries later. As we will see, the former enables us to understand the process that led to this latter. It was actually at that earlier time that a crucial change occurred in the ways in which power and society were conceived. Ultimately, the *Sattelzeit* was the result of an attempt to answer the dilemmas raised two centuries earlier, around 1600. But to fully grasp the nature of the historical-conceptual inflection of the time, we must turn back to the reception of Aristotle's *Politics* in the West in the thirteenth century, since the whole political debate for the next six hundred years hinged on the ancient theory of the forms of government.[13]

The text of *Politics* was translated at the request of Thomas Aquinas in 1269, and it was he who made the comments that established the canonical interpretation of this work. Analyzing the process through which Aristotelian theory was assimilated, we can observe how an element that was alien to that theory, and to the ancient world, was introduced into it: the political.

This can be observed by comparing Aristotle's original text with the successive reinterpretations of it. *Politics* begins with a criticism of Plato, in which Aristotle underlines what he considers the fundamental difference between the political and the domestic realms, a difference that, he alleged, had altogether escaped Plato's notice. The criticism that Aristotle levies against Plato is that the latter thinks of the republic as a kind of large household, and of political power as nothing more than parental power expanded to encompass the entire city. Aristotle, instead, stresses that the difference between the two realms is one of nature and not just of magnitude or scope, because the goals that each pursues is different. As he states: "Some people think that the qualifications of a statesman, king, householder, and master are the same, and that they differ, not in kind, but only in the number of their subjects. For example, the ruler over a few is called a master; over more, the manager of a household; over a still larger number, a statesman or king, as if there were no difference between a great household and a small state."¹⁴ Aristotle thus underlines the specificity of politics. Still, the idea of "politics" is difficult to translate. It opposes the idea of *oikonomia*, which refers to the domestic sphere and relates to those goals that are specific to each individual. Politics, by contrast, relates to the polis, and refers to those goals that apply to all its members. In fact, what Aristotle calls "politics" would be better translated| as "the social"—that which is common to all. It does not relate to what we understand today as politics. For Aristotle and his contemporaries, distinguishing between the political and the social was not feasible, and this is expressed in the difficulties he encounters when he intends to define monarchy.

Aristotle asserts that of the three forms of government (monarchy, aristocracy, and democracy), only two are original: aristocracy (or, more precisely, oligarchy, because it is the government not of the best but of the rich) and democracy: "There are generally thought to be two principal forms: as men say of the winds that there are but two—north and south, and that the rest of them are only variations of these, so of governments there are said to be only two forms—democracy and oligarchy."¹⁵ To him, monarchy was nothing more than a version of aristocracy. He concludes that the best form of government is what he calls *politeia*, a combination of democracy and aristocracy. This is so because, in Aristotle's opinion, the art of politics consists of combining social elements. "The reason why there are many forms of government," he states, "is that every state contains many elements."¹⁶ In the end, the art of politics is about avoiding conflict between the many and the few, the rich and the poor, and ensuring that no social group is excluded from the process of political decision making, which would generate dissent and would threaten the stability of the polis.

In this context, the monarchy does not appear as a separate "element" incarnating a principle of its own. In fact, if we think of the art of politics in terms of social balance, monarchy has no place, for it represents no social constituency or any specific social interest but only the preeminence of a particular individual. "A royal rule, if not a mere name, must exist by virtue of some great personal superiority in the king"—which, Aristotle said, no longer existed in his time.¹⁷ If Aristotle could think of monarchy as nothing but a version of aristocracy, it is because neither he nor his contemporaries could conceive of the principle of the political as such. This began to change during the time of Aquinas.

In the thirteenth and fourteenth centuries, the emergence of scholastic thought accompanied a transformation of the regimes of exercise of power. The transition from the late Middle Ages to the Renaissance involved a series of changes, as a result of which the old feudal monarchies gave way to the corporatist monarchies.[18] This entailed a fundamental shift of the premises upon which monarchical power was founded. Feudal monarchies rested on the assumption of an essential continuity, a linear link, between the domestic and the political realms. Royal authority was seen as the prolongation of the system of hierarchies and subordinations in the social body, having its starting point in parental authority. The monarch was a kind of communal father. In fact, there was no fundamental difference—save for scope—between the type of power exercised by the monarch and that of the dukes, marquesses, viscounts, and so on, who possessed absolute power within their domains, which sometimes were larger even than those of the king himself. The king was nothing more than a *primus inter pares*.[19]

Between the thirteenth and the fifteenth centuries, however, national monarchies became affirmed, subordinating feudal powers under a centralized authority.[20] Along with this, there emerged the first parliaments and courts, where the different estates of the realm were represented, profoundly changing the ways in which power was conceived. The monarch thus became separated from the social body; his function was to establish justice, which is to say, to mutually articulate the estates of the realm.[21] The implicit assumption here is that there was not one single law but, rather, a plurality of sources of right, since each estate had legislative powers, and the function of the monarch was to harmonize them. In this sense, royal power came to occupy a peculiar place vis-à-vis society. His position was neither entirely internal nor entirely external to the community. Rather, he placed himself at the intermediary edges that joined together the different estates of the realm and allowed them to become mutually compatible.

Scholastic thought emerges within the context of the political transition from feudal to corporatist monarchies and, more specifically, of the battle for supremacy between the papacy and the empire.[22] In this dispute, Aquinas takes the side of the papacy, but his political doctrine was an integral part of a larger philosophical project. If Aquinas returned to Aristotle, it was because this allowed him to resolve the great Christian theological problems that had not existed in the ancient world: How could a God, now placed in a relationship of transcendence with regards to the world, govern the latter from within it? How could He inscribe His designs in the spontaneous functioning of things? In sum, it allowed Aquinas to approach the issue of the divine oikonomia (the right disposition of things) by reinterpreting Aristotle's concept of Nature and associating it to the idea of divine providence (some students of Aquinas's philosophy even claim that he "invented" the concept of Nature, with an uppercase *N*).[23] With Aquinas, Nature became the means through which God operated in the world.

This opened up the field for a divine oikonomia based on the distinction between first causes and second causes. God governs the world but does so via His agents, which are parts of the nature of things. The system of goals implemented by God in the world is imprinted in them, constituting immanent principles. The word *Nature* is, precisely, the name for that system of ends immanent in the world.

On the political plane, God's modus operandi is through his agent, the monarch, who represents this divine principle in the social world:

> It is thus necessary to consider God's actions in the world in order to deduce that which is convenient for the king to do. Universally speaking, God performs two tasks: the first is to create the world; the second is to govern it. These are two tasks also performed by the soul in the body. First, it is the shape of the body; second, it governs and moves it. Both things are proper of true office, since the king is chosen to rule, and due to said ruling he is called king.[24]

Yet, as to the specific problem of the forms of government, Aquinas neither explores this idea nor gives it any importance whatsoever. He says he finds the Aristotelian theory regarding such a topic far too complicated: "It would be laborious to write and boring to listen to if we attempted to refer to all the diverse politics, since each city has its own."[25] But if he does not find it worth discussing, it is because, even though he accepts the possibility of the existence of legitimate forms of government other than the monarchy, this latter seemed to him the most "natural," since it corresponded with the idea of unity of God in the world, and of the father, in the domestic realm:

> Thus a king who rules over an entire city or province is a king *par excellence*, and he who rules a family is not a king but a father. Due to a similarity between the two, sometimes a king may be called the father of the people. From this we can conclude that the king is he who directs the people of a province or a city towards the common good.
> In addition, that which is best comes from nature itself, and the most natural and perfect unity is that of man; thus, the most natural ordinary government is ruled by a single man.[26]

At this point, Aquinas brings up a fundamental aspect (which is present in Aristotle's work), although he does not actually elaborate it: that, though the republic and all forms of "civil government" would be perfectly legitimate, nevertheless, they lack the capacity to reform laws. Only the monarch has legislative power. Civil servants must limit themselves to honoring and observing the existing legislation.[27] The idea that only the king has legislative power will soon become the cornerstone for the conception of that which, for Aristotle, was unthinkable: monarchy as incarnating a specifically political principle.[28]

However, it is one of the challengers to Aquinas's thesis who moves forward in this direction: Dante Alighieri, a Guelph who defends the authority of the emperor above that of the pope. The first book of *De monarchia* begins with a seemingly strange statement that caught many of his readers' attention. The text, titled "Whether Temporal Monarchy Is Necessary for the Well-Being of the World," states:

> Now, inasmuch as among other abstruse and important truths, knowledge of temporal Monarchy is most important and most obscure, and inasmuch as the subject has been shunned by all because it has no direct relation to gain, therefore my purpose is to bring it out from its hiding-place, that I may both keep watch for the good of the world, and be the first to win the palm of so great a prize for my own glory.[29]

Taken literally, this statement is clearly false. By the time Dante wrote it, there was already a large tradition of treatises on monarchy, and he was familiar with them. What does he mean, then, when he says that, until now, no one has spoken about monarchy? The explanation has to do with how he defines the fundamental theological-political problem: understanding the process of reduction from diversity to unity: "That in every class of objects the best is the most unified, the Philosopher [Aristotle] maintains in his treatise on simple Being. From this it would seem that unity is the root of goodness, and multiplicity is the root of evil."[30]

This brings us back to the question of divine *oikonomia*: how God produces a world out of the plurality of created beings—a question that leads him down the same path as Aquinas, to the reformulation of the Aristotelian idea of Nature:

> Thus, since God is ultimate perfection, and since heaven, his instrument, suffers no defect in its required perfectness (as a philosophic study of heaven makes clear), it is evident that whatever flaw mars lesser things is a flaw in the subjected material, and outside the intention of God working through Nature, and of heaven; and that whatever good is in lesser things cannot come from the material itself, which exists only potentially, but must come first from the artist, God, and secondly from the instrument of divine art, heaven, which men generally call Nature.[31]

Dante's postulate would be at the basis of the Renaissance system of knowledge: the presence of an invisible thread linking beings and things, connecting them all, and thus constituting the great chain of being.[32] However, at that point, Dante introduces an exception that returns us to the initial question of why, in his opinion, the subject of "temporal Monarchy... has been shunned by all." Among created beings there is always necessarily one whose transcendental content is immediately apparent, one whose profane form and sacred essence are fused together and serve to hold steadfast the link among the different parts. "A dual order is therefore discernible in the world, namely, the order of parts among themselves, and the order of parts with reference to a third entity which is not a part."[33]

Following the judicial principle that no one can be both a judge and a petitioner, he who administers justice to the community cannot be a part of that very community. The figure of the monarch thus emerges as occupying a singular place, as "a part that is not a part," but at the same time as the incarnation of the whole, a "third entity" at once internal and external to society. This is linked to the aforementioned change that is being produced in the regimes of exercise of power. With the shift from feudal monarchy to corporatist monarchy, the monarch begins to separate from society, despite remaining a constitutive element of it. In sum, at that moment, it begins to become clear that *the relationship between subject and monarch is not of the same order as that of subjects with one another.* This gives monarchy a meaning that, as Dante wrote, had yet to be analyzed, simply because it did not exist previously.[34]

We can see here how the Aristotelian theory of the forms of government begins twisting to pave the way for a concept that, until then, was completely alien to it: of monarchy as expressing a principle that is specific to it. And it is symptomatic of how the political then begins to emerge as something different from the social. But the definitive step in that direction was taken only at the end of the sixteenth century and the beginning of the seventeenth century, accompanying a new break in the regimes of political power, which would then depart from the corporatist matrix that had prevailed during the preceding three centuries.

THE STRUCTURE OF BAROQUE THOUGHT

With the emergence of absolute monarchies, the king ceased to be a mere arbiter among the different bodies. He would now have a completely different nature from his subjects. As long as he shared the divine essence, he cut all ties with other mortals and placed himself in a situation of transcendence and preeminence with respect to those over whom he exercised power. This would represent a crucial political shift.[35]

In Spain, this transition accompanied the imperial crisis that began toward the end of the reign of Phillip II. The loss of Spain's colonies in Europe marked a watershed in this process, but this also related to a broader phenomenon that encompassed the entire European continent. The shift toward absolutism was closely associated with the dissolution of the universalist ideals of the old feudal empires and the affirmation of a system of national monarchies. We can call this a turn from Renaissance monarchy to baroque monarchy. The baroque actually represented a fundamental reconfiguration in the matrix of Western thinking and the emergence of a new political and social language. It ultimately entailed a kind of *Sattelzeit* that predated by two centuries the one ana-

THE THEOLOGICAL GENESIS OF THE POLITICAL 11

FIGURE 1.1 El Greco, *The Burial of the Count of Orgaz* (1586–1588).

lyzed by Koselleck. A painting by El Greco, *The Burial of the Count of Orgaz* (El entierro del conde de Orgaz) (1586–1588), expresses very well the structure of baroque thought (see figure 1.1). A brief analysis of the painting shows how that structure subsequently became manifest at a more specifically political level.

FIGURE 1.2 El Greco, *The Sleeping of the Virgin* (1565).

In this painting, El Greco takes on a traditional, sacred motif: the death of the count and the ascent of the soul to heaven. There is a spirit of elevation in this search for reaching, after death, the final communion with the divine. But here we see something new and striking. This novelty becomes more obvious if we compare it with an earlier painting by El Greco, *The Sleeping of the Virgin* (La dormición de la Virgen) (1565), composed in the post-Byzantine style that he learned in his youth and which probably inspired the design for *The Burial* (see figure 1.2).

As we can clearly observe, there is a split in *The Burial of the Count of Orgaz*. A horizontal line sharply divides the top from the bottom, separating the divine from the mundane. The levels actually adhere to very different logics, which is expressed in El Greco's well-known tendency to stretch and stylize figures. This takes place here in two different fashions: while the bodies below the horizontal line curve downward, as if overwhelmed by the weight of their material existence, the ones above wind upward as they rise, seeking their unity with God.

The typically Renaissance idea of the interpenetration between the sacred and the profane, expressed in the harmony and beauty of forms and bodies, has definitively disappeared. The proliferation of figures, characteristic of the baroque's mannerist impulse, sharpens the division in the middle area of the painting and leaves no open path to pass from one level to the other. Nor can the members of the cortege have a direct vision of God. The only individual who is looking upward and can observe Him has separated from the cortege. He is the figure at the bottom right: the priest who presides over the religious service. In his vestments are reproduced the folds of the sacred; the same folds are found in the garments of Christ and in the shroud that is waiting to receive the soul of the dead count.

The presence of the priest introduces a new sense of depth. Indeed, we almost feel that we could walk across the painting between the priest and the cortege. *The Burial of the Count of Orgaz* is actually the first painting to portray different planes and create a tridimensional effect, a technique that would be typical of the baroque and would find its best expression in Velázquez's *Las Meninas*. The depth effect produced by the introduction of the priest also reveals another altogether new aspect, the introduction of a new element: the figure of the mediator as the only one who is now able to reestablish communication between the sacred and the profane and restore to the world its lost unity. Even though such a figure has a long tradition in Christian thinking, the nature of the function that it now must perform definitely is new. From the moment that communication between the two planes is broken, the restoring of contact demands the intervention of a third factor that does not completely belong to one realm or the other but is not completely alien to them, either; one that, at once, participates in both and neither dominion.

It is, in the end, the figure of the mediator that, from then on, comes to occupy the center of the political stage—and that also becomes particularly problematic. It is in this figure that the tragic sense that underlies and defines the seventeenth century becomes condensed: once God has retired from the world, this figure finds itself always torn by its dual nature, at once sacred and profane, universal and particular.[36] He actually internalizes and makes manifest the cosmic schism (represented in El Greco's painting) that occurs at the moment in which God retires from the world and becomes absent from it, that He becomes a *Deus absconditus*.

This enables us to better comprehend what Ernst Kantorowicz mentions in his classic text about the king's two bodies. As he points out, in connection with the English Civil War, the argument that was used to legitimize the execution of Charles I was this idea regarding the monarch's dual body: his mystic body, which does not die, and his earthly body, which does die. The revolution would not be waged against the anointed monarch but only against his deficient earthly incarnation. The truth is that between both bodies of the king lay an unbridgeable abyss. As he demonstrates in his analysis of Shakespeare's *Richard II*, the monarch, "a kind of God that suffers more of moral grief than do his worshippers," will find himself irredeemably split, and that is why he becomes a tragic figure.[37] "In the baroque," says Walter Benjamin, "the tyrant and the martyr are but the two faces of the monarch. They are the necessarily extreme incarnations of the princely essence."[38]

This represented a crucial shift in the modes of understanding of the political realm. However, the problem of the king's two bodies was just an expression of a broader phenomenon that exceeded the royal persona (although it is true that it was in the king that it became more clearly manifest). Baltasar Gracian's *Criticón* (The Critic)—which some consider, after *Don Quixote*, the most important work in the literature of the Spanish Golden Age—illustrates well the problematic nature of the mediating agent.

The main character is Andrenius, man himself (in Greek, *andros* means "man"), who lives in a state of pure nature until he is rescued and brought into the "civil" world. It is then that he discovers the perversion of man. Thus the other protagonist of the story, his guide, Critilo, introduces him to this world:

> This new lecture seemed strange to Andrenius, whose judgment not being improved by experience, made him to reprove Critilo, wondering that he did not rather advise him of the dangers of the woods and cruelty of beasts then with so much inveterate hatred to inveigh against men.

"Was not our danger greater," said he, "whilst our want of habitation drove us to the dens of tigers, nor did you fear them, much less should your courage abate with the sight of men"

"Yes," sighing, answered Critilo. "For if men be not beasts, it is because their inhumanity exceeds theirs, whose irrational soul is not capable to invent such extravagant inequities."[39]

Here, we may observe an idea that was later adopted by Thomas Hobbes: that man is the wolf of man, and the world a stage of disgraces. In our secular realm, the human essence finds itself separated from its body, which has been abandoned to its purely material state. Things have become tricky, and deception has become functional to life:

Nature has dealt subtly, if not fraudulently with man, by decoying him into the world in a condition of ignorance; for he enters in obscurity, and blindness, and begins to live before he is sensible of his life, or knows what is to live . . . I am persuaded were it not for this universal policy, none would upon such conditions adventure to tread this deceitful world, were they forewarned of those difficulties they were to undergo. For who being first acquainted with these infallible inconveniences, would rashly precipitate himself into this feigned kingdom and true prison . . . ?[40]

The hiding of the truth, its abandonment of the world, is at the same time a problem and a requisite for its functioning, that is, for the articulation of a universe of symbols that supports and renders meaningful our secular, collective life.

As in the painting by El Greco, here we can observe a fundamental split in *El Criticón*, this time chronologically unfolded. On the one hand, we have the original, prelapsarian place where Andrenius lived before being introduced to the world; on the other hand, there is this other, earthly realm, made up of artifices and conventions, lacking in values, where God never makes Himself known.[41] Andrenius still manages to get through the trials of his worldly existence and arrive at the Island of Immortality. For Gracian, it is reason that allows us to transcend the mundane.[42] Nevertheless, what makes this relationship truly problematic is the fact that, while reason serves as a guide, that guide must materialize and become incarnate in the world. It is here that the mediating figure appears. On each island where he arrives, in each place he goes, Andrenius finds someone who guides him so that he may better navigate the hostile environment and escape from lies. However, in this world full of deceit, the guides are also unreliable; false guides will dress in the garments of truth to disguise those they must lead.

> For this guide or conductor of Fortune directed her always contrary to her intentions; if she desired to bless the head of the virtuous with her presence, the unlucky boy wantonly led her to the house of the vicious; when necessity or convenience required her haste, he stopped her progress; when slowly she should move, he fixed her wings to fly; and so shuffled, changed, and confounded her actions.[43]

The problem now has become how to discern the true guides from the false guides. For this purpose we would need a kind of second-order guide (a guide of the guides). Yet, this guide of guides may also be deceitful, and on and on. Ultimately, once that natural link to truth and value has been broken, it is always necessary to interpose a new mediating figure who will also become problematic, and so on ad infinitum.

The same thing happens with the idea of truth. For the baroque, there is certainly one single, universal truth, but what we always have in front of us are, inevitably, interpretations of it, which are not necessarily reliable and which demand, in turn, to be interpreted, and so back and forth. And the same can be said of justice: every positive law presupposes it but is nothing more than an interpretation of it, which, in turn, has to be interpreted, and on and on. Here we find that which underlies and confers its mannerist dynamic upon the baroque. The breach that has opened between the high and the low, the interior and exterior, is in constant need of being closed, but once this is achieved, it will necessarily open again on another level. In this way, the abyss will never cease to reproduce itself at all levels of reality.

From this, there derives the folding structure that, as Gilles Deleuze points out, defines the baroque system of knowledge and differentiates it as much from the Renaissance as from the Enlightenment systems.

> Dividing endlessly, the parts of matter form little vortices in a maelstrom, and in these are found even more vortices, even smaller, and

even more are spinning in the concave intervals of the whirls that touch one another . . .

A fold is always folded within a fold, like a cavern in a cavern. The unit of the matter, the smallest element of the labyrinth is the fold, not the point which is never a part, but a simple extremity of the line . . . Unfolding thus is not the contrary of folding, but the fold up of the following fold.[44]

As we shall see, that structure of the fold also underlies the political thought of the baroque period. It is the cosmological principle that replicates itself at all levels of reality and results in a kind of eternal oscillation between two principles.

The folding operation entails two procedures, scission and mediation, to be reproduced over and over. On the one hand, the break with the Renaissance principle of continuity between the high and the low—the idea of Nature as a substance that goes through and unifies all beings and things, and, in turn, immediately communicates them with God—defines a dualistic worldview. As we have seen, the entire structure of baroque culture will be determined by the opposition between the external and the internal, the superior and the inferior, and the impossibility of communication between the two planes. Baroque facades, and the proliferation of forms and figures that are characteristic of them, have to do with this vocation toward clearly delimiting both dominions. Simultaneously, on the other hand, it is necessary for communication between the two to exist. The baroque will thus be a thinking of the scission but also of the mediation between these two planes, which becomes both necessary and impossible—and the more one thing, the more the other, too.

Once God has abandoned the world, we find ourselves trapped in a realm of mere appearances, devoid of meaning. But that is exactly what pushes us to relentlessly seek Him. That absence of values is also what prevents us from ever reconciling with the world: if we could find in it the minimal vestige of Him, a small trace of the divine, something of unconditioned value, we could reconcile with it and forget Him. For the baroque, it is, paradoxically, through His radical silence that God speaks to us and compels us to continue to seek him.

This new awareness about the insubstantiality of the world, which was a central problem of the entire seventeenth century, in a Spain that had already begun its decline, will express itself in an accentuated manner. It is here that we find the second of the perplexing figures that appear in El Greco's painting: that of the boy in the bottom left corner, who is, in fact, El Greco's son.

Here the artist uses a motif of the era. In the paintings of those years, it was common for references to the artist's own métier to appear as a means by which the representation's problem would become it itself represented and brought into question. As we have seen, *The Burial of the Count of Orgaz* is a profoundly dramatic scene portraying an event of a cosmological dimension—the communion of the human soul with the divine substance. However, it is telling that this boy, who seems completely unaware of the drama that is taking place behind him, is also a figure who looks directly at the observer of the painting.[45] In doing this, he becomes yet another mediating figure, one who acts as a link between the interior of the picture and the world outside it. Ironically, it is this figure, who seems alien to the drama, who calls our attention to it: with his left hand he makes a gesture inviting us to look at what is taking place inside, behind his back.

There is a strange effect here. One cannot but help to look at the eyes of this boy who looks so insistently at us. Yet, from the moment we join eyes, the dramatic character of the scene fades away; its tragic sense becomes diluted in his gaze. This phenomenon has to do with a problem that is characteristic of the baroque but becomes more noticeable in the Hispanic world of the seventeenth century: the problem of representation.[46] It was in that period that the break in the mystic union between the invisible and the visible, which we observed in the Renaissance, allowed the system of re-presentation to become visible as such.[47]

This problem of representation, symbolized by the figure of the child, expresses the break in the natural link between words and things, between the external signs and the internal essence.[48] In the same way that the priest, the one who mediates between the high and the low (and the first of the problematic figures), must situate himself outside of the cortege to do so, so too does this other figure, the boy who introduces us to what is presented in the picture, place himself outside the very system of the representation. He must stay apart from the drama to which he is introducing us, thereby revealing the artificiality and the conventionality of its mode of expression, the radical absence of that which finds itself re-presented within the system of the representation. It is also here where a problematic that is actually eminently political is manifest.

What emerges then as puzzling is the issue of the symbolic (representative) nature of political power *qua* the visible manifestation of the community, the point at which it becomes present to itself and constitutes itself as such. Spanish neoscholastic political thought, and that of Francisco Suárez in particular, illustrates the type of inflection that was produced in the seventeenth century, finally opening a new field, which eventually, during the past century, would be referred to as the political.

NEOSCHOLASTIC THOUGHT AND THE EMERGENCE OF THE POLITICAL

In *The Kingdom and the Glory*, Agamben takes on Eric Peterson's idea of the presence of a political theology within the traditional Christian universe of thought. Its basis is the definition of the monarch as the mediating figure, the agent through whom God operates in the world (the incarnation of the principle of divine oikonomia). However, it was still a strictly theological problem, not a political one. As we will see, the issue of vicariousness becomes a specifically *political* problem when the question of oikonomia translates to the political realm, giving rise not to the question of how God operates in the world or how He inscribes His will in its interior but of how the monarch, who has now become projected on a transcendental sphere, operates within society and inscribes his will in society. The problem of *political* oikonomia, which is no longer that of *divine* oikonomia, emerges only in the seventeenth century, along with the affirmation of royal absolutism. At that juncture, the monarch appears as the (paradoxical) figure of the mediator who must restore unity to a community that no longer possesses the principle that constitutes it as such, that is constitutively disjointed ("out of joint"). Here is where theology becomes *political* theology.

Defensio fidei (Defense of Faith), by Francisco Suárez, illustrates the nature of the inflection thus produced in the regimes of exercise of power and how this will open the way for the emergence of the political in the West. This text was written, upon the request of Cardinal Bellarmine, to refute the thesis of the "apostate" king of England, James I, who would systematize the idea of the divine rights of the king, meaning that sovereignty was transmitted to the king directly by God. In confronting this assertion, the Jesuits, as agents of the papacy sent to combat the Protestant Reformation, developed the idea that sovereignty was not granted directly to the monarch by God but, rather, through the people's intercession. In other words, God gives sovereignty to the people, and the people transfer it to the monarch.

That theory of a social contract had then a specific meaning. As we saw, all neoscholastic thought is about scission and mediation. But the discussion about the divine right of kings assumes, at first, the stance of an epistemological question. The first argument that James I uses to discredit papal authority involves the right of men to exercise their natural reasoning in the reading of the sacred texts, without waiting for the pope to tell them what they should think. For Suárez, however, this reintroduces the original theological problem that we observed in Dante's discourse—how to transform plurality into unity—rendering it unsolvable. To Suárez, James's proposal tosses us into the realm of diversity (opinions), destroying all authoritative criteria and all possibility of truth: "Or how can each of the faithful, with the prudence or modesty which Paul requires, prefer not only himself to the doctors of the Church in understanding Scripture, but count even his own senses alone as certain knowledge, and leave behind whatever diverges from it as the uncertain opinion of men?"[49] Following James I's proposal, every single person could put his or her own personal opinion in place of the truth, thus destroying the very concept of it. In a case when two contradictory interpretations emerged, there would be no way to resolve those differences. Each person could believe what he or she wished, turning the world into a reign of personal whims. "The danger is much greater, therefore, if each believer place the foundation of his faith in his own interpretation and in his own human sense, for thus not only will the Gospel of God become a Gospel of men, but there will be as many Gospels of Scripture as there are heads of men."[50]

In the same way that in the painting by El Greco there is no means of communication between the high and the low, if we accept that everything is based on opinions, we can never access a single truth. To do so requires the intercession of a third external factor that mediates between both terms and that can reduce plurality to unity (opinions to truth). Here we find replicated the idea of a divine oikonomia and of the Trinitarian mystery: between the Father and the Son, a third figure is needed, the Holy Spirit, which serves as a force merging the two into a single substance. In the realm of beliefs, Suárez states that the third term, which reduces opinion to truth, plurality to unity, can be none other than *faith*.

Suárez offers two arguments to demonstrate this. First, he states that James I, in his assertion that pure natural reasoning can be used in the interpretation of the sacred texts, actually contradicts himself. Indeed, the title of book I, chapter 11, section 18 is "The Exhortation of the King to the Sectarians About the Unity of Faith Contains Within Itself a Contradiction." On page 43 of the prologue of his document, James I condemns "heretics" (the Puritans who do not accept his authority), but in doing this, claims Suárez, James's argument becomes self-contradictory. If he considers natural reasoning to be the basis of truthful knowledge, then why does he deny his subjects this right, which he claims for himself? What gives him the authority to impose his own interpretation of Scripture and condemn those that do not agree with it?[51] Thus, James I cannot avoid invoking a certain principle of kingly authority (since, without it, anyone—including those who questioned his legitimacy—could opine anything he or she liked), but he could no longer provide an argument to justify that principle, thereby undermining his own position.

In the end, with his argument supporting the free exercise of natural reasoning, James I had destroyed all sense of authority that would permit the assertion of his opinion over all others. This is where Suárez's second argument appears: "Or perhaps, because Christ does not exist there in a natural and visible way and is hidden under the sacramental appearances, is he then, at last, not to be adored as if he were an object for bodily eyes? But this only happens to those who for faith use merely their senses, who, to be sure, would not adore Christ in visible appearance because they do not see the divinity of the same."[52] What Suárez is saying in this paragraph is that it is not through the exercise of reasoning that we will achieve the truth of Christ but the other way around. Those who do not believe in Christ, he states, will not be able to recognize Him, even if He were to appear before their very eyes. To be able to recognize Him it is first necessary to believe in Him, in his existence. One must have faith. Faith, Suárez says, precedes reason as a path to truth.

Suárez does not actually discredit the use of reason, but he affirms that it can only function within the boundaries established by faith—only there does reason become effective. His argument is as follows: James I says that he wants to gain access to the truth of the sacred texts via reasoning. To Suárez, this means that he is presupposing that the texts already contain the truth, and this involves a leap of faith. It is not the *result* of an exercise of natural reasoning but, rather, its *premise*. If James wants to exercise natural reasoning to gain access to the truth deposited in the sacred texts, it is because he already has faith in them; if he did not, then the exercising of natural reasoning would be pointless. There is an implicit faith incorporated within reason, and only within the boundaries established by the former can reason be displayed.

> For it cannot be that he believes the things which are written in those books with greater faith than he believes that those books are canonical, that is, are the word of God, since the very word of God is the reason for believing the rest. But if he believes with sure and indubitable divine faith that in those books is the pure word of God, or that those books are canonical, we ask further why he believes it; for he cannot believe it because it is written in them, both because it will scarcely anywhere therein be found expressed with complete clarity, and also because, even if it did occur, we would ask about this word itself why he believes it to be divine, or written at the direction and with the inspiration of God. Therefore, he must confess that the rule and foundation of believing this particular truth at least, namely that those books are the divine Scripture, is not Scripture itself, and hence that there is a word of God that is not written in the canonical books, which is what we are now calling tradition.[53]

Once again we see the Trinitarian scheme reproduced in the realm of the relationship between opinions and truth. Only through the intercession of this third term (faith), which acts as a mediator between the two, can plurality (opinions) be reduced to unity (truth). Now, it is this same structure, present in the epistemological realm, that Suárez will transpose to the political realm.

Going back to the theological question, Suárez returns to Aquinas's reading of Aristotle and his statement that there are two ways in which

God operates, but Suárez introduces a particular twist. He says that there is a power that is immanent in all things and another power that acts in addition to it. The former is necessary; the latter is not. What he means is that when God operates directly in the world, the end (the final form) is something that is inscribed in the nature of the thing in question, which is why the thing must necessarily be as it is and cannot be another way. Thus, we can recognize the immediate ways in which God operates because its opposite is simply self-contradictory; that is, it collides with its own definition or concept.

Now, along with these self-evident truths exist others that are not self-evident, which opens up an array of alternative choices, introduces latitude, an element of discretion. This is where Suárez returns to Aristotle's theory of the forms of government. Every political community presupposes an authority; it does not exist as such if there are no relationships of power and obedience. Society is only constituted when there is someone to give an order and someone to observe it. But the ways of exercising this authority are varied, and this is the point where the different forms of government come in; monarchy is not the only possible form of government.

Here we enter the realm of the conventional. The existence of an authority belongs to the realm of natural law, is of natural order; it cannot be otherwise. However, the ways in which this power is exercised permit different possible variables. This, Suárez states, is the "axiom of theology": "From these considerations finally it is concluded that no king or monarch has or has had (according to ordinary law) directly from God or from divine institution a political principality, but by the medium of human will and institution. This is the distinguished axiom of theology."[54] All theological-political thought is, as we have said, the thought of scission and mediation.[55] Between God and the monarch a third element is needed, which is the community or the people that confer authority on the monarch.

By this, Suárez means that God did not give power to any man or woman in particular but to the community as a whole. Sovereignty is a natural law, an essential element for the constitution of community, but the figure of the sovereign is something conventional. God does not decide who will be monarch. Even the forms of government are changeable. God did not institute that there must be a monarch. Once we delve into the realm of the conventional, that of secondary causes, in which things do not operate in a preestablished fashion, we need something or someone that mediates between the essence and its manifestation and can produce a definite effect. In this case, the community as a whole is that which occupies the place of the mediator between God and the monarch, conferring sovereignty on the latter.

It bears clarifying that when Suárez and his contemporaries speak of "the people," they are not referring to any material reality; it is a purely political principle. The people, or the community, as a political principle, embodies all of the sovereignty that exceeds that of the sovereign himself. It materializes the postulate of the existence of metapositive limitations to the authority of the sovereign.[56] The community is simply the name for all that is beyond the reach of the sovereign himself, that which the sovereign cannot alter without becoming the opposite: a tyrant. In the end, the need for mediation implies the idea of a constitutive *excess* of sovereignty with respect to the sovereign, that is, an excess of the community with respect to the royal persona.

James I rejected this doctrine, stating that, in reality, it established an anarchic principle. If the people conferred sovereignty on the monarch, then they could remove it at any time, thus making it impossible to establish any authority; that is, if the people disobeyed the monarch whenever they thought of a reason to do it, there would be no sovereignty and no sovereign. How does Suárez reply to this argument? It is true that all neoscholastic thought is associated with the idea of the legitimacy of tyrannicide.[57] However, it is important to remember that it is a doctrine of power, of obedience, not of resistance. Here we find the crucial aspect of Suárez's thought, which is not actually the contractual doctrine, as it is usually interpreted retroactively, because in that case Suárez could be viewed as a precursor to the ideas that would later be developed by the Enlightenment. The true nucleus of Suárez's argument is not there but in another aspect.

In *Defensio fidei*, Suárez offers an initial response (which is also the best known, and which he would further elaborate in *De legibus*) to the objection that his doctrine brings with it anarchic consequences: the postulate that once sovereignty has been conferred, the pact is irrevocable. But presented in this way, his argument seems weak. In fact, Suárez still cannot do without establishing some kind of limitation on royal power: The people must obey the monarch unconditionally, as long as the monarch is a legitimate monarch. But if the sovereign violates justice and renounces the sacred values established by God, he ceases to be a monarch and thus can be legitimately dethroned.

> But there must be sufficient agreement about such a right either by ancient and definite instruments or by immemorial custom. Also by the same reasoning if the king turns his just power into a tyranny by abusing that power in manifest destruction of the city, the people will be able to use their natural power to defend themselves, for of this never did they deprive themselves. But outside of these and the like cases never will a people, relying on its own power, be permitted lawfully to revolt from a lawful king, and so all basis or occasion for sedition ceases.[58]

Suárez recognizes that, in all other cases, the people cannot rebel, but even then he imposes limitations. When the monarch becomes a tyrant, all obligations toward him disappear. The revoking of the pact is produced not by the people but by the sovereign, but this does not alter the deeper question.

Presented in this way, we do not seem to have made any progress. The conclusion of his argument is not different from the point from which it wishes to distinguish itself. There is, however, a second—and much more important, albeit much less noted—argument that gives this first consistency. The core of the problem is not whether rising against a tyrant is legitimate. As we have seen, this is acceptable, and indeed necessary, not only in Suárez's opinion but also in the opinion of all of the thinkers of his time.[59] Rather, the issue is *who decides when a king has become a tyrant*. This is the bottom line of modern politics, where its traumatic nucleus lies.

Suárez's argument completes itself this way. One the one hand, the sovereign requires that, to constitute himself as a sovereign, the community transfer sovereignty to him, but, conversely, *the community does not exist as such when separated from the body of said sovereign*. Without an authority, the community does not exist. They are born together, one presupposing the other, because it is only in the body of the monarch that the community finds its principle of unity and from which it takes its consistency.

> This power and the community are formed by the consent and the will of each and every individual. And thus, from these wills emanates power. Before men met together as a political body, this power existed; but it did not exist, totally or partially, in each and every one of them; and not even in the rough conglomerate of men . . . and so this power can never come immediately from those very men . . .
>
> Secondly, this power is inexistent in human nature until men join together in a perfect community and unite politically. This power does not exist in each and every *separate* man, nor in the conjoined multitude of them without order or union of the members of a body.[60]

There is a simultaneity of the institution of power and of the community. Both mutually presuppose each other, and neither can exist in isolation: "There cannot truly be a body with no head, unless it is mutilated, monstrous."[61] This is the reason that, as Suárez stated before, once the community has invested the monarch, it cannot strip him of his sovereignty: because nobody other than the monarch himself (no private individual or particular state) is entitled to speak or act on his behalf. It is only this (usually omitted) second argument that renders the former consistent.

Once again we are faced with the problem of mediation (the Trinitarian scheme). Just as the community is needed to intercede as a third element between God and the monarch, there is, conversely, a need for an intermediary agent to intercede as a third element between the community as a whole and the plurality of subjects. This third element is none other than the sovereign. Such a sovereign is not necessarily the monarch, but it is a political authority that makes possible the reduction of that plurality into a single unit. Until there is such an authority, what we have is a simple conglomerate of beings; a community proper does not yet exist.

This means that *a community is never immediately one, immediately congruent, with regards to itself.* The principle of unity that constitutes it as such comes to it from an external source. This is what "the political" designates. The constitution of the social cannot be reduced to the balancing mechanisms inherent in society. It involves the reference to an agency placed beyond it and from which it takes its consistency, a supplement. Thus, distinguishing between "politics" and "society" finally becomes possible. The terms now cease to overlap, since each serves as a respective index of what the other presupposes but cannot encompass, the place where it finds the conditions that make it possible and that at the same time threatens to destroy it.

Just as the community is in an excess relation with respect to the sovereign, inasmuch as that represents the source of its legitimacy but, at the same time, prevents the actualization of its very concept (impedes doing away with the principle of the legitimacy of tyrannicide that renders it impossible), conversely, sovereignty is in an excess relation with respect to the community. The former confers on the latter the principle of unity, which constitutes it as such and also demolishes its very concept by introducing in it power relationships; that is, the constitution of the community demands its dissolution, the partition of it between those who govern and those who are governed. In sum, the concept of community is an impossible one, a self-contradictory one, which contains an aporia that is intrinsic to it.

The field of the political that then emerged would be articulated by that dual excess. On the one hand, we have the community, which indicates all of sovereignty that exceeds the figure of the sovereign—what we can call the social principle. But, on the other hand, we find the opposite excess (the political principle), which indicates all of the sovereign that exceeds the community and constitutes it as such. These two principles finally become detached, establishing a mutual relation, which is at the same time inseparable and conflictive. That dual excess is also what transforms both into political concepts, that is, limit notions—not in the sense that they constitute some type of unreachable ideal (something too good to be true, which can only be approximated asymptotically), but in the sense that the moment of its achievement is also the moment of its destruction.

The concept of sovereignty illustrates this paradox. On the one hand, it excludes the possibility of any limitation, because if a limit were imposed upon a monarch, that would imply the presence of a superior power that could judge him, thus unmaking him as sovereign. On the other hand, it implies the existence of a limit that the sovereign cannot trespass without becoming its opposite, a tyrant. That is, if he were to become truly sovereign, ipso facto he would cease to be a legitimate sovereign. The moment of the actualization of sovereignty is also that of its own destruction. This is so because the very concept of it contains an implicit aporia, insofar as it simultaneously excludes and entails the idea of the pact: without the pact, sovereignty cannot be established, but with the pact, it becomes unfeasible. And, as we have seen, the same happens with the concept of community: it demands political power as its condition of possibility and also as that which dislocates it (that is, introduces power relations). This means that the community can constitute only at the price of destroying itself as such.

This leads us back to our original question: What is the meaning of that great political-conceptual inflection produced during the seventeenth century? What is it that appears and marks the break in the regimes of exercise of power in the West—the idea of the sovereign or that of the pact, the theory of the state or the foundations of democracy (the so-called classical republicanism)? Different authors opt for one or the other, depending on their historical perspectives or ideological affinities, hoping they can find the epitome of the origin of political modernity in either Suárez or Jean Bodin (or perhaps in John Locke or Hobbes). But, in doing so, through this typical procedure of the history of ideas, they lose sight of the nucleus of the transformation then produced. A conceptual history of the political—the mark that distinguishes it from the old tradition of the history of ideas—consists of moving beyond the realm of ideas, of the diverse possible options, and analyzing *how the terrain within which those options could take shape was historically articulated.*

Ultimately, what underlies the opposition between sovereignty and pact is a much more crucial phenomenon: the emergence of the political, that is to say, the opening of a new field that unfolds itself on the basis of that constitutive incongruence of the community with regards to itself and that establishes the arena in which political debates and practices will, from then on, take place. It is woven and held taut by a dual excess. At one extreme, there is the "community," as the name designating everything that belongs to the sovereignty but exceeds the figure of the sovereign himself (which we can term the principle of the social). At the other extreme, we find an opposite excess (the principle of the political), meaning everything inherent to political power that exceeds the community and constitutes it as such. Following the breakdown of the idea of the immediate communion of society with itself, its conformation as such can only be the result of a *work*—namely, the work of politics. Society cannot realize itself without appealing to an external factor to supplement this constitutive void.

However, in this way, this third factor does nothing more than internalize that fissure, thus reenacting the constitutive scission of the social in another plane. It is the figure of the mediator, which is embodied successively in various forms (the monarch, the congress, the law, the nation, the party, and so on), that will become placed, again and again, at the center of debates, the locus where the traumatic core of modern politics would find its fullest manifestation. Regardless of the expression it assumes, the mediator will always be torn by its own dual nature: human and divine, particular and universal, profane and sacred, conventional (artificial) and objective (transcendent). Even so, we cannot do without it because of the problem that has been raised—or, rather, that which has *become* a problem (how to reduce the plurality of particular wills to a single, unified, general will, the problem of articulation)—will never be settled. Upon losing sight of this phenomenon, the history of ideas is inevitably condemned to oscillate between one term or another (between sovereignty and pact, reason and faith, etc.), while never reaching an understanding of what underlies and drives that oscillation.

More specifically, what the history of ideas makes difficult to understand is the actual structure of baroque political thought, its characteristic habitus. The idea of the deepening of the absolutist aspects seems insufficient as an answer, because it reduces political-conceptual differences to mere matters of degree or emphasis. In fact, the identification of the king with God was by this time an old topic.[62] The traditional idea of the monarch as the incarnation of justice already implicitly had that identity. Nor was the pact a novel idea. Its model was the biblical covenant between God and the people of Israel. The crux of the political-conceptual twist occurred not at either of these extremes but in the paradoxical link now established between them. It was not the concepts that changed; what was new was the kind of logic that articulated them: the folding logic.

At this point, we must reformulate the previous question: Was Suárez for or against imposing limits on royal authority? Not surprisingly, historians of ideas cannot come to an agreement regarding this. Some emphasize his absolutist ideal and see in him the embodiment of an archaic Hispanic political tradition, whereas others point out his "democratic vein," turning him into a predecessor of Rousseau.[63] In this way, both views lose sight of what constitutes the true nucleus of his thought. According to what we have seen so far, Suárez's response to the above question is both yes and no. Monarchical power *is* and *is not* absolute. This does not mean that the monarch is absolute in some respects and limited in others, but, rather, that he is and is not simultaneously limited in *all* regards. Ultimately, what defines and characterizes baroque thought is its paradoxical nature. The inability to choose one option over the other is not simply a matter of indecisiveness but, rather, is the expression of a more radical, objective undecidability. If, to the baroque, one cannot opt between sovereignty and pact, between state and society, or between reason and faith, it is because both terms are contradictory but at once inseparable.

This explains the "folding" structure observed by Deleuze. As he states, "The baroque refers not to an essence but rather to an operative function, to a trait. It endlessly produces folds."[64] As we saw above, the same thing that Deleuze observed about the idea of matter also applies to political concepts. This is profoundly significant, since it tells us about a more general structure of thought, a characteristic procedure. Political concepts continuously fold in upon themselves, only to find, within, their opposite. Like the concept of pact to sovereignty, these latter constitute the foundations of the former and at the same time are what threaten to destroy them. This folding generates, in turn, a new scission of the concepts. They split into two different ones in order to expel contradiction from within, and so on and so on, thus triggering the mannerist dynamic that is characteristic of the baroque.

As we will see in the chapters that follow, the impasse that emerges from the simultaneous exclusion/presupposition of sovereignty and contract will make the concept of sovereignty fold in upon itself, making room for a new antinomy—this time between sovereignty and government. The idea of government will now be defined in opposition to the concept of sovereignty; the two become mutually detached, thus establishing the latter as a political category. It, in turn, will only end up finding within itself that upon which it is founded and yet also makes it impossible: the idea of public opinion. And so on and so on with all social-political concepts. Ultimately, this problematic structure, this paradox that comes from the simultaneous necessity and impossibility of choosing between antonymic terms, is what confers on the seventeenth century its tragic mood. As Lucien Goldmann puts it:

> *Paradoxical,* because it conceives of all reality as a clash and opposition of contraries, of a thesis and an antithesis simultaneously opposing each other but inseparable, and whose mutually irreducible nature cannot lessen any worldly hope; *tragic,* because man can neither avoid nor accept paradox, because he is a man only insofar as he, while affirming the actual possibility of synthesis, makes of it the axis of his existence, even while always remaining aware that not even this statement can escape paradox.[65]

Faced with this simultaneous necessity and impossibility of choosing, the subject will inevitably tear apart, reproducing within itself that cosmological scission depicted by El Greco. This sets the stage for the universe of the modern tragedy, which we will explore in chapter 2.

2

THE TRAGIC SCENE

The Symbolic Nature of Power and the Problem of Expression

> *The absurd is born of this confrontation between human
> need and the irrational silence of the world.*
> —ALBERT CAMUS, *THE MYTH OF SISYPHUS*

When analyzing Hobbes's political philosophy from the perspective of the rhetorical tradition in which it was written, Quentin Skinner underlined the centrality of the use of "paradiastole." This rhetorical device consists of the ability to redescribe actions or events, attributing to them opposite ethical contents. Thus, virtues could be made to appear as vices, and the other way around, which seemed profoundly disturbing, since it seemed to undermine the possibility of moral judgments. It was closely associated, in turn, with the technique that marked the culmination of an education in the humanities: argumentation *in utramque partem*—the capacity to argue in favor of two contending parties in an equally convincing manner. Skinner thus provides a stimulating and original view of Hobbes's thinking on the subject, and the challenge that it raises: "His solution has the great merit of confronting the problem in a uniquely uncompromising fashion. His final word is that, if we wish to overcome the threat of paradiastole by fixing our moral language unambiguously onto the world, we can only hope to do so by fiat. His conclusion remains deeply skeptical, and does little to uphold the dignity of moral philosophy. For all that, however, he may be right."[1]

Seen from this perspective, however, Hobbes's fundamental contribution would have consisted of merely bringing a new solution to an old problem, thus missing the meaning that these rhetorical devices got in the context of the conceptual universe of the seventeenth century. The crucial point is this: How did it happen that, in that epoch, paradiastole became a specifically political problem and not (or not only) a moral one? As we will see, the resurgence of tragedy as a dramatic form is an expression of it and can enlighten us on the issue.

THE POLITICAL UNDERGROUND OF TRAGIC AMBIVALENCE

In the tragedies of the period, we may observe a systematic appeal to the devices of paradiastole and argumentation *in utramque partem*, that is, different characters defending opposite views with the same persuasive force.[2] In Shakespeare's *Richard II* (whose protagonist, as we have seen, Ernst Kantorowicz takes as the model of the king's two bodies), we can find some of the finest literary elaborations of this technique.[3] A good example occurs in the scene in which Bolingbroke justifies his rebellion against Richard by invoking the injustice of his sentence of exile, while York replies by reporting the crime he had committed by returning from exile without permission. And both characters were actually right.[4]

This ambivalence effect is repeated in all of Shakespeare's plays.[5] According to William Empson, "the total effect is to show a fundamental division in the writer's mind."[6] Yet the consistency of this tendency in the seventeenth century reveals much more than subjective indecisiveness. The "fundamental division in the writer's mind" replicates an even more fundamental division, which is intrinsic to the baroque worldview. As a matter of fact, the rebirth of the genre of tragedy is one of its characteristic expressions.

In effect, the link between the baroque's political thinking and tragedy is not contingent.[7] The two follow the same basic structure. Every tragic hero confronts an unsolvable dilemma. Typically, the choice is either to marry the person he loves but should not marry or to marry the person he must marry but does not love. This is the way of staging that fundamental schism inherent in the baroque's worldview: by means of the contradiction between love and honor (justice and law).[8] If the hero wishes to act in pursuit of superior, transcendent values (love, justice), he must violate social conventions (honor, law). Conversely, if he decides to observe social conventions, he must set aside the values on which those very conventions are founded.[9]

This replicates the fundamental political problem that at that moment was igniting political-philosophical debates and was implicit in the issue of tyrannicide. Faced with the enthronement of a tyrant, the subject had two options: to seek the restoration of justice and rebel against the tyrant, at the cost of violating the law and destroying the community (sinking it into anarchy), or to behave as a good citizen, paying his natural lord the required obedience, at the cost of betraying his own moral conscience and accepting an "Antichrist" as a ruler. (During the Wars of Religion, this dilemma was not merely a philosophical problem but also a burning question.)

After the emergence of the political, when the sphere of justice, of transcendental values, severed its ties with the world, subjects could not help but internalize contradiction; they became condemned to live split lives—as citizens (legal subjects) and as Christians (moral subjects)—playing the two roles simultaneously without ever managing to fuse them.

In tragedies, the hero finally decides to take either the side of love or the side of honor (justice or law), but in doing so, his ethical universe will dramatically shrink.[10] The oblivion of justice or the ignorance of law is thus the condition for action. By giving the primacy to law (the state) over justice (the community), Hobbes behaves as a tragic hero.[11] But Locke also does so when, at least in some parts of his work, he moves in the opposite direction.[12] In any case, from the perspective of a conceptual history of the political, the respective positions these authors took (which is the subject matter of the history of ideas) are relevant only insofar as, in their mutual opposition, they allow us to recreate the array of choices they had available to articulate their positions. What matters here is to understand how that array was established and, eventually, how it was reconfigured.

Ultimately, both Hobbes and Locke were actually right. If we frame their thinking within the baroque conceptual universe, it was true that, as Hobbes stated, only law provided an objective ground on which to judge the legitimacy of authority. If everybody claimed the right to act according to his own free, unconditioned consciousness, if "no man dare to obey Sovereign Power, farther than it shall seem good in his own eyes," no regular government could ever be established (that is, we would never have escaped from the state of nature). But Locke was also right when he stated that, if individuals could not judge authority, if they became deprived of their sovereign rights, authority would, ipso facto, be without foundation, since "slaves could never have a right to compact or consent."[13]

To properly understand the positions Locke and Hobbes adopted, we must transcend them and gain access to the traumatic core that lay behind them. The goal is to disclose the underlying questions, the soil of problems, that at that moment were fueling political debates and demanded to be answered. While the position of the actors is a subjective matter, having to do with the ideas of the agents, the soil of problems refers us back to the objective grounds of those ideas, the framework within which they could become articulated and from which they took their concrete meaning. Only this constitutes a properly historical-conceptual concern.

That remainder of undecidability (the fact that the opposite views are equally tenable) is ultimately what defines the properly political nature of the issues at stake. Only this makes it understandable why these issues eventually became matters of political debate, as well as their link with tragedy and the tragic universe. All tragedy is the narration of the events that preceded the hero's decision to act, the dilemmas he faced at the moment he was called upon to do so, and the depiction of his radical inability to solve that dilemma. It is the function of the chorus to remind us of this. The chorus knows the ultimate irresolution of the contradiction in the midst of which the hero is placed, and how his decision entails the suppression of one of the terms of the contradictions: either the violation of law or the betrayal of justice. As a consequence, he cannot continue to live; the tragic hero is condemned beforehand to die, ignorant of why he must do so, of what he did wrong.

But if the chorus does know this, it is because it is not an actor in the drama and only remains as a mere observer and a commentator on it.[14]

The gap between justice and law thus unfolds itself, giving rise to another fold and articulating a new contradiction—between knowledge and action—an opposition of which Hamlet, the Dionysian man, according to Friedrich Nietzsche, has become the symbol par excellence. As he stated in his classic work *The Birth of Tragedy*:

> In this sense, the Dionysian man resembles Hamlet: both have for once penetrated into the true nature of things—they have *perceived*, but it is irksome for them to act; for their action cannot change the eternal nature of things; the time is out of joint and they regard it as shameful or ridiculous that they should be required to set it right. Knowledge kills action, action requires the veil of illusion—it is the lesson that Hamlet teaches, and not the idle wisdom of John-o'-Dreams, who from too much reflection, from a surplus of possibilities, never arrives at action at all. Not reflection, no!—true knowledge, insight into the terrible truth, preponderate over all motives inciting to action, in Hamlet as well as in the Dionysian man.[15]

Action requires ignorance, self-deception. Yet from the moment that the constitution of the community demands a work (which is, in fact, the work of the political), action is necessary, decision is not dispensable. In sum, communal life is erected upon justice (truth), but she is the daughter of illusion (ignorance, self-deception). This explains the proliferation of masks, dreams, and ghosts in the plays of the time; the mental breakdown of characters, which drives them to madness (the confusion between reality and illusion);[16] and the passion for artifice.[17]

The intermingling of illusion and reality actually constitutes the true core of *Richard II*. In the momentous scene depicting the king's confusion after his dethronement, he is unable to understand how the very same people who, just a few moments earlier, adored him as a sacred person, a vicarious God now despise him and look down on him as if he were a common villain.[18] Even more astonishingly, in that same act, the vulgar character Bolingbroke is suddenly turned into a king and, incredibly enough, everybody now bows down to him as if he were really such a one—as Richard had been up to that moment and now, abruptly, has ceased to be. To be a king, to be a subject, they are mere conventions, illusions, is Richard's conclusion. "Think our former state a happy dream; /

From which awaked, the truth of what we are," he tells his disconsolate wife (*Richard II*, act 5, scene 1). We all are only characters in a play, actors performing a role.

This leads us back to our original question: What was the ultimate sense of the break produced in the seventeenth century? In chapter 1, we gave a first answer to that question: that crucial turning point consisted in a new awareness that the community was never immediately one with itself; that the principle which gave it unity came from without; that is, that the process of reduction of plurality to unity was the result of a labor and required the action of an agent, the intercession of a mediator, the intervention of an external factor. Yet this is not the whole answer. We can now complete it by introducing an additional element that only makes explicit what was implicit in the previous formulation. The fundamental discovery of the baroque was the *symbolic* nature of that mediating instance, the representative (illusory) character of political power.[19] This must be understood not in the more obvious but banal sense that power manifests itself in symbols, but in the sense that power *is* symbolic in its nature.

This entails a fundamental reconfiguration of the modes of conceiving political power. It was now seen as an invisible force (*vis*), an immaterial fluid, like life, that circulates through the social body, animating it.[20] The king is merely the visible manifestation of it, the expression of a social force that exceeds his figure, the symbol of something whose source lies elsewhere. That was what, in those very years, Pedro Calderón de la Barca expressed even more potently, in Segismundo's celebrated monologue in *Life Is a Dream* (act II, scene 19):

> We live, while we see the sun,
> Where life and dreams are as one;
> And living has taught me this,
> Man dreams the life that is his,
> Until his living is done.
> The king dreams he is king, and he lives
> In the deceit of a king,
> Commanding and governing;
> And all the praise he receives
> Is written in wind, and leaves

> A little dust on the way
> When death ends all with a breath.
> Where then is the gain of the throne,
> That shall perish and not be known
> In the other dream that is death?
> Dreams the rich man of riches and fears,
> The fears that his riches breed;
> The poor man dreams of his need,
> And all his sorrows and tears . . .
> What is life? a tale that is told;
> What is life? a frenzy extreme,
> A shadow of things that seem;
> And the greatest good is but small,
> That all life is a dream to all,
> And that dreams themselves are a dream.

The bearer of the scepter simply performs a role in a play. But insofar as everybody accepts him *as if* he were a king, he actually becomes one with the role he assumes. And so do community and individuals come to life. In this world, nothing is real; it is a world of figures, of conventions, of "as ifs."[21]

The mercantilist theories that emerged at this time are good examples of this entirely new worldview. By then, it was clear that, unlike gold or silver coins, paper money (which had become more common) has a merely representative character. It allows us to acquire goods but in itself has no worth. It is just printed paper, but we take it *as if* it really had the value it represents. The point is that, although it is certainly an illusion, it does not simply exist in the minds of men and women; it is inscribed in their social practices and is intrinsic to them. It is not merely a mirage, the result of a subjective delusion; it operates in actual reality. To the extent that it is a collectively shared convention, it somehow gets an actual entity—for instance, nobody would throw bills away. Ultimately, the whole economy stands and works on the basis of that illusion. The symbolic that the baroque discovered is no longer a world of "ideas" but a *constitutive dimension of politics and society*.[22]

In effect, as Calderón so acutely observed, the king dreams of being a king, but so do the banker and the beggar, the nobleman and the peasant. All roles in society are merely that—masks, illusions. "*Totus mundus agit histrionem*" (All the world's a stage), as tradition holds was the motto of Shakespeare's Globe Theatre. Illusions are ethereal, diffuse, ungraspable, but they are what organizes society, shapes it. Thus, we cannot escape from them. Even though the tragic hero knows that they are merely illusory, he himself is trapped in the world of interpretations, the "as ifs," without ever being able to disclose the mechanism that produces them.

In *Art and Illusion*, E. H. Gombricht provides a good analogy to illustrate the nature of tragic contradiction: the Gestalt test.

> We can see the picture as either a rabbit or a duck. It is easy to discover both readings. It is less easy to describe what happens when we switch from one interpretation to the other. Clearly we do not have the illusion that we are confronted with a "real" duck or rabbit. The shape on the paper resembles neither animal very closely. And yet there is no doubt that it transforms itself in some subtle way when the duck's beak becomes the rabbit's ears and brings an otherwise neglected spot into prominence. I say "neglected," but does it enter our experience at all when we switch back to reading "duck"? To answer this question, we are compelled to look for what is "really there," to see the shape apart from its interpretation, and this, we soon discover, is not really possible. True, we can switch from one reading to another with increasing rapidity: we will also "remember" the rabbit while we see the duck, but the more closely we watch ourselves, the more certainly we will discover that we cannot experience alternative readings at the same time. Illusion, we will find, is hard to describe or analyze, for though we may be intellectually aware of the fact that any given experience *must* be an illusion, we cannot, strictly speaking, watch ourselves having an illusion.[23]

Here we find the real, and truly problematic, question King Richard asks after awakening from his dreams: What is "the truth of what we are"? The answer is: "Nothing." Stripped of our masks, we find only our inner void, cosmological vacuum, the *kenoma*. Only death, a purely physical and meaningless death, can awaken us from our illusory existence—"For in that sleep of death what dreams may come" (*Hamlet*, act III, scene 1). If there is a meaning in life, only worms know—"Your worm is your only emperor for diet" (*Hamlet*, act IV, scene 3)—because they have no illusions; having illusions is what differentiates men from worms. Life is a dream, "a tale / Told by an idiot, full of sound and fury, / Signifying nothing" (*Macbeth*, act V, scene 5), but beyond dreams there is nothing, only the ghosts reside there.

The scene that follows the one previously cited, in which Richard II looks at himself in the mirror, clearly illustrates this.[24] Once detached of the symbols of his power (his *corpus mysticum*), Richard can finally see himself as a man (his *corpus verum*).[25] But what he sees is . . . nothing.[26] When stripped of his royal cloak, his being fades away; he becomes a nonbeing, "a thing . . . of nothing."[27] Then he throws away the mirror and it shatters into pieces, as he himself is shattered: after he loses the principle that provided unity to his being as the representative of his community "and know[s] not now what name to call [himself]" (*Richard II*, act 4, scene 1), he becomes formless, like music with no metric rhythm. Imprisoned within the world of contradictions, his mind becomes populated with opposing impulses; he has as many "intermix'd" thoughts as he has subjects.[28]

> I have been studying how I may compare
> This prison where I live unto the world:
> And for because the world is populous
> And here is not a creature but myself,
> I cannot do it; yet I'll hammer it out.
> My brain I'll prove the female to my soul,
> My soul the father; and these two beget
> A generation of still-breeding thoughts,
> And these same thoughts people this little world,
> In humors like the people of this world,
> For no thought is contented. The better sort,
> As thoughts of things divine, are intermix'd
> With scruples and do set the word itself
> Against the word:
> As thus, "Come, little ones," and then again,
> "It is as hard to come as for a camel
> To thread the postern of a small needle's eye."
> Thoughts tending to ambition, they do plot

Unlikely wonders; how these vain weak nails
May tear a passage through the flinty ribs
Of this hard world, my ragged prison walls,
And, for they cannot, die in their own pride.
Thoughts tending to content flatter themselves
That they are not the first of fortune's slaves,
Nor shall not be the last; like silly beggars
Who sitting in the stocks refuge their shame,
That many have and others must sit there;
And in this thought they find a kind of ease,
Bearing their own misfortunes on the back
Of such as have before endured the like.
Thus play I in one person many people,
And none contented: sometimes am I king;
Then treasons make me wish myself a beggar,
And so I am: then crushing penury
Persuades me I was better when a king;
Then am I king'd again: and by and by
Think that I am unking'd by Bolingbroke,
And straight am nothing: but whate'er I be,
Nor I nor any man that but man is
With nothing shall be pleased, till he be eased
With being nothing. Music do I hear?

[*Music.*]

Ha, ha! keep time: how sour sweet music is,
When time is broke and no proportion kept!
So is it in the music of men's lives.[29]

Ambivalence turns into subjective fragmentation and leads to madness. Only the symbolic figure, the character (hence the repeated comparison of life with theater), prevents the dissolution of his personality and introduces a principle of order in the midst of contradiction. Only the masks, although illusory, can provide us with an identity. That is why we cannot escape them. Because there is nothing behind them. They are the true threads that weave the social fabric. And the illusion of sovereignty provides the basic matrix of all the others. Hence, after his dethronement, along with the royal figure, it is the entire kingdom that inevitably crumbles down and shatters, and only a new illusion of legality could prevent it.

The same kind of final collapse can be seen in *Hamlet*. Hamlet, as we know from the beginning, must kill the usurper Claudius, as the ghost of his father compels him to "revenge his foul and most unnatural murder" (*Hamlet*, act I, scene 5). Only in this way can Hamlet reestablish justice and reconstitute the community. Yet, when he finally does so, the scene ends with the unintentional murder of his mother, Gertrude, that is, with the destruction of his kingdom—at that moment, Hamlet's traditional enemy, Fortinbras, the prince of Norway, is crossing the frontiers and occupying his dominions.[30] The reconstitution of the community, the reestablishment of justice, which necessarily entails the violation of law, rebellion against the established authority, turns into its opposite: the dissolution of communal life (the killing of the queen mother).[31] She could not survive the death of the king. At that juncture, the kingdom has become a body with no head, a dissected figure, a monster. "The whole play," says John Hunt, "looks like a dissecting room, stocked with all of man's limbs, organs, tissues, and fluids."[32] She was already dead before actually dying; only a new fiction of sovereignty could reconstitute her identity, but this is inevitably precarious and ephemeral.

We now can go back to our initial question—What is "the truth of what we are"?—and observe the consequences of the discovery of the symbolic nature of power. In the first place, the illusory (representative) nature of political power underscores the disjointed character of it, that it is never perfectly congruent with itself. It contains, within, a gap. That is, it represents a social force that can never become fully present in it but only re-presented. Just as justice can never become fully embodied in the law, neither can the sovereign fully express sovereignty. The social force that is symbolically represented by political power, the community, is in a surplus relation with respect to the sovereign, and this explains its eventual break. The sovereign contains within himself an unrepresentable excess that cannot be comprehended within the frameworks of the state, a dark side that is its (hidden) properly political substance. "The people" (the community) is only the name designating that excess, the inner gap of political power. It is not a sociological concept; it does not refer to any empirical reality; it just serves as the index of both the foundation and the ultimate impossibility of sovereignty, of its ethereal and ghostly nature.

But the symbolic and illusory nature of political power, the ultimate impossibility of it, does not mean that it is not an effective factor in the constitution of the community. Quite the contrary. Only with the sovereign does the community find the principle of its unity. Here we meet the second consequence: it is in the symbolic realm that the community finds its conditions of possibility. The symbolic constitution of power actually provides the matrix for the entire mechanism of the social conventions (subjective roles) that make up communal life. Yet the crucial point is that, in the very act of providing consistency to the community, political power also disrupts the homogeneity of the social space, introducing a cleavage in it, in the form of power relations.

This means that the community, the people, as the condition of possibility of political power, is, just like the sovereign, something ghostly, ethereal. Like political power, the community contains within itself a gap that must be filled symbolically. But, just as the community functions as the source of legitimacy and, at the same time, the limit of political power—at once its foundation and that which always threatens to destroy it—so too does political power function as the condition of possibility of the community and, at the same time, the index of its ultimate impossibility.[33] Ultimately, political power is the specter of community, representing, as Molly Smith has described it, its "darker world within." The *political* that at that moment emerges is, in the end, *nothing but the intermediary space opened by this double impasse.*

To sum it up, on the one hand, only illusions, empty conventions, give meaning to our secular existence, insofar as what lies beyond them is nothingness, only death. Yet, the same illusions that give our lives meaning are also destructive of it—like "much drink," which, as the porter in Macbeth describes it, is "an equivocator with lechery: it makes [a man], and it mars him; it sets him on, and it takes him off" (*Macbeth*, act II, scene 3). Illusions engender life and bear death within, and the two are inextricably tied in them, as the ghosts, the living dead, which are neither alive nor dead. Tragic drama becomes such, according to Gombrich, insofar as it exposes what is unavailable to us, insofar as it transcends illusions and penetrates the mechanism that produces them. More exactly, it shows the perverse core that the mechanism simultaneously performs and hides. In sum, tragic dramas expose the fundamental matrix of the fold structure that, according to Deleuze, is typical of the baroque and by which the one (the community, the state) always folds upon itself to find within its secret, hidden being, its specter: the Two, the *numerus infamis quia principium divisionis* (infamous number that gives rise to divisions), according to Pseudo-Dionysius's definition.

TRAGEDY, POLITICS, AND THE INVENTION OF THE SUBJECT

At this point, we must introduce a distinction. Taking on a concept elaborated by the romantics, Walter Benjamin, in *Ursprung des deutschen Trauerspiels* (The Origin of German Tragic Drama), distinguishes between the symbol and the allegory. It is allegory that provides the form of expression that is most appropriate to tragedy. Quoting Georg Friedrich Creuzer, Benjamin states: "The difference between symbolic and allegorical representation is explained as follows: 'The latter signifies merely a general concept or an idea, which is different from itself; the former is the very incarnation and embodiment of the idea. In the former a process of substitution takes place ... In the latter the concept itself has descended into our physical world, and we see it itself directly in the image.'"[34] For Creuzer (and Benjamin after him), the romantic ideal of representation, or *Darstellung*, takes form of symbols, which are the sensitive expressions of the Idea. Here, the idea and its expression are one; the substance is not beyond its manifestation but is the actual way in which it expresses itself. For the baroque, by contrast, a thing never coincides with its representation; an insurmountable gap separates the two. The represented thing, the essence, works as the absent cause of the phenomenal forms of its expression. Yet the conditions of possibility of phenomena—like the mechanism that produces optical illusions in the Gestalt test, for Gombrich; or sovereignty, for Bodin; and, later, the subject, for Immanuel Kant—do not lend themselves to representation. The counterpart of the intelligibility, measurability, and manipulability of the phenomenal world is thus the radical ungraspability and impenetrability of the ultimate causes. Hence the role of allegories. "Allegories," says Benjamin, "are, in the realm of thought, what ruins are in the realm of things."[35]

Allegories represent nothing but the very impossibility of representation. And, as Georg Lukács remarked, the expression of this paradox as such is the crucial aspect that distinguishes tragedy from modern realism: "Realism is bound to destroy all the form-creating and life-maintaining values of tragic drama... Drama is bound to become trivial if its lifelikeness conceals that which is dramatically real."[36]

The realm of the conditions of possibility of phenomena actually has an ambiguous ontological status. The transcendental, in the Kantian sense, is neither an essence nor a mere appearance; the conditions of the possibility of phenomena are always contained in them but are never present in the phenomenal world. In sum, in the seventeenth century the opening of the field of the theological-political, and the consequent emergence of an economy of power, provided the basis for the conception of a new realm of reality, a somehow paradoxical one: It is neither transcendent nor immanent but both at the same time. It is never present but always re-presented, and yet it does not lend itself to representation and can be expressed only allegorically. It is, in sum, indefinable, unnamable, a spectral presence, at once constituent and threatening.

As Lukács wrote, this transcendental realm is expressed in tragedy in the intermingling of life and death.

> Every ending is always an arrival and a cessation, an affirmation and a denial all at once; every climax is a peak and frontier, the point of intersection between life and death. The tragic life is, of all possible lives, the one most exclusively of this world. That is why its frontier always merges into death. Real, ordinary life never reaches the frontier; it knows death only as something frightening, threatening, meaningless, something that suddenly arrests the flow of life. Mysticism overleaps the frontier and thus robs death of any value as reality. But for tragedy, death, the frontier as such, is an always immanent reality, inseparably connected with every tragic event.[37]

In other words, the distinguishing feature of tragedy is the undecidability between life and death. In a world deprived of meaning, tragic heroes "are dead a long time before they actually die."[38]

This is an eminently political problem, which leads us back to Hamlet. He somehow knew that the killing of Claudius also entailed the destruction of the kingdom, that is, the death of his mother queen. Hence his hesitation, and his raptures of madness. Because he also knew that, even so, he could not avoid doing it. That was the tragic dilemma he faced. He could not accept Claudius as a king without becoming an accomplice to his crime. But to avenge his father's death, Hamlet had to commit a new crime, thus becoming indistinguishable from his stepfather. In this world, justice is a poisoned gift: "This even-handed justice / Commends the ingredients of our poison'd chalice / To our own lips" (*Macbeth*, act I, scene 7). The ideal of justice, which provides meaning to life, at once destroys it: "Feed'st thy lights flame with selfe substantiall fewell" (Sonnet 1, line 6).

We observe here two different forms of undecidability. Hamlet has no certainty regarding the culpability of Claudius in the killing of his father, and only a dubious interpretation of a scene during the performance of a play proves it to him. Yet the spectator knows it, because Claudius confesses it from the very beginning. As for Gertrude, the question of her complicity in the king's murder is left undecided in the play. We find no hint about whether she was involved in the assassination of her husband. In the case of whether Claudius was guilty of killing his father, we find a situation of subjective, epistemological uncertainty—the hero does not know the truth, but he eventually could do as the spectator actually does.[39] In the case of Gertrude's guilt, we are faced with objective, ontological uncertainty. It is not simply a matter of the lack of the relevant information. There is no way of verifying it.

In effect, we cannot blame the entire kingdom for the dethronement of the king, yet she is not innocent either. *She is and is not guilty.* Regardless whether the kingdom (Gertrude) participated in the event, she is a participant from the moment she pledges obedience to the usurper. Hamlet cannot forgive his mother for marrying Claudius when the corpse of his father was still warm. However, there is nothing irregular in Gertrude's attitude; she, like her kingdom, simply accepted the coming of a new king, the same way she had accepted the previous king and will accept all the kings to come, as is her duty. In fact, not doing so would mean civil war.[40]

If the question regarding Gertrude's (and the kingdom's) guilt is undecidable, it is because it is not really about whether she took part in the killing of her former husband but, rather, about the *meaning* of that event, that is, whether avenging him and killing Claudius was an act of justice or actually a new crime. The former question, regarding her actual participation in the killing, could eventually be answered; not so the question about the meaning of that action, whether it was an act of justice or a crime, as *it is both things at the same time* (a crime and an act of justice). "Fair is foul, and foul is fair," intone the witches in *Macbeth* (act I, scene 1). And, eventually, the participation of the kingdom in this deed would not alter that point; the people's support would not turn a crime into an act of justice, just as the lack of support would not turn an act of justice into a crime.

Regardless, Hamlet cannot and will not participate in that "traitorous" action (accepting a usurper as a legitimate king), though this comes at the price of indefinitely prolonging the chain of crimes: to avenge a crime, he will bring about a new usurpation, which, in turn, will demand to be punished with a new crime, and so on ad infinitum. This is the basic structure of Shakespeare's historical tragedies (with perhaps a few exceptions, such as *Henry V*). They are normally written in medias res, tracing a circle with no beginning or end. In *Richard II*, the final scene actually replicates the first. In it, Bolingbroke tries to wash away his guilty conscience, exiling Exton for a crime Bolingbroke himself had ordered— "I hate the murderer, love him murdered. / The guilt of conscience take thou for thy labor" (*Richard II*, act V, scene 6)—as Richard II had done at the beginning of the play, with Mowbray, thus sealing his own tragic fate. We can foresee here that the same will happen to Bolingbroke and, probably, to the perpetrator of his death and all of his successors. "Blood will have blood," asserts Macbeth (*Macbeth*, act III, scene 4).[41]

In this chain of usurpations, all receive their deserved punishment. Queen Margaret can console herself by saying, "Thy Edward he is dead, that stabb'd my Edward: / Thy other Edward dead, to quit my Edward" (*Richard III*, act IV, scene 4). However, this punishment happens without justice ever being reinstituted. Once natural law is violated, it cannot be artificially reestablished. "From this instant," states Macbeth, after committing his first crime, "There's nothing serious in mortality: / All is but toys" (*Macbeth*, act II, scene 3). To consider it a just punishment or a crime thus becomes simply a matter of perspective.[42] That was the objective basis for the reactivation of the rhetorical figure of paradiastole, and it explains how this then gained a new meaning, becoming an eminently political, and not a merely moral, problem (the question posed above in reference to Skinner's view). It tells us not of Hobbes's (or whoever's) ideas, but of an objective, historical-conceptual development that was characteristic of the seventeenth century (or, more precisely, of the classical age, according to Foucault).

In tragedies, the hero struggles to distinguish justice from its opposite, but with his action he ends up collapsing the two. This is the perverse mechanism in which Macbeth finds himself trapped.[43] He wants to commit the crime that would put an end to the whirlwind of criminality unbound after his first crime. "This blow," he expects, "Might be the be-all and the end-all here" (*Macbeth*, act I, scene 7). He longs for the time when the dead were dead and did not come back to life as specters (act III, scene 4):

> Ay, and since too, murders have been perform'd
> Too terrible for the ear: the times have been,
> That, when the brains were out, the man would die,
> And there an end; but now they rise again,
> With twenty mortal murders on their crowns,
> And push us from our stools: this is more strange
> Than such a murder is.

Seeking a way out of that eternal cycle, Macbeth precipitates himself into a new crime, only to reproduce that cycle. He would thus become the symbol of one of the worst assassin-tyrants in the history of literature, yet we cannot say he is personally perverse. He faces moral dilemmas about his crimes and complains, "Better be with the dead, / Whom we, to gain our peace, have sent to peace, / Than on the torture of the mind to lie / In restless ecstasy" (*Macbeth*, act III, scene 2).

Remorse is what differentiates Macbeth's character from that of his wife, Lady Macbeth, whose counterpoint structures the whole play. Unlike Macbeth, she cannot see the ghosts; she has no sense for that. She believes that blood can be washed away with water. For her, morality is simply a human contradiction. It consists of seeking a goal but rejecting the means to attain it, as we saw in *Richard II*'s Bolingbroke, when he stated, "I hate the murderer, love him murdered." If Macbeth hesitates and turns pale at the sight of the dead coming back to life, it is simply, as his wife tells him, because he does not dare "to be the same in thine own act and valor / As [he is] in desire" (*Macbeth*, act I, scene 7).[44]

In fact, Macbeth intends to gain some distance from his role, although it is seemingly absurd. By doing so, he would lose all identity; he would become a figure deprived of personality, a selfless self, a ghost. To be and remain a king, he must kill all the competitors—an endless endeavor, ultimately doomed to failure, but which he cannot help but attempt: "Whiles I see lives, the gashes / Do better upon them" (*Macbeth*, act V, scene 8). He is fated to do what he does (the witches have prophesied it). In the end, he is only the puppet of an impersonal mechanism that he cannot control. Macbeth does and is what his role (*officium*) determines him to do and to be, and he cannot do and be otherwise. His tragedy lies in the fact that he is lucid about it. He knows that he is driven by a force superior to his own (a force of which he, as a king, is representative but which exceeds his own power), and he can do nothing to change it. If he did not do it and kill his enemies, another person would do (would kill him and all of his enemies), and this person would then be the king.

In any case, a similar thing occurs at all levels of society. This is the meaning of the famous scene featuring the "porter of hell-gate" (*Macbeth*, act 2, scene 3). Kings kill adversaries, just as tailors cheat customers, and so back and forth. In this scene, Shakespeare actually expresses a concept that James I elaborated in his work "Basilikon Doron" (1599 and 1603), in which he details the perverse aspects that are intrinsic to each social category, the dark side of every profession.[45] As the porter of hell affirms, "I had thought to have let in some of all professions that go the primrose way to the everlasting bonfire" (*Macbeth*, act II, scene 3).

We find here Shakespeare's expression of the emergence of an entirely new worldview, which is distinctive of seventeenth-century culture. Hitherto, it was thought that the difference between a tyrant and a good king depended upon the ruler's moral condition. If he was a pious, generous man, he was a good king; if he was perverse, ambitious, he was a tyrant. After the Reformation, this view became untenable, as categories became contingent. It no longer seemed feasible to say who was a pious man and who was not, because the person whom some considered pious was, to others, the Antichrist, and the other way around. Things themselves have become obscure. Like the illusions to which it is attached, for Shakespeare, *evil is an objective phenomenon, which exists in the world*; it does not refer to the moral condition of the agents but to the structure and functioning of human societies. The owner of a company, for example, could be a good man who wants his workers to be prosperous and happy. Yet, whatever his internal wishes, he must be an exploiter. As kings must be tyrannical, the company owner must pay low salaries, otherwise he will be driven to bankruptcy. What is wrong with him has nothing to do with the personality of the eventual bearer of the role of the owner but with the mode in which capitalist production works; it cannot be explained by the ethics of the subject in question but by the way in which our world, in which the owner is merely a participant, is organized.

We may call this a theory of the "objective evil," which is the direct result of the breakdown of the anthropocentric universe. This position—heartbreakingly expressed in King Lear's discovery that we live in a merciless world that lacks any concern for our welfare—entailed a complete reformulation of the issue of tyrannicide. To be a tyrant or to be a good king now says nothing about the moral qualities of the individual who holds the scepter. James I explained the issue in the clearest terms in his imprecation against the Puritans. As he states, the "sectarians" questioned him not for being a bad king but simply for being a king: "I was oftimes calumniated in their popular Sermons, not for any euil or vice in me, but because I was a King, which they thought the highest euil."[46] Unlike Kantorowicz's interpretation, James affirmed that what the Puritans impugned was not his self but his role, his investiture as king rather than any actions he may have taken, his mystical body rather than his mortal body. For the Puritans, James's perversity was thus independent of the king's personal moral makeup and had no relationship to what he did, had done, or had ceased doing but to what he represented as a social figure. And, therefore, he could do nothing to change it.

As we have seen, in the baroque world, illusions (the masks, the roles) were not merely subjective ideas; they were a constitutive part of social practice. They cannot be considered an expression of merely personal delusion; instead, they are a dimension intrinsic to actual reality. We see now that the same should be said of evil, insofar as, in tragedies, illusion and evil are inextricably associated: evil is the result of the illusory (conventional) nature of our mundane existence. Now, although the conclusion here converges with *Richard II*'s, we have drawn, in an unnoticed fashion, a full circle. We find here the opposite perspective from the one described earlier.

In *Richard II*, all misdeeds resulted from the pursuit of justice, of the attempt to realize (to make present) justice in our world, where it is inevitably re-presented, subject to interpretations, which are contradictory by nature. In *Macbeth*, on the contrary, misdeeds spring from the disregard of justice and the individual's plain identification with his role, with the mask (*officium*, the "as ifs"). Roles (life) are dreams. Justice is nothing, a void (death). But the two contain evil within.

At this point, we can finally observe the particular concept of the subject that underlies the tragic view, and its eminently political nature. Harold Bloom's now-iconic phrase, "Shakespeare's invention of the human,"[47] is normally understood in the sense of the emergence of bourgeois individuality or the romantic concept of *Bildung*—the self's construction of its own being. But this way of understanding that expression implies an anachronistic transposition, the retroactive projection to the seventeenth century of a concept of the self that would be elaborated only much later, in the nineteenth century, and that was far removed from the worldview of the times (and, certainly, from Shakespeare's).[48] The subject here is, ultimately, the vanishing mediation between two illusory entities, the self and the mask; the spectral presence that emerges at the impasse (the ontological void, the cosmological gap) produced by the simultaneous contradiction and indiscernibility of justice and law, love and honor, death and life.[49] In sum, "subject" is just a name pointing to the new phenomenological field that had at that moment made its appearance: the political, that ghostly entity, which simultaneously provides an illusory identity to the community (life) and destroys it (precipitates death), revealing it as merely illusory (a dream), and whose formless, anomalous, inner structure would be made visible to us in tragedy.

As we will see, Racine's tragedies express the way in which the chain of usurpations and the impossibility of justice become the constructive principle of love stories,[50] revealing further aspects of the seventeenth-century concept of the subject as the empty name of the political, of its fold nature, and of the reasons for the ultimate impossibility of it (the subject, and, finally, the community).

THE LOGIC OF THE FOLD STRUCTURE AND THE SPLIT SUBJECT

The typical modus operandi in love stories is the forward projection of passionate drives and the resulting deferral of love. In Racine's *Andromache*, for example,[51] Orestes loves Hermione, but Hermione loves her husband, Pyrrhus, king of Epirus, who loves Andromache. But Andromache cannot love Pyrrhus because she is still in mourning for her dead husband, Hector. The basic scheme can be represented as: A $\Rightarrow$ B $\Rightarrow$ C $\Rightarrow$ ... N. The question this sequence raises is, What is the reason for this permanent deferral; why does not anyone love the "right" person? The answer is, Because this is the playful structure of history. In the reversal of passionate impulses (A $<=>$ B), there is no room for history; like the "I Am that I Am" of God in Genesis, it starts and ends at the same point.[52]

In this string of unrequited attachments, in their permanent state of maladjustment, everybody receives (as also happens in the chain of usurpations in the realm of politics) his or her deserved punishment: C takes revenge for the sufferings B inflicts on A, as C, in turn, is punished for it by D, and so on. The problem in *Andromache* lies in the fact that, for the narrative to make any sense, it should reach an end point where the different relationships are sorted out.[53] But, as it is, the sequence is here prolonged well beyond the earthly plane, which prevents closure.[54] The figure of Hector, the dead husband, works here as a spectral presence that never appears on the stage but drives the development of the story from the shadows, the world beyond, thus preventing any logical conclusion.

This leads, in turn, to a further split: the figure of Hector is duplicated in that of his son Astriamax (who also never appears on the stage but whose ghostly presence also governs the development of the plot). If Andromache refuses to love Pyrrhus, he has said he will kill Astriamax. Thus, Andromache finds herself in a double bind: to save the boy, she must betray her love for her dead husband, which would mean killing him twice, but to remain faithful to Hector, she must sacrifice his only progeny. Either way, she becomes the unintended accomplice in a crime. Either way, in order to live in the world, she must renounce love; that is, she must live a meaningless life—become a kind of living death, carry on a ghostly existence—with no expectations for the future. This reveals the paradoxes of the conceptual universe in which Racine's play takes form.

In the world of tragedies, time is not productive. Productive time is a nineteenth-century concept, a concept of the "age of history," as Foucault calls it, and its emergence would involve a radical break with the "age of representation" of the seventeenth and eighteenth centuries. Its emergence is the distinguishing mark of Koselleck's *Sattelzeit*. In the world of the baroque, instead, time and history (understood as the opposite of nature) is the story of decay and perdition, of the absence of God (of justice), of His radical silence. But what throws the characters back into the world (into tragedy) is, paradoxically, their continuing attempt to escape it, to persist, against all odds, in their search for love (justice). It is in their struggle to find meaning for their worldly existence—which, without love (justice), becomes meaningless, a machinelike existence—that they will find death (the cosmological void). This empty, unproductive dynamic is the one that underlies the paradoxical development of the tragic universe.

As Racine's tragedies show, the only means of escaping from the world and its useless rotation is the self-depletion of desire. The best example is the figure of Hippolytus, in *Phaedra* (perhaps Racine's major work). He is a perfect ascetic, an asexual being. But he cannot stay in that condition. It is not long before he finds himself in a situation of intense passion, which overwhelms him and ends up destroying him. His tragic destiny is set up when his stepmother, Phaedra, confesses her love for him, after receiving the news that Hippolytus's father, Theseus, the king of Athens, has died. Only later do we learn that this was a false rumor. After the supposed death of her husband, Phaedra thinks that she is finally in a position to realize her incest-like love for her stepson without compromising her honor.

What Phaedra is drawn to in Hippolytus is his total lack of emotions. But, at the very moment that she expresses her repressed passion, Hippolytus abandons his asceticism and admits his love for Aricia, thereby setting into motion the tragic denouement, triggering the game of forward projection of passionate drives. Thus, Hippolytus becomes a mere link in the chain. Rather than liberating him from the world, elevating him and giving him distance from it, love throws him into "the tempest," "the raging tide," turning him into a "case of blind conceit," an abject.

> You see before you a most sorry prince,
> A signal case of blind conceit. I wince
> To think how I, Love's enemy, long disdained
> Its bonds, and all whom passion had enchained;
> How, pitying poor storm-tossed fools; I swore
> Ever to view such tempests from the shore;
> And now, like common men, for all my pride,
> Am lost to reason in a raging tide.
> One moment saw my vain defenses fall:
> My haughty spirit is at last in thrall.
>
> Racine, *Phaedra*, act II, scene 2

We see here the fundamental problem of the age of representation: the problem of expression.[55] In the same way that truth (the ideal of oneness) cannot become manifest in the world (the realm of diversity) without turning into its opposite—mere opinion—love, which is the striving for communion, cannot become manifest without giving rise to discord. Once justice has abandoned the world into which transcendental values have disappeared, love, whenever it intends to make itself present in it, inevitably gets trapped in the play of mundane contradictions and becomes defiled by crime and death. As Aricia tells Theseus: "Our sacrifices anger Heaven at times; / Its gifts are often sent to scourge our crimes" (Racine, *Phaedra*, act V, scene 3). At that point, Hippolytus, like Richard II after losing his crown, seems also to lose his identity:

> I seek myself, and find myself no more.
> My bow, my javelins and my chariot pall;
> What Neptune taught me once, I can't recall;
> My idle steeds forget the voice they've known
>
> Racine, *Phaedra*, act II, scene 2

He becomes a split subject, suffering from a "horrible duplicity." We find here a fundamental aspect of the "fold logic" that is typical of the age of representation: the duplication of characters. Just as, in *Andromache*, Astriamax was a stand-in for Hector, here Phaedra actually sees in Hippolytus the image of his father:

> But no! He is not dead; he breathes in you.
> My husband still seems present to my view.
> I see him, speak with him . . . Ah, my lord; I feel
> Crazed with a passion which I can't conceal.
>
> Racine, *Phaedra*, act II, scene 5

We observe the hidden pattern behind the chain of passionate drives. A (Phaedra) loves B (Hippolytus), who loves C (Aricia). But C is no other than A projected as an illusory image by B. Just as we obey not the actual body of the king but his mystical figure, we never love the actual figure of our beloved but only the idealized image we create of him or her (C), which never coincides with the actual person (like Dulcinea del Toboso and Aldonza Lorenzo, in *Don Quixote*).[56] What matters here is not the loved one, as he or she truly exists, but, rather, what that person means to us, what he or she produces in us. The beloved provides us with an identity, as kings do for the community, and makes us a subject. Yet, at the same time, it dissolves our selves, which then become (like seventeenth-century kings, for Kantorowicz) inevitably split, cleaved between our actual and our illusory bodies.

The main premise that creates the possibility of history is Iago's maxim "I am what I am not" (*Othello*, act I, scene 1).[57] The subject (like the community, for Suárez) is never one with himself; he has as many different identities as the roles he plays. He has no underlying principle of unity to avoid dissemination.[58] He is nothing but the torn space between two existential voids (love and honor, justice and law, community and state). And this generates the (typically) mannerist dynamic of duplication and proliferation of characters.

To keep playing the game, to preserve their illusory identity, characters must continuously fold in upon themselves to engender a new persona that externalizes their inner fragmentation and thereby restores their identity. But this new self will now internalize scission, generating the need for a new duplication, and so on. This is the case with Aricia, another of Phaedra's personae, who, like Phaedra, loves in Hippolytus the idealized image of his father, Theseus. As she confesses,

> I find in him far nobler gifts than these—
> His father's strengths, without his frailties.
> I love, I own, a heart that's never bowed
> Beneath Love's yoke, but stayed aloof and proud.
>
> Racine, *Phaedra*, Act II, Scene 1

In other words, she loves the one who cannot love her. The burgeoning passion in Hippolytus's soul, which enables him to return Aricia's love, also makes that love impossible, because it debases the idealized image of him, making him share his father's "frailties." Thus, instead of elevating him, love throws him back to the world. This experience of abjection results, in turn, in a new duplication.

This new scission is the opposite of the former. Whereas Aricia incarnates the idealized image of Phaedra, Oenone, her maid, represents her material body. In the same way that Exton is blamed by Bolingbroke for his own misdeeds, and Mowbray by Richard II, Oenone is accused by Phaedra of lying and unloosing the tragedy, and is finally driven to death. In fact, Oenone's only sin was to counsel Phaedra to disclose her love for Hippolytus, thus freeing her repressed feelings. Ultimately, Oenone allows Phaedra to objectify the dark side that inhabits her, thus giving a positive presence to and controlling that spectral aspect of herself. The price for this is the self's alienation, which can no longer recognize itself in the game of its own outward manifestations.

Thus, paradoxically, the subjects can gain an (illusory) identity and overcome inner fragmentation only by dissolving themselves in the inarticulate sequence of the roles they eventually perform. The subjects are all the characters in which they become incarnated, and none of them, at the same time. They create all of them, remaining always an ungraspable, spectral, nonpresent presence, inhabiting a transcendental realm that does not lend itself to representation, to conceptualization, and that can only be alluded to allegorically.

Yet the attempt to avoid the self's alienation has even worse consequences. The desire to preserve the integrity of the inner self, which is inhabited by infinitely opposite impulses, and the inability to expel contradiction from it, inevitably leads to madness. Its best literary expression is one of Cervantes's Exemplary Novels, "The Lawyer of Glass" (El licenciado Vidriera). Its protagonist is a talented student who develops an obsessive desire to avoid being contaminated by the world and ends up cutting off all ties with it. Believing that he is made entirely of glass, he allows no one to touch him, because he thinks that (like Richard II and his mirror) he would break into pieces. Freed of the weight of his material body, he becomes absolutely sharp. He knows everything about everything; however, although he is always asked for advice, nobody can understand him. Only a mediating figure (a character who serves as a translator) can reestablish communication between the inner self and the external world and thus avoid madness, at the price of splitting the subject (introducing incongruence with itself), alienating it (creating the self's misrecognition of itself in its own realizations). Yet this is no longer possible here, because, in his obsessive desire to preserve the integrity of his self, the *licenciado* refuses to expel contradiction (he is the only hero in Cervantes's novels who does not appear as part of a pair, the only one in whom the figure of the hero's alter ego is absent). As a result, he becomes a disjointed person, with his mind and his body living separate, autonomous lives.[59] And this also has a political expression. *Punishment Without Revenge*, by Lope de Vega, shows this homology, the analogous mode in which the fold logic displays on both planes, the private and the public.

THE OIKONOMIA OF PASSION AND THE ART OF GOVERNMENT

Punishment Without Revenge is the only piece by Lope de Vega that we know he labeled "tragedy." In the declining Spain, after the loss of her European colonies, the tragic sense dissolved and turned into tragic-comedy.[60] As we saw in chapter 1, this phenomenon is closely tied to the intensification of the problem of representation. In the plays, the proliferation of mutual misunderstandings, the break of communication among the characters due to the lack of a common language, prevents the development of truly tragic situations. As a result, the tragic genre folds upon itself to find in its core its opposite, the comic element that inhabits it. What it says to us is that the true tragedy behind tragedies is the radical lack of true tragedy. Tragic parody reproduces the living experience of a worldly existence, which has become merely a theater of shadows and masks, "a tale / Told by an idiot . . . / Signifying nothing" (*Macbeth*, act V, scene 5). Thus, tragedy is revealed as the opposite genre to comedy but at the same time contains it—just as (public) punishment is the opposite of (private) revenge but contains the latter within it, as the ironic title of Lope's play informs us.

This explains the impulse, intrinsic to the culture of the baroque (as we observed in El Greco's *Burial of the Count of Orgaz* in figure 1.1), for the sharp demarcation of the boundaries between the high and the low, the internal and the external, the superior and the inferior, the transcendental and the mundane, the natural and the conventional, the public and the private, and so on. It is an impulse that becomes increasingly obsessive (producing the mannerist proliferation of figures) as it is confronted with the evidence of the radical impossibility of unmaking the inextricable mixture of the opposites. Even so, it is also true that distinguishing the two is not dispensable if we intend to live a life in common, which leads us back to the symbolical nature of power. As Lope's work also shows, that distinction, which is materially unfeasible, can be, and must be, established on a symbolic level.[61]

The literary works of the times reproduced, on the level of the narrative forms, the kind of logic at work in the state power, which was then emerging in the West. Lope's *Punishment Without Revenge* illustrates it.

The first thing that Lope presents to us is the dark side of the public figure of the duke of Ferrara, who displays his private vices in the outer world, while in the interior of the palace he behaves with decorum, as the public official he is. The play begins with a scene in which the duke, covered by a black cloak, wanders at night through the streets, in search of illicit adventures. The only other scene that takes place outside the palace occurs when the duke's son, Count Federico, meets by chance the young woman who, unknown to him, is his father's fiancée, Cassandra. The two immediately fall in love.

As soon as Cassandra reaches the duke's palace, she and Federico realize that their love is impossible and agree to avoid contact. At that moment, the count becomes a kind of zombie,[62] an unanimated being, thrice alienated: from God, from his beloved, and from his own self (*Punishment*, act II, 1917). Yet the duke continues his adventures, while refusing to have relations with Cassandra. Actually, the marriage has been forced upon the duke by the court. His wedding is a state affair—he needs a legal successor because Federico was born out of wedlock. Federico aspires to succeed the duke, and the duke supports his son's pretensions. One possible reason for the duke not having relations with Cassandra is to avoid a pregnancy and the birth of a legitimate heir. In any event, the duke's refusal to have relations with his wife will bring catastrophe to the palace.

The turning point of the play comes when the duke leaves on a military campaign in support of the Papacy. The long-expected romance between Cassandra and Federico can finally be consummated, and their relationship soon becomes public at the court when Aurora, Federico's fiancée, sees the couple together through their reflection in the bedroom mirrors. Looking glasses thus serve to communicate both realms: they replicate actions, making public what is intended to remain private (ultimately, as we have seen, love relations are official concerns in the court).

It is clear to everyone in the court that Cassandra and Federico were made for each other, that their love was fated to be consummated because it was responding to a force superior to any human norm: the law of nature. As Lucrecia (Cassandra's maid) tells her, "By nature's law and all that's fair, / There is not a scrap of doubt you and / The Count would make a better pair" (*Punishment*, act II, 1098). Conflict emerges, however, when the duke returns to Ferrara and is seen as a kind of saint-hero because of his services to the pope. His rehabilitation introduces a sudden twist in the plot (peripeteia). It is only at this moment that we become aware of the perverse situation generated by the romance between Cassandra and Federico. No matter how intense their mutual feeling, or how irregular has been the duke's former life and his relation with Cassandra, Federico has dishonored "the bed and the house"—he not only possessed the material body of the duke's wife but also, in so doing, prevented the possibility of the duke having a legitimate successor.

The disturbing event results from the introduction to the court (the realm of law, of the symbolic, in Lacanian terms) of an outer factor:

Cassandra's arrival. She cannot imagine a world without love; that is, she confuses her imagination with reality, and, in this fashion, she internalizes contradiction. After the rehabilitation of the duke, she becomes unable to distinguish between him and the count. For her, Federico is "like a portrait" of his father (*Punishment*, act III, 2655).[63] Her mind is the stage where the "confused truths" that produce thoughts compete (act II, 1545). She is driven by the "clear confusions" of the imagination, which, "more than telling me arguments, have left me thoughts" (act II, 1545). That is, her whole being is an oxymoron (the confused clarity of the truths anterior to any thought). Yet the disorder is not merely in her mind; it is in the very logic of history. As one critic said, "Father [law] and son [love] are linked by the fatal symmetry of repetition."[64] It actually is its propelling force, that which separates history from nature.

Cassandra knows that social norms have no rational foundation, that they are arbitrary and indeed perverse insofar as they necessarily stand in opposition to natural law: "Alas honor, fierce enemy . . . your inventor was not a lawyer, but a barbarian legislator" (act III, 2809). Otherwise, they simply would not be necessary. She is convinced that "if it's love, then it's not treason" (act III, 1840). Yet her character also shows that if love is separated from honor, if imagination is detached of its material body and becomes ethereal—"a spirit without a body" (act I, 969)—it turns into a mere justification, a mask to hide (like the duke's black cloak) and excuse all kinds of licenses. In the end, the couple's romance has created chaos in the court and confusion of roles, and, as a result, public punishment is called for. The duke's elimination of the young couple is not personal revenge but an official act of justice. He says:

> The justice I now seek comes not
> From any sense of private hurt
> But from God's love. For this is His
> Revenge, not mine, and I am but
> The instrument of punishment divine.
> I act not as a husband wronged,
> But as a father called upon to thus
> Avenge a hideous sin and so demand
> A punishment without revenge.

It is in any case what each
Of us by honor's law is clearly told.

Punishment, act III, 2843

However, to distinguish itself from private violence, legitimate violence must assume a ritualized form. It can only take place on a public stage—honor is, by definition, a public matter. As Lope says in *Los comendadores de Córdoba* (act XI): "Honor is a thing that resides in the other. No man is honorable by himself, since the honor of man is received by him from the other."[65]

Here we find one of the classic topics of seventeenth-century dramaturgy. Just as baroque painting sought to incorporate its own métier within the picture, to represent representation itself (thus revealing it as such and breaking the representative effect), theatrical pieces often included a play within the play. We have already seen how Hamlet tried to make his stepfather confess his crime during the presentation, within the court, of the play that Hamlet himself had written (the "mousetrap"). Thus, the protagonist also becomes an author, thereby placing himself simultaneously inside and outside the play.[66]

Hamlet's position is closely related to the role of the chorus in classical tragedies: "You are as good as a chorus," Ophelia tells him (*Hamlet*, act III, scene 2).[67] Yet, unlike the classical chorus, Hamlet's point of view is not necessarily reliable. He does not have a perspective on the totality of events, no possibility to grasp the meaning of it. (As we have seen, he could eventually know whether Claudius was or was not guilty of his father's murder, but he was radically unable to understand the role his mother had performed in this event.) This is the result of the disappearance of the chorus and the internalization by the system of representation of the figure of the public (the spectator, the people).[68] At this point, this figure also reveals its ambiguous, inherent duality. It too becomes cleaved.

Punishment Without Revenge reveals the logic operating behind this process of the folding of the people (the community). Theatricality occupies a central place in the play; it undoes a seemingly unsolvable dilemma. The duke cannot kill his own son. Federico is, in fact, the only person for whom the duke shows a deep feeling. Killing Federico would amount to killing himself. Yet he must do so to save his house and restore order (honor). Failure to do so would annihilate him, if not physically then, indeed, symbolically: "If he takes me out the honor today, tomorrow he will take me out my life" (*Punishment*, act III, 2890). The duke then plots a farce. Replicating the initial scene, he uses a cloak to hide the body of Cassandra, whom he has tied and muzzled, and then calls for his son, telling him that he has captured an enemy who has broken into the palace. Federico, as a good son, stabs the covered body, and as soon as he does, the duke shouts for the members of the court to arrest his son for killing Cassandra. He explains that Federico has done this because he wanted to prevent the birth of an inheritor to the title. Thus, "Federico is punished for a crime he did not commit in revenge for a crime he did."[69]

The farcical scene serves a fundamental function in the economy of power. Through it, the sovereign's innocence is saved, and the guilt for the misdeeds of power is transferred to its mediators (courtiers and lackeys).[70] The point in *Punishment Without Revenge* is that the courtiers know that the duke's action was only a farce, yet they participated in it. Indeed, they perform a role in it, and they could not do otherwise, in order to keep the action going and to restore order in the house. As witnesses, they are necessary participants to make punishment legitimate, thus turning private revenge into public justice.

This is another common topic in seventeenth-century tragedies. The people (the public), who are represented in the plays as various characters,[71] always perform a twofold role. They embody contradictory demands—love's desire and honor's duty. Ultimately, this shows that the contradiction is not in the actors but in the world. And we, the spectators, do not escape it.[72] This is the point where the system of representation directs our eye (like El Greco's son) to that which lies outside of its framework, the communicating point between the interior and the exterior of the proscenium. The duke is certainly treacherous, perverse. He permanently blames himself and cannot forgive himself for the death of his son. Yet Lope here makes us experience our own perversity as spectators. We, the courtiers and the lackeys (the spectators), participate in the game of hypocrisy. We fervently desire the consummation of Cassandra and Federico's love, and then later, after the return of the duke and his rehabilitation, we accept, and even demand, their punishment.[73] In the end, we share with the duke the responsibility.

This expresses on an aesthetic level the disturbing emergence, during the seventeenth century (along with absolutism), of a new, broader, and seemingly paradoxical phenomenon: the violence exerted by a central power is different tout court from that produced by landlords and feudal noblemen, whose violence is then reduced to merely personal revenge. The courtiers and lackeys in Lope's play behave as Hobbesian subjects (Hobbes's use of the theater as the model for politics is well known).[74] They are aware that the artificial persona of the Leviathan is only an artifice, that the sovereign is not really a sovereign, and that his opinion is only a private opinion (as a matter of fact, even after his "rehabilitation," the duke continues to have his illicit adventures).[75] But they are also aware that they must obliterate this fact and accept his opinion *as if it were a truth*—the expression of general will, the incarnation of those transcendent values that make collective life possible.[76]

In any case, this conventional solution is inevitably precarious. Ultimately, it hides a perverse core, insofar as it works merely as a mechanism to render legitimate the crimes of a private subject, once he is turned into a public authority. And it is here that the theatrical metaphor reveals its deepest meaning. Theatrical representation was, by the seventeenth century, a wholly secular event, pure entertainment, which had relinquished the kind of ritual efficacy of the sacred drama. In theatrical representation, there was transposition without transubstantiation.[77] In the theater, unlike in the Mass, the mystical body is not present in its image; the vicarious relation between the two is a pure artifice. The performer enacts the authority of the king, but he cannot ratify it. It is a game of "as ifs," which everybody knows to be so, and therefore no one can take it as real.

We find here the truly troublesome aspect of conventional vicariousness expressed in theatrical representation: it was not clear who or what the actor was supposed to represent.[78] For the representative illusion to be produced, performance must create not only the illusory characters on the stage but also that transcendental reality that lies beyond it. Performance thus has a double dimension. Whereas *Richard II* reveals the symbolic (artificial, conventional) nature of the figure of the sovereign—only an illusory device can convert a common man into a king, a sacred figure—*Punishment Without Revenge* leads us one step further. It reveals that the same thing happens with the principle that authority supposedly incarnates: only in the symbolic realm, through an illusory device, is the justice effect produced, that is, can personal revenge be converted into official punishment.[79] The production of justice, then, is a play displayed entirely on the surface of the system of representation (artifice). In sum, if subjective identity can be achieved only through the identification with a principle, that principle is not a given; it must be established and defined, which sends us back to the symbolic level, the artifice.[80]

It is here that the system of representation reveals its true meaning. It must generate the illusion of transcendence out of immanence, of values out of matter, of nature out of artifice; in short, it must create its Other (that which founds representation, being itself unrepresentable). It is the mechanism for distinguishing what had become indistinguishable: an act of justice and a crime, punishment and revenge. And for this illusory justice effect to be effective (for the audience to really accept an act of revenge, a crime, as a deserved punishment, an act of justice), oblivion must be reduplicated. Courtiers not only must obliterate the true nature of the duke's action (a heinous crime, a filicide) but also must forget the very act of oblivion. Nietzsche's idea of the contradiction between knowledge and action must be interpreted as referring to a second-degree symbolic reality—the need to ignore ignorance. And here we find the rationale behind the duplication mechanism of representation (the representation of representation itself) in Lope's play. It reveals the hidden logic at work in the game of conventional rituality, of artificial vicariousness.

For the reduplication of oblivion to take effect, it is necessary to partition the symbolic field, to make an incision in the secular realm of conventional rituality (representation) separating the spheres of being and praxis. Here, again, we encounter that problem that runs through the whole age of representation: the problem of expression. Like truth, like love, power (the realm of unity) cannot be realized in the world without dissolving itself, without becoming involved in the play of contradictions that is life, that is, without throwing itself into society and fusing with the realm of pure diversity, opposition. In short, it must turn into its contrary, transforming from the principle that provides unity to society (as we know, only political power can make the community one) into the origin of discord and chaos.[81]

Here is where the resort to theatricality (artifice, convention) becomes functional. The true goal of the farce plotted by the duke is to detach his public persona from its own actions, to distinguish the authority he enjoys from its eventual realizations. He condemns crimes but he himself does not inflict punishment. Instead, he moves his subjects to do so, like a playwright with actors. State authority (as it will finally emerge out of the Wars of Religion) can thus take on the appearance of a merely formal entity placed above dissent; it can be free of finding itself trapped in the midst of contradiction. But this "innocence" is achieved at the price of discharging the state's guilty conscience onto the very subjects (the audience, the courtiers) who now assume the responsibility for mundane conflicts, for social dissension. From the seventeenth century on, as we saw in chapter 1, in connection with the issue of tyrannicide, the subject will have to carry with himself the weight of his guilty conscience, which will lead, in turn, to an internal scission.[82] The subject will inevitably become torn by contradictory demands, cleaved by his dual nature as a moral subject (a Christian) and a legal subject (a citizen).

In any case, for this second-degree oblivion mechanism to work, it was first necessary that state authority itself split and that the spheres of sovereignty and government became clearly distinct from each other. Ultimately, the scission between these two entities provided the basic matrix for the whole series of dualistic oppositions that, at that moment, became established (and which El Greco's painting depicts). Thus, we finally get to the point where all the preceding considerations converge: the true nucleus that underlies the entire baroque universe. Just as the subject of the age of representation was merely the mediating agent between two voids—between justice (ghost) and norm (mask)—the political field was the gap opened through the play of opposition and inseparability between sovereignty and government. This marked the emergence of a new regime of the exercise of power, which oscillated between the margins of justice and *oikonomia*. As we will see in the next chapter, the consequences of this scission, which occurred in the very heart of political power, would be both unexpected and disturbing.

3

THE DISCOURSE OF EMANCIPATION AND THE EMERGENCE OF DEMOCRACY AS A PROBLEM

The Latin American Case

Absolute monarchy, commonly and rightly credited with having prepared the rise of the nation-state, has been responsible, by the same token, for the rise of the secular realm with a dignity and a splendor of its own. The short-lived, tumultuous story of the Italian city-states, whose affinity with the later story of the revolutions consists in a common harkening back to antiquity, to the ancient glory of the political realm, might have forwarded and could have foretold what the chances and what the perplexities would be that lay in store for the modern age in the realm of politics, except, of course, that there exists no such foretelling and forewarnings in history. Moreover, it was precisely the use of absolutism which for centuries clouded these perplexities because it seemed to have found, within the political realm itself, a fully satisfactory substitute for the lost religious sanction of secular authority in the person of the king or rather the institution of kingship. But this solution, which the revolutionaries soon enough were to unmask as a pseudo-solution, served only to hide, for some centuries, the most elementary predicament of all modern political bodies, their profound instability, the result of some elementary lack of authority.

—HANNAH ARENDT, *ON REVOLUTION*

In *The Origin of German Tragic Drama*, Walter Benjamin elaborates on the ways that baroque tragedies enacted a paradox that was contained in the concept of the modern sovereign. It is a very different one from that observed by Carl Schmitt in connection to Hobbes's concept of the sovereign as "he who decides on the [state of] exception."[1] According to Schmitt, in a conventional universe, only the decision of the sovereign can provide a foundation for a normative system on which communal life could rest. The paradox here is that, for a regular legal order to be established, there must be someone outside that order, someone who is placed beyond its norms. The person who establishes that order should be in the position of changing it, which is the very definition of sovereignty. To put it in another way, to put an end to violence, it is necessary to have one who can exercise violence with no limitations. Otherwise, we will not escape the state of nature. Yet, in this fashion, the sovereign instance would remain a vestige of that state of nature in the heart of the political community—"the beast," in Benjamin's words, the ever-present trace of the conventional nature of its institutive act, tainting that very order with an undeletable seal of arbitrariness.[2] Benjamin, in turn, underlined what he considered a second and more important paradox resulting from the first, which the baroque tragedies exposed:

> The antithesis between the power of the ruler and his capacity to rule led to a feature peculiar to the *Trauerspiel* [tragic drama] which is, however, a generic feature and which can be illuminated only against the background of the theory of sovereignty. This is the indecisiveness of the tyrant. The prince, who is responsible for making the decision to proclaim the state of emergency, reveals, at the first opportunity, that he is almost incapable of making a decision . . .[3]
>
> The sublime status of the Emperor, on the one hand, and the infamous futility on the other, create a fundamental uncertainty as to whether this is a drama of tyranny or a history of martyrdom.[4]

The tragic fate of the sovereign, determined by his dual nature (at once sacred and profane), is expressed in the fact that this renders absolute decisiveness necessary but impossible. This is the ghost that haunts him: the insurmountable disproportion between his human finite condition and the task he must perform. This is the crucial difference between indecision and undecidability. The latter is related not to the presence of contradictory values that are, at the same time, necessary (the tragic dilemma), which demands a decision, but also, and more fundamentally, to the dissolution of the very subject who must decide.[5] Yet it makes manifest more than just a subjective frailty in the person who occupies the position of sovereign. As Hannah Arendt remarks, this unstable mixture of absolute power and extreme weakness (the two being the same thing)[6] expresses a structural condition of the political field: its constitutive incongruence, resulting from the overlapping of transcendence and immanence in an enclosed realm, which is, by definition, at once finite and infinite (that is, framed but endlessly divisible, a mannerist realm).[7] This is the core dilemma that underlies the entire culture of the baroque: how to reestablish the relation between law and justice, legality and legitimacy, once the link between the two terms (the finite and the infinite) has been broken. This leads us back to El Greco's *Burial of the Count of Orgaz* (figure 1.1) and, more specifically, to a fundamental feature of its design, which is expressive of the new spatial sense of the baroque: the artificial generation of the sense of depth that transcends the flatness of the two-dimensional plane of representation.

In fact, the dichotomous universe that El Greco's picture portrays is not really so. The figure of the mediator introduces an anomaly. His presence breaks through the two-dimensional surface, framing the spheres of the sacred and the profane by a three-dimensional space, within which they become inner circumvolutions of it. In this invagination process, intertwining finiteness and infiniteness, there is no ultimate ground. This results in the feeling of the "profound instability" that Arendt observes was characteristic of the absolutist monarchical system. The groundless space produces a perpetual movement of folding and unfolding at different, successive levels, which is expressed in the replication of the three-dimensional design in the interior of the central motif, framed by the triangle delineated by the figures of God, in the upper vertex, and the priest and the boy at its base. The dynamic of the scene is defined by the function of the two vectors indicated by the sight lines of the characters (see figure 3.1).

The sense of enclosure of the space is emphasized by the downward-turning heads of the characters outside the central triangle in which the scene takes place (the witnesses), all of whom are looking at that cen-

FIGURE 3.1 Vector diagram for El Greco's *The Burial of the Count of Orgaz*.

tral triangle, focusing our attention on it. Yet, in this self-enclosed design, we find two points of exception, represented by the figures placed at the inferior vertexes of the triangle—those of the mediators (the priest and the boy), who are looking at what lies beyond that central frame. However, the two look in opposite directions. The sight of the priest indicates the presence of an ascendant vector, which expresses the will for transcendence inscribed at the center of the profane sphere. Yet the eyes of the boy, which are directed not only beyond the frame within the picture but beyond the picture itself, reveal this effect of transcendence as such, an effect generated at the interior of the system of representation, a figurative device, the illusory nature of which is emphasized by the plastic effect produced by the artificial light emanating from the torches carried by the cortege.

Here we find expressed the crucial, and eminently political, point: how to produce an effect of transcendence out of immanence. This is the key issue for an archaeological approach to the political. The different regimes of exercise of power are, essentially, specific modes of production of transcendence effect out of immanence, diverse mechanisms for the artificial generation of a sense of meaning in a secular world, a justice effect on which communal life could rest, once it had become deprived of its natural foundations.

Despite the very different forms they take in the context of the diverse regimes of exercise of power, there is one common aspect shared by all the different mechanisms for the generation of justice effect. This leads us back to El Greco's painting, and a particular detail of it: the proliferation of characters who are placed outside the central triangle in which the main scene takes place and who observe it—the witnesses. In order for the mechanism that produces the justice effect to work, the intervention of the witnesses is always necessary. They are constitutive factors of the political field, structural elements in it. In a world in which justice has become radically absent, they must participate in creating the illusion of a sense of meaning out of appearance, of a sense of legitimacy out of legality. In the specific case of the baroque political machine, the intervention of the witnesses is the condition for the operation of a new scission by means of which political power can expel contradiction. *Punishment Without Revenge* illustrates the working of the mechanism of production of the effect of transcendence out of immanence in the age of representation, as well as the role of the witnesses in setting this mechanism in motion.

As we saw in chapter 2, the replication of the folding procedure gives rise to a new scission. The subjective split, expressed in the figure of the king's two bodies, then becomes externalized and turns into an objective split in the political realm. Only this division of the political field allows the sovereign's simultaneous necessity and impossibility of acting, remarked on by Benjamin—the fact that the sovereign must act but cannot act, cannot make justice effective in the world without being immersed in the midst of contradiction, that is, without turning from the expression of the unity of the community into an object of dissent—to be projected, respectively, into two different planes: being and praxis, sovereignty and oikonomia. The sovereign no longer acts, but, as an author, he moves people to act. Here again we can see the operation of the folding logic characteristic of the baroque. For the mechanism of production of the transcendence effect out of immanence to become effective, the foundation of power must cut ties with the practice of it; that is, the king must turn into a *rex inutilis*, which is the defining feature of the regime of exercise of power in the classical period, one articulated by tension between the two margins of sovereignty and government, justice and oikonomia.[8]

We can now finally understand the meaning of the expression "the theological became political." This does not suggest that the monarch became identified with God; rather, it is the other way around. It is God (the *Deus absconditus*) who became identified with the absolutist monarch, a monarch who had removed himself from worldly politics and become, as Baltasar Gracián stated, a "hidden majesty":

> For to see him [the king] is to be affected by his own will, and he will never want to, since the sole being of this prince is to be unknown; the way his ministers take to give a view and prospect of him is to blind you first. Consider but awhile how blind you are . . .
> Andrenio turned his eyes, and looked toward the palace, to see if he could espy any glimpse or appearance of the hidden majesty, but he perceived that it was all in vain, for the windows were shut, the lattices obstructed, and the glass so thick as no sight could penetrate it.[9]

The scission between sovereignty and government indicated the fundamental difference between the political processes in the British Isles and on the Continent. As Ernst Kantorowicz wrote, the metaphor of the king's two bodies is fully applicable only to the specific case of seventeenth-century Britain. The solution tried on the Continent was very different. This is illustrated by the usual translation of the ancient Latin motto *Dignitas non moritur* (The investiture never dies) into French as *Le roi ne meurt jamais* (The king never dies).[10] The figure of the king was identified with the *dignitas*, with his sacred body, his investiture. But this is the other side of the drastic separation that had been established between *dignitas* and *officium* (justice and role, being and praxis). The mystical and the material bodies of authority would eventually become incarnate in two different instances of power.

We can see the old theological issue of the Trinitarian mystery (the presence of a third term mediating between the other two and reestablishing its unity) resurfacing, but this time located in the new secular, realm. The identification of the figure of the king with God would cause the issue to be reformulated in political terms. The question of how God inscribed His will in the world would now be reframed as how a *king*, placed above and outside his realm, makes his will manifest in *society*, how he regulates the latter from within it. It is here that the issue of government emerges. At this juncture, the quintessentially political problem shifts: it is no longer a matter of justice but of oikonomia (the right disposition of things).[11] The traumatic core of politics thus moves from the orbit of primary causes to the orbit of secondary causes (mediation).

Sovereignty and government are based on two different logics. Sovereignty, like parental authority, belongs to the realm of nature. Its function is to produce justice. Government belongs to the realm of artifice. It puts into action a kind of practical (rational) knowledge. Thus, the two represent two different forms of the arcane—the knowledge of which is supposed to confer preeminence upon its possessor. The sovereign displays a kind of knowledge of an ecstatic nature—insight into the mind of God, the superior vision that allows him to disclose the secret design of Creation. Ministers, by contrast, possess a technical knowledge, which is not given but, rather, acquired. Finally, the sovereignty and the government have two different objects as their respective focuses. The object of sovereignty is the people; it refers to the mystical communion between the people and its natural lord, which constitutes the community. The government, by contrast, has the population as its target (this was the time in which censuses and statistical records began to be systematically carried out).[12] While sovereignty is in charge of preserving the natural order that makes communal life possible, government is focused on the daily needs of the subjects, their material well-being.[13] Thus, the split between sovereignty and government would be closely associated with a crucial shift in the regimes of exercise of power and the dramatic expansion of the functions of public authority, which resulted in the development in the West of what Michel Foucault labeled "biopolitics."[14]

Sovereignty and government were thus born together, and they refer back to each other. Only the absolutization of royal authority opened up the field for the emergence of government—the administration of political power, the modes of exercising authority and making it effective and present in society—as something different from sovereignty—the foundation of authority, the source of its legitimacy, the transcendent values it incarnates. As we have said, this is associated with the affirmation of centralized, national states and the development of bureaucratic apparatuses,[15] which, in turn, resulted in a radical shift in the Western mind with regard to the ways of thinking about politics.

Political theory would then reproduce the cosmic split depicted by El Greco. The old tradition of the "mirror of princes," designed for the education of future kings, is replaced by a political literature that moves in two different directions. On the one hand is a political philosophy concerned with the elaboration of a *theory of sovereignty* and dealing with the issue of the foundations of power, its limits, and so on. On the other hand is an *art of government* concerned with the practical problems resulting from the actual exercise of power, its praxis.[16] The members of the diplomatic service (the first group, along with the military, that underwent a process of professionalization) were generally the ones who wrote the treatises, which were destined for ministers and governors and were aimed at teaching them the right way to administer the state.[17]

While the art of government took as its premise Machiavelli's idea of the reason of state,[18] it redefined this ideal.[19] Vicente Montano's *Arcano de principes* is a good example: following Machiavelli's teachings, he even encourages the artificial prolongation of wars as a means of preventing overpopulation.[20] However, we can also see in Montano's proposal the traces of the changes in the context of production of these texts vis-à-vis its Machiavellian model.

The art of government was supposed to be a kind of knowledge at once theoretical and practical.[21] Medical practice would provide the model for it, which leads us back to Montano. His proposals for the expulsion (or actual annihilation) of part of the population when it grows excessively replicates, in the field of politics, the fundamental medical technique of the times—bleeding—by means of which the body is supposed to get rid of poisonous humors. However, the crucial aspect in Montano's "Malthusianism" is not this but his definition of the humor causing social diseases: it is a man with no attribute, an abstract being. What matters to Montano is no longer the moral qualities of the subjects (their republican virtues), as in the Renaissance political tradition, but merely their number. Thus, the people become exclusively identified with their role as consumers of goods. Should their number grow excessively, in an economy always on the edge of self-sufficiency, the effect would be to push prices up, generating inflation, starvation, and, finally, the financial ruin of the kingdom.

Although Montano was aware of the unethical premises of his proposal, the problems that it raised for him were not moral but, rather, strictly political. Given the controversial nature of the principles discussed, it did not seem wise to make the material public, and Montano decided not to publish the book. Its very title—*Arcano de príncipes* (Princes' Arcane)—illustrates the problem. In fact, the widespread dissemination of treatises on the art of government coincided with the growing number of books dealing with the issue of the *arcana imperii* (mysteries of the state).[22] But, in the following century, when the Spanish empire was already in sharp decline and the monarchical system had begun to face challenges on many fronts, this genre of books would fall into disrepute. As Fray Luis de León pointed out, their detailed knowledge about the secrets of government made their possessors much more dangerous than Machiavelli and his followers, the much-decried "politicians."[23]

Even so, because the intended reader of these books was not the king but a segment of society—public officials and those aspiring to be so—the books had to be made public if they were to achieve their goal. In any case, their authors could not help feeling that they were entering dangerous territory, that they were disclosing hidden, sacred things. They could say, after Virgil, "Acheronta movebo."[24] The truth is that, in the following century, the specters that haunted baroque thinking would prove dramatically real. The contradictions raised by the new art of government—or, more precisely, the folding of the political realm that produced its scission—would become manifest, although it was in the Spanish colonies that their final consequences would be felt.

It was not a coincidence that the revolutionary movements that spread throughout the ultramarine possessions of Spain in the second half of the eighteenth century, although very different from one another, all raised a common battle cry: "Long life to the king; death to the bad government." Historians have interpreted this expression as characteristic of the traditionalist mental makeup of the lower classes of the period.[25] Yet what we have seen so far alerts us to what is wrong with this view: it dehistoricizes concepts, thus missing the fact that this battle cry actually was not that old. It was uttered for the first time in the seventeenth century (in the period we designated as *Schwellenzeit*), during the rebellions in of Catalonia and Portugal (1649), Naples and Palermo (1647–1648), and Andalucía (1650–1651).[26] Ultimately, it was an expression of the secularization process, and the tragic dramas of the time are revealing in this regard. As Benjamin asserts, "It is quite appropriate to the secularization of passion plays in the baroque drama that the official should take the place of the evil."[27] In the end, the battle cry doesn't tell us about the people's supposed reliance on traditional motifs but rather about the changes operating in the conditions of the visibility of objects. Only the set of oppositions established by absolute monarchs could make the government visible to the subjects (including the popular sectors) as a distinct sphere of reality, placed between sovereignty and society and serving as the mediating instance between the two.[28]

The separation of the two spheres of being and praxis, of primary and secondary causes, was aimed at protecting the newly emerged states from the vicissitudes of actual political practice, placing them in a position of transcendence, externality, vis-à-vis the contradictions that tear society apart. Yet, as in the Trinitarian mystery, scission always demanded the intervention of a mediating instance, an agent communicating between two realms, the heaven of sovereignty and the earth of society: governmental action. And, once again, it is the latter that becomes problematic, thus triggering the folding logic, which now would operate on a new terrain: the oikonomia of power (the realm of artifice).

As we will see, the political categories at stake would then fold in upon themselves to find, in their interior, their opposite, thereby setting in motion the reduplication mechanism that was destined to expel contradiction from within, generating a new opposition that, in turn, demanded the action of a mediating agent, and so on. In the same way that the emergence of sovereignty gave birth to that concept, which at once institutes and dislocates it (the social pact), the cognate concept of government also would fold in to find, inside, its condition of possibility-impossibility: "public opinion," or the *law of public consent*. Here we find the paradox that underlies the art of government, and which Montano's text explains: the very principle on which government rested (public opinion) would end up undermining it.[29] But, for this to happen, the categories at stake must first undergo a series of meaningful reconfigurations. It would eventually pave the way to what Reinhart Koselleck labeled

Sattlezeit, the pivotal period in which all social and political concepts became redefined. This is the origin of the so-called age of democratic revolutions, which brings the tragic scene to its close. Though tragedy would not disappear, it would be displaced into a realm of shadows, surviving only as a spectral, mute un-presence in public discourse.

JOAQUÍN DE FINESTRAD AND THE PATHOGENESIS OF MODERN POLITICS

The year 1780 was of great importance in the Spanish colonies. It was a year marked by unprecedented agitations in an empire that had remained amazingly stable for three centuries. The events in the Kingdom of New Granada are illustrative.[30] It witnessed a major uprising under the motto "Long life to the king; death to the bad government." The so-called *comunero* rebellion put the capital under siege, and it only ended because of the intervention of the local archbishop, who signed a peace agreement with the rebels. Once disarmed, the rebels were decimated. Not long afterward, a royal entourage (*visita real*) was sent to the region, with the object of pacification. Joaquín de Finestrad, a Capuchin friar who was a member of the group, wrote an essay, "*El vasallo instruido*" (The Educated Vassal), describing the lessons he drew from this experience. Although it is clearly a defense of the monarchy, his book enables us to observe the series of fundamental changes in the conceptions of power and society that were produced during the eighteenth century. It also shows how, in their attempt to secure power, absolute monarchies ended up opening the doors to revolution.

Unlike the traditional procedure in the history of ideas, our search is not for the alleged precursors of the ideal of independence, which necessarily entails a retrospective, anachronistic projection. Indeed, nothing is further from that than the writings of Finestrad. He was persuaded that the *comunero* revolt had disrupted "all good order" in the region: "Limbs have transmuted to a head; subjects into rulers; faithful to partisan."[31] This destruction had darkened the eternal norms of justice that ruled their community, the principles of natural subordination upon which every society is founded, making it impossible for the subjects to discern them.³² This is the ruinous consequence, according to Finestrad, of the population's "pretension of taking the right of war." The insurrection reveals, to him, that the people have lost sight of the fact that the monarch, as the living expression of the mystic body of the republic, constitutes the condition of possibility of the community and that, without him, it will crumble down. "If the body of political society loses its being, the nation is destroyed; despite the continued existence of those by whom it is made up, it can no longer survive."³³

The subjects are not the ones who are entitled to judge whether the monarch has strayed from his mission. "Private men," he says, "do not enjoy public authority; they have a sovereign who may form their claims and represent their oppressions."³⁴ In that case, the vassal would be constituting himself as simultaneously an involved party and the judge. "Are the vassals either elevated to the high hierarchy of absolute judges entitled to resolve the disproportion of the established norms, or do they see themselves comprehended by them? If one embraces the latter, how, then, do they dare to condemn those norms as unjust, cruel, and tyrannical? How do they sentence them with abolition?"³⁵

For there to be justice, it is necessary that there be a mediating instance placed above the contending parties, under whom the parties are subordinated. The principle of justice is associated with the preeminence of jurisdictional power; it constitutes the basis on which the idea of communal life rests. "Lacking superiority," Finestrad says, "leads to the lacking of the defense of the respective rights of men."³⁶

This concept allows Finestrad to neatly distinguish the principles that preside over these two orders: the monarchical principle, for sovereign authority; the aristocratic principle, for the government. It is not the king's personal qualities that are the basis for his preeminence and the ground on which his authority, as the incarnation of justice, rests. "The right to judge the masses," Finestrad maintains, "is not given to the most just, the best warrior, the most political, and the wisest as a reward to his deeds and virtues."³⁷ These are, however, indispensable qualities that must be present when elevating a vassal to the rank of public official. Interpreted in this manner, the monarchies of the ancien régime would be "mixed governments," in the classical sense of the term; that is, they would combine two diverse principles (the monarchical and the aristocratic) into a single system.

The Aristotelian theory would prove itself highly functional here, though only so long as the radical distinction between sovereignty and government was maintained. Only such a distinction could solve the contradiction that this theory raised between the postulate of the presence of a plurality of legitimate forms of government and the assumption of the naturalness and uniqueness of monarchical power. That contradiction actually ceased to exist from the moment that sovereignty and government referred to two different instances. Monarchical power was natural and unique, although the ways in which it could be exercised adopted different forms.

This distinction sets into motion the political-theological machine that tragedies lay bare. As Roland Barthes said, in connection with Racine's plays, the idea of an unjust God (power) is not unthinkable yet unbearable. Hence, man accepts blaming himself for evil in the world. Only this allows him to preserve the idea of the beatitude of God.[38] Similarly, the preservation of the sacred (transcendent) character of the king demanded that the subjects assume the weight of the actual practice of political power, the material *government* of the world, which then became a purely practical, worldly matter.

However—and this is the fundamental lesson of the revolt, for Finestrad—once the distinction is made between the mystic body of the king (sovereignty) and his corporal organ (government), the two cannot remain separate without undermining the foundations upon which the monarchical regime rests. From this distinction came a disturbing consequence. As we have seen, sovereignty could not be questioned without demolishing the foundations upon which the community itself was founded. But the government could be contested, as long as it accepted different forms, and, therefore, could be modified through another conventional arrangement.

This seemed to lend support to the motto "Long life to the king; death to the bad government." We thus get to the nucleus of Finestrad's text, the fundamental problem he intends to solve. Although his political concept, as we have seen, was premised on the ideal of the radical separation of the realms of sovereignty and government, he believed that it was now necessary to fuse the two again if the monarchical order wanted to survive.

Faced with the rebels' challenge, Finestrad, who was himself a public official, insisted on the necessary presence of public officials, not only as a practical matter but also as a conceptual one.[39] No political power could exist without them. Ultimately, their authority could not be challenged, because they were the living incarnations of the sovereign.

> Who can deny that the voice of the ministers is that of the sovereign? It is known that sovereignty was inherited from God Himself, who constituted the sovereign as absolute in the mortal plane. He alone cannot attend to the governing of the kingdom or the nation. He needs wise ministers who enjoy the gift of governance . . . They are the sure aqueducts and safe canals of the Government and the instruments at its service. His orders merit the same respect and veneration as those of the king because they represent the character of the sovereign himself. The images of God, despite being material paintings, are objects of patriotic cult and of the same religious devotion deserved by God Himself, just due to the respect and relationship they hold with the original. To think the contrary is to commit the grave mistake of the iconoclasts, cruel opponents of the sacred imagery.[40]

The relationship between the officials and the king is the same as the relationship between the king and God; the overlap between the archetype and its image is the same. In their role as representatives of the sovereign in society, officials share his sacred essence. It is from this mystery of vicariousness that the two take their very being. The link between them cannot be broken without destroying the two instances that it unites.

In effect, according to Finestrad, by questioning the decisions made by the colonial officials, the rebels were not questioning their authority as individuals, as *private* persons, but as *public* persons. Given that the king had given these officials their power and was the ultimate source from which their authority emanated, questioning the officials was equivalent to questioning the monarch himself. To Finestrad, making a radical distinction between the sovereign and government was "monstrous." It was tantamount to the creation of, on the one hand, a lame king, with no way of enforcing his power, and, on the other hand, a government without any authority, which no one has any obligation to obey.

Conserving the life of the king but leaving without vital breath his ministers is to make of the royal person only a vain shadow of his royal name. In monarchies, to separate the prince from command means to create a monstrous government with no head, that is to say, that the legal authority of the ministers is not real, and that their orders are not immediately originated from the public authority . . . If the government is in charge with independence of the royal persona, then there is no obligation to respect, obey, or venerate it, because it is regarded by its vassals as independent from the king, and thereby the ministers are private people, who do not represent the character of the king, and cease to act on his behalf. Under this assumption, neither the king nor the government can be obeyed; each individual lives just following their own whims, remaining free to gather together and revolt . . .

It cannot be ignored that the insult and injury brought upon the image end up addressing the prototype . . . It is not illogical, then, that to say death to the government is to say death to the king, and plotting against the former entails tyrannizing the latter. A king without ministers is the same as a body without a soul: it boasts no activity nor life, being but a cold corpse.[41]

Ultimately, according to Finestrad, if anarchy was to be avoided, it was necessary to close the distance between sovereignty and government. However, this would make the problem of vicariousness reemerge. The distinction between sovereignty and government had opened up the field for a political theology within which all subsequent attempts to fuse them would inevitably become inscribed.

In effect, the distinction between sovereignty and government gave rise to an "economy of the arcane," hitherto unknown. The type of technical knowledge that was necessary for the exercise of government, unlike that of justice, radically escaped the doxological realm; it was not publicly available, although in a way much different from the traditional arcane. Actually, the traditional concept of the arcane contained an ambiguity. On the one hand, it was assumed that only the king had an insight into the order of justice, into the design of Creation, and this provided the basis for his preeminence. On the other hand, however, implicit in the transcendent character of the eternal norms of justice was the idea of their transparency. Their a priori nature (the norms of justice are supposed to be eternally valid, simply because the opposite ones are self-contradictory) made them immediately evident, at least for those whose discerning faculties were not diminished by passions. This is why, to be a good subject (unlike being a good citizen), it was not necessary to be educated, but only morally fit. This is what is expressed by the concept of *synderesis*, the innate knowledge of the basic principles of morality.[42] The vassal must participate in the moral universe that constitutes the community of the faithful. Yet this could eventually make it feasible for the subjects to judge the justice of the titles of the monarch (whether he was a legitimate king or a tyrant), rendering the problem of tyrannicide always present—there was no means to do away with it.

In the sphere of government, this was no longer so. With its emergence, the norms that presided over communal life lost their self-evident character, given their conventional nature. Therefore, the grasping of them demanded intellectual capacities that were not engraved in the hearts of men by God but that needed to be acquired and, as a consequence, were not available to all. In this fashion, the distinction between sovereignty and government did not do away with the mystical connotations of the arcane but, rather, added to it a new, rational basis that functioned as a fundamental supplement to it. And it entailed a radical reformulation of the problem of tyrannicide.

The accusation levied by Finestrad against the commoners illustrates how this standoff had now changed. The rebels, he pointed out, claimed that the amount of taxation established by the government was unjust. But how could commoners evaluate its fairness? How did they know how much was needed to build a fleet, develop the production of a new crop, build a cathedral, and so on?[43] Here we find the dualism between sovereignty and government replicated in the realm of the arcane. The bifurcation of it paved the way for an economy of the arcane, which displayed itself between two borders. The obligation to pay taxes, which belonged to the realm of natural right (subjects could not refuse this obligation without destroying the natural order), now became a purely formal principle. But the formalism of that principle was now opposed by the materiality of its content—that is, the amount of taxes to be paid—which was not preestablished and was not determinable using moral principles of justice alone, as was traditionally thought. The latter now became exclusively a matter of government:

> The determination of natural and divine law is a privilege proper to the king. Yet the duty and the obligation of nature and religion that vassals have to feed our monarch is confusing, vague, and has no determined quantity. Neither nature nor religion make mention of the amount of the contribution ... The providence of the determination of the contribution to be imposed upon the fortunes of the subjects is an effect of the human law, as Saint Thomas teaches, and as such is reserved for our prince, by way of his wise government.[44]

As we can see, far from opposing Catholic monarchy, the Enlightenment served to reinforce the esoteric character of the exercise of power.[45] This allowed Finestrad to reframe the question of tyrannicide. He certainly rejected the principle of the legitimacy of tyrannicide. In fact, as he said, he had sworn an oath "to teach and enforce the doctrine against regicide as an indispensable circumstance to obtain the degree in the year '77."[46] Nevertheless, following the old social contract tradition, he could not unequivocally disavow the need to establish limits on royal power. Thus, immediately after writing this passage, he acknowledged that a king who was guilty of "tyrannical oppression" could be deposed:

> I agree that one may tyrannize a prince who, due to lack of legitimate titles, attempts to occupy the throne by force of arms, one who without being called by God nor chosen by the kingdom, nor by hereditary right, nor by justice of war wants to take the scepter, subordinating public authority to his personal interests, oppressing the people with taxation superior to their means, machinating against the republic and injuring majesty with his tyrannical action. In this case, he is an unjust invader of society, and usurper, and there is no doubt that in such sad circumstances the kingdom is authorized to resist him, to displace him, and even to condemn him to death with the goal of defending its innocence, interests, life and liberty, redeeming itself through the natural right resulting from his tyrannical oppression, provided there is no other means left for that to be accomplished.[47]

Finestrad resolved this contradiction by affirming the existence of a radical asymmetry between *legitimacy of origin* and *legitimacy of exercise*. Even though some of the causes he listed—"oppressing the people with taxation," "machinating against the Republic," and so on—actually refer to questions having to do with the exercise of power, Finestrad insisted that only the illegitimacy of origin was a permissible reason to dethrone a king.[48]

This is where the sharp distinction between the being and the praxis of power (between the monarchic principle and the aristocratic principle) is revealed as extremely functional to the monarchy. The legitimacy, or lack thereof, of a monarch's titles refers to the sphere of justice and thus could be evaluated clearly by vassals. On this level, as the neoscholastics could verify, the problem of tyrannicide was unsolvable. On the contrary, the exercise of sovereignty (the government) did not belong to the orbit of natural law, and, as a consequence, it could not be evaluated by subjects, inasmuch as the kind of knowledge involved was possessed only by those initiated in the art of government.

This takes us to what constitutes the nucleus of the program of reform Finestrad proposed—and which the title of his book, *The Educated Vassal*, already suggests. He stated, "The deplorable decadence suffered in splendor by this people recognizes no other origin than the lack of public schools."[49] His plan for public education was oriented toward two goals. The first goal was to disseminate the spirit of obedience among the local population. "Where ignorance reigns," he stated, "so are ignored the right of nature, religion, and politics." But he immediately switched targets: the ultimate cause of the people's revolt, he wrote, lay not so much in the turbulent spirit of the population as in the government's inexperience in controlling it. Thus, the second goal in his plan for educational reform was the "public teaching" of the art of government, its dissemination across the kingdom.

> What assurances can have the government that ignores the undeniable truths through which it is leading the people in its care? How can it implement the means of contention if it ignores the principles of conjuration? . . . How can it foment the subordination of vassals to the crown and its ministers that govern in its royal name if it lacks instruction in such specific points? . . . Public teachings administer such precious luster upon the royal ministers as upon the vassals. They are an indispensable step toward rising to a height of wisdom that is suitable to the work of their ministry, to the accurate execution of it.[50]

In Finestrad's view, the two tasks—instructing governors and educating subjects—were closely associated, and this connection had a theological-political premise. The need to instill in the population the habit of obedience brings us back to the subject of "glory"—that is to say, the third of the elements composing the Holy Trinity, which permits the linking of the other two, the Father and the Son, thereby rejoining the divine essence with its material body.[51] In the same way that the mystery of the Eucharist (the transubstantiation of the bread and wine into Christ's body and blood) demands the pronouncement of the "Amen" by the faithful (*con-sensus*), the transubstantiation of divine essence into its mundane incarnation, the king, demands the acclamation of the monarch by his people. It has the function of producing the mystical union between the sovereign and his subjects, thus constituting the republic. Without the act of confirmation, there is no authority; the king is a head without a body. The people cannot be mere spectators of a scene of which they are not part. Like the courtiers in Lope de Vega's *Punishment Without Revenge*, they are an active factor in the institution of justice.

In Christian iconography, the mystical union of the king and his subjects is expressed by the duality of the figure of the lamb (see figure 3.2). The lamb is the symbol of the people, the flock of Christ; and, at the same time, Christ is the lamb—in the Bible and in the Mass, He is said to be "the lamb of God." Ultimately, if the subjects did not somehow participate in the king's divine essence, if the eternal principles of justice were not already imprinted in their spirit, the mystical body of the republic could never be constituted. This is, precisely, what the concept of *synderesis* comes to express.

However, the problem that torments Finestrad—and the critical point that separates his work from the Christian evangelical genre[52]—is replicating the principle of acclamation on a governmental level. How can the mechanism of glory be reproduced at the level of artifice?

If Finestrad believed that only public education could infuse the population (which is now distinct from the Christian people, albeit still that) with the habit of obedience, it is because of the nature of the knowledge here involved. This, as we have pointed out, is no longer a purely ethical matter but entails certain faculties of discernment. Thus, in order to understand the reasons for the government's actions, and to give their consent to those actions, the subjects must, in some way, share the officials'

FIGURE 3.2 Jan van Eyck, *The Adoration of the Mystic Lamb* (1432).

rational capabilities. Here we see the link between both aspects of Finestrad's project of reform: what assures the obedience of the subject is also what guarantees the wise exercise of government and the correct behavior of the officials in charge.

Ultimately, the double function Finestrad assigned to public education expressed the dual nature of the public officials themselves, which emerged from the innermost part of the society that they would rule. The public official thus represented a duplicate of transcendence and immanence. In other words, the economy of the arcane opened up out of an aporia. On the one hand, the formation of the government led to the issue of justice (on the level of the legitimacy of exercise) being taken out of the reach of society, thus reinforcing the esoteric nature of power by providing a rational supplement to the idea of the arcane. On the other hand, however, because its origin was placed within society itself, the formation of government necessarily entailed the diffusion of that knowledge through the population, which meant the break with the idea of the arcane.

The problem with glory, with the mediating instance that makes the mechanism of vicariousness effective, is that, after being brutally displaced from the political stage of sovereignty, that is, reduced to a purely moral question and relegated to the internal forum of the citizen, it would resurface as a political question on the level of governmental action. And its second coming would occur in an exacerbated manner, due to the allegedly conventional nature of the knowledge upon which it was now based. We may say that public opinion is to governmental action as social contract is to sovereignty: a correlative, in the realm of "artifice," of the principle of *synderesis* in the realm of "nature." Governmental action thus discovered in public opinion its hidden, traumatic core, that which institutes it and also permanently threatens to destroy it.

That aporia, typical of the new economy of the arcane, would find its material expression as soon as the journalistic system, which was then emerging, assumed the task of disseminating that technical knowledge throughout society. Even when its purpose was to serve the monarch by promoting the prosperity and the correct functioning of the kingdom, the press would in fact end up breaking the government monopoly on knowledge and thereby open up its action to public judgment. And Finestrad himself was somehow aware that he did not escape this aporia. Actually, he fell into a kind of performative contradiction in his writing: although he never sought to undermine royal investiture, he questioned the actions of ministers, which is to say, he set himself up as the judge of their actions. "It is the love for my homeland," he wrote, "that leads me to publicly express what I feel in this case. Far from penetrating the politics of our wise government, whom I venerate with the most profound respects without inquiring as to its motives, I offer my way of thought so that it may be experienced over time."[53] As we have seen, he largely blamed the ministers and their lack of familiarity with the art of government for the rebellion. But, following his own precept of identifying the ministers with the king, this would be tantamount to questioning the monarch himself. Here we can see how the emergence of an economy of the arcane had opened a political field, a public realm of publicity, within which Finestrad's own discourse would inevitably become inscribed. Though his language was the opposite of that of the *comuneros*, the effect was nearly the same; namely, he made himself the judge of the government's action. Whether he accepted it or not, he found himself trapped in the governmental machine and the web of the paradoxes that were implicit in the new economy of the arcane resulting from it.

The presence of that new realm of publicity thus ended up undermining the very logic upon which absolutist order was founded. Yet it would be erroneous to attribute the formation of it merely to the emergence of journalism, since that event must still be explained. It would be more appropriate to invert this affirmation. It was first necessary that the assumptions about the nature of the knowledge upon which political action was founded was detached from ethics and removed from the natural plane, that the realm of power was split between the sovereignty and the government, the being of power and the praxis of power, for something such as a "public opinion" to emerge. In sum, this would become possible only at the moment when theology became *political theology*.

The economy of the arcane resulting from the bifurcation of the arcane into two realms (mystic and rational) actually replicated another, more fundamental economy, which was located in its very core: the economy of vicariousness. As we have seen, for Finestrad the ultimate goal was to end the rift between sovereignty and government. But such a rift was not something that could simply be reversed or sent back to its point of origin. The attempt to fuse the body of the king with the voice of the officials only transferred the dualism between nature and artifice to another plane, without eliminating it.

Finestrad wrote that the king and his ministers were inseparable:

> The ministers of the king are living images of his royal person, earthly vicars of him, the soul of the people; despite the fact that they have the character of vassals qua private persons, they still are public persons qua minister of the king, for which they deserve the same veneration and obedience that is due to the prototype, whose character and legal authority shines brightly in them with more clarity than the light of the sun in the stars.[54]

But this raises a number of fundamental questions. How is it possible that the sovereign became incarnate in the royal officials, that the latter became vicars of the king, his representatives, the means by which he makes himself present in the world? That is, how can the official participate in the superhuman essence of the monarch, given the official's mundane nature? The *comuneros* stated that they owed obedience to the king because he participated in the divine essence. As Finestrad put it, "Obedience and respect that we owe to God, the same shall we owe to the monarchs, for they are living images of Him."[55] But why obey an official who is no more than a man like them? This is what the rebels were not willing to accept.

In the end, the fusion between sovereignty and government could be achieved only at the price of reopening that fissure on another plane. When the breach in the king's two bodies had been closed by means of the partition of the very structure of the political field, it reemerged on the side of the artifice, in the problem of the official's two bodies. The split between sovereignty and government (which marked the crucial difference between the political processes in the British Isles and those on the Continent) unfolded now into the dual nature of the public official, who was at once a private person and a public person. He would live, as Shakespeare's Richard II did, sundered by his dual body. In hindsight, we can see the folding logic at work.

In truth, the problem did not reside so much in the distinction between sovereignty and government as it did in their simultaneous distinction and inseparability, in the material impossibility of completely detaching one from the other. As Finestrad noted, the questioning of the ministers actually entailed a direct questioning of the king. And this, too, had conceptual roots. The truly critical point, but one that Finestrad could not observe, is that if sovereignty and government could have become fused, the result for the monarchy would have been even more devastating. As we have seen, only the meticulous preservation of the distinction between the king and the government permitted the idea of the plural and conventional nature of the forms of government to be reconciled with the assumption of the unity, singularity, and naturalness of royal power. This ultimately served to protect monarchical authority from the vicissitudes of political practice. It was achieved by detaching the issue of the foundations of power from its own activity, like the characters in tragedies who recover their identity through their self-duplication, which is also their self-alienation—the impossibility of recognizing themselves in their own realizations, in their own outer projections of themselves, in the different roles they perform.

In any case, in its very attempt to reunite sovereign and government, the absolutist discourse ended up easing the way for an unexpected outcome, which the insurgents would bring about in the following decades. For that outcome to be possible, however, the insurgents first had to perform an operation on said discourse, undermining its core assumption: they had to move royal sovereignty from one realm to another, locating it on the same conventional plane as that on which government was located. The fusion between sovereignty and government would finally be produced, but not *on the side of nature*, as Finestrad intended. At that moment, it could only be produced *on the side of artifice*. Monarchy then became, as the ancient Aristotelian doctrine postulated, just one of the three possible forms of government.

Conversely, sovereignty, as a mystic principle and the incarnation of divine justice, now would belong exclusively to the only natural entity that was supposed to exist: the nation. Toward the end of the eighteenth century, a variety of authors could thus publicly proclaim an idea that just half a century earlier would have been unthinkable. The subjects could now conceive of the presence of an opposition between, on the one hand, a natural nation that existed independently of royal investiture and, on the other hand, a royal power that represented a purely conventional type of authority.

At that point, Francisco Martínez Marina could write with certainty:

> Paternal authority and the patriarchal government, without a doubt the first and for many centuries the only government among men, does not have any similarities nor connection with political authority, nor with absolute monarchy, nor with any of the legitimate forms of government adopted by nations in different times and eras . . . Under the first consideration, parental authority comes from nature, precedes all convention; is independent of any pact, invariable, incommunicable, and legal, circumstances that are in no way applicable to political authority, and even less so to absolute monarchy. This genre of government was produced by time, necessity, and freedom of consent to men; it is variable in its shape and subject to thousands of vicissitudes.[56]

This enables us to understand why the royal vacancy produced in 1808 could bring about the consequences that it did: *sovereignty was a vacant place even before the royal vacancy was produced.*[57] What had been inconceivable to Francisco Suárez had now taken place: that "beheaded body, mutilated and monstrous" had finally come to life.[58]

The most notable expression of this political-conceptual reorientation occurred in Spain and was the emergence of the "historical constitutionalist" current. Its starting point was the discourse of acceptance, at the Academy of History, by Melchor Gaspar de Jovellanos.[59] According to

Jovellanos, the evils that afflicted the Hispanic empire had their origin in the departure from the traditional Spanish constitution by the action of despostism (that is, by ministerial action). "By chance, does Spain not have a constitution? It has it, without a doubt, because what other thing is a constitution but the set of fundamental laws that fasten the rights of the sovereign and of the subjects, and the healthy mediums of preserving one another? And who doubts that Spain has these laws and knows them? Are there any that despotism has attacked and destroyed? Then restore them."[60]

This will bring with it a new reconfiguration of political discourse. The bifurcation between two genres (the treatises regarding the art of governance and of political philosophy), which had displaced the traditional mirrors of the prince, now gave way to a new kind of studies that took the nation as its subject matter. These studies were oriented toward discovering the traditional constitution that despotism had supposedly violated. Thus we complete a full circle: the idea of sovereignty, which emerged at the end of the sixteenth century, gave way, two centuries later, to exactly that which it had originally come to exclude as a possibility, the idea of *national* sovereignty.[61] This new entity, the nation, then assumed all the attributes that had been proper to the absolutist monarchy and were now detached from it.

The conceptual violence implicit in this change did not pass unnoticed, even by the historical constitutionalists. Jovellanos himself felt obligated to establish a terminological distinction. As he explained, speaking of "national sovereignty" was simply absurd. All sovereignty assumed the presence of subjects. To say that something (an individual or a community) was "sovereign of itself" was nonsense. "It is a necessity to confess that the name of sovereignty is not suitable to this absolute power; because sovereignty is relative and in the same way as it assumes one part authority and majesty, it also assumes one part submission and obedience; thus, never can it be said with rigorous propriety that a man or a people is sovereign of itself."[62] Thus, this author proposes to go back to the old concept of "supremacy," which he distinguishes from sovereignty.

> Because the power that a nation possesses when it constitutes itself as a monarchy is very different from the power it grants a monarch to preside and govern it, it is clear that these two powers must be denoted by

using two different words, and since the word *sovereignty* is taken to denote monarchical power, a different word is necessary to denote the power of a nation ... This is why I believe that we can denote it better by calling it *supremacy*, since even though this denotation also possesses several definitions, it is indubitable that national *supremacy* is in this case higher and superior to all that which in politics is called *sovereign* or *supreme*.[63]

It is evident, however, that the notion of sovereignty excluded this concept by definition. By placing another sovereignty (the "national supremacy") above it, the word was emptied of meaning and was simply translated into another term that collected all those attributes that had been stripped from the former.

As we can see, the problem of vicariousness in the plane of the government (the opposition between the two bodies of the official—his mystical body as a public persona and his material body as a private persona), which the plight of the commoners put on the table, hides a much more fundamental split. *It was the mystical body itself that had now become torn.* The official was simultaneously called to obedience by two opposite systems of norms, two diverse sources from which his authority would emanate. The antinomy between the state and society finally gave way, unexpectedly, to a paradoxical situation: the presence of two contradictory sovereignties, that of the monarchy and that of the nation. Their clash then became inevitable.

THE INVENTION OF THE PEOPLE

We can see here the final (and somehow paradoxical) consequence of the broader cosmological split portrayed in El Greco's *The Burial of the Count of Orgaz*: how the theological problem of the divine oikonomia, studied by Agamben in *The Kingdom and the Glory*, turned into a properly political problem, which ended up undermining the foundations of the ancien régime. Yet, to observe it, we must introduce a diachronic perspective, a chronological sequence, which is completely absent from Agamben's perspective. It demands a study that is both conceptual and historical, because only this allows us to perceive the series of torsions within the frameworks of the theological universe that would eventually prepare the way for the modern project of political emancipation.

What we have seen so far reveals the conditions that allowed the emergence of the concept of the nation as an entity that exists independently of sovereign authority, and why it undermined the very logic upon which the ancien régime rested. But this still does not make clear how that nation took empirical form, how it materialized, and how it expressed itself in the political arena—in other words, how it turned from being merely a principle into an effective political factor.

The power of territorial bodies actually had ancient roots on the Iberian Peninsula. As different authors have indicated, while the courts were no longer convened after 1664, the councils acted as the representatives of territorial bodies (particularly of cities with votes.). Charles Jago and Irving Thomson show that the courts were actually eliminated as a result of pressure from the cities that saw them as more susceptible to the influence of royal power.[64] In *Teoría del estado*, José Antonio Maravall explained it this way: even though the Hispanic monarchy was never a parliamentary monarchy like the British one, it was, in any case, a "councilary" monarchy.

Beyond the representative instances (the courts and councils), there were two fields in which the power of territorial bodies was effective: taxation and justice. The creation of the Service of Millions, in 1601, after the defeat of the Spanish Armada, gave local governments control of taxation—they were then in charge of collecting and administrating the tributes. Cities also reserved the power to administer justice in the first instance, invoking the principle sanctioned by King John II in 1442, at the request of the courts of Valladolid, that royal ordinances would not be valid in controversies among peers. This sustained the image of the kingdom as a "community of cities," cities that constituted "perfect societies," self-contained and self-sufficient communities.

However, it is also true that in the course of the seventeenth century the crown developed an important system of royal finances, which increasingly depended less on tributes collected by local governments. The Cortes of Madrid's imposition, in 1632, of the *estanco* (royal monopoly) on salt initiated the dismantling of the Service of Millions. In the course of the following century, not only did the royal treasury affirm a financial system independent of the tribute by the cities, but also monarchical power increasingly intervened in the internal organization of local governments, imposing a host of regulations and controls on taxation and administration. The institution of the *Visitas Reales*, the *Juntas de Propios y Arbitrios*, and so on, were aimed at countering what was then being called the "venality" of urban oligarchies.[65]

In the American colonies, this process of centralization became much more noticeable after the Seven Years' War and the occupation of Havana in 1762. José de Gálvez's visit to the viceroyalty of New Spain (comprising the territories of contemporary Mexico and Central America) was an example of the crown's attempt to intervene in urban corporations, and the resistance that it generated. Particularly irritating was the establishment of the General Accounting of Finances, which controlled the finances of municipalities and villages, and the naming of honorary regents in city councils (*cabildos*). This coincided with the proliferation of charitable foundations, by means of which the central administration assumed the protection of the lower strata of the population, and with an attempt at territorial rationalization, which was expressed in the division of cities into police districts and the appointment of majors and local judges, who were also in charge of collecting census information.

Such measures drastically expanded the functions of the crown, whose mission was no longer limited to preserving justice and maintaining equilibrium among the diverse bodies that constituted the kingdom, but now also included administering its oikonomia. The transcendent nature of this government with respect to society was expressed, however, by successive regulations restricting officials from establishing relationships with the local population. (Many officials complained that, in order to follow the government's rules, they should simply stay at home).

Representatives of the territorial bodies reacted, in turn, by denouncing the corruption and ambition of the colonial administrators. Eventually, events in the Spanish Empire were similar to what had earlier taken place in the British Isles and that Edmund Morgan defined as "the invention of the people."[66] In defense of their corporate interests, local governments invoked "the people" or even "the nation." They began to speak on the people's behalf and to invoke their representation. It was these invocations of the people that the monarchy could not accept. In 1753, New Spain's viceroy firmly rebuked the consulate for "taking up the word of all the people" and thus assuming a "representation," which was a direct threat to the rights of the king. As Annick Lempérière has pointed out, with regard to the viceroy's denunciation, the consulate, as a professional guild, did not have the right to represent the people but only to exercise a royal dispensation.[67] And the same occurred with other groups, representing different strata of society. They had the right of representation before the king, but they could act only on behalf of the interests of their particular group. Only the king was authorized to speak in the name of society as a whole, because he was the only instance in which the plurality of the groups that constituted society in the ancien régime found their principle of unity.

In fact, with their invocation of the people, these organs dislocated the logic upon which the entire political system rested. Finestrad eloquently shows this. As he says, with the rebels' act of rising up as the spokesmen for the common good, they had created a "two-headed monster":

> They pretended to be the heads of the kingdom and claimed for themselves all the power, majesty, and sovereignty that belongs to the entire body of the state, creating a horrible two-headed monster that left its beauty withered and tattered, spoiled the perfect concordance among the members and the mutual relationship that intervened between them and the head, which must be the only one to represent all the actions of the nation.[68]

By making a distinction between the body of the people and the figure of the king, the rebels opened a fissure within the very principle of justice. The determination of its locus then became a matter of controversy—was the locus of justice in the nation or in the sovereign? This distinction was thus even more challenging of monarchy than the distinction between the king (sovereignty) and the ministers (government). The paradox is that, in its battle against urban corporations, the monarchy also invoked the people (or the nation) and claimed to represent it. Royal authorities assured the people that they sought to liberate them from the oppressive rule to which they were subject under the local oligarchies.[69] The point is that, even though "the people" that both sides in this controversy invoked was just a vague entity, no less ethereal than the God supposedly incarnate in the monarchs, the uprisings in the colonies in the 1780s (and some time earlier, on the Peninsula) gave "the people" or "the nation" the aspect of an empirical reality. What had thus far functioned as a pure principle was finally, toward the middle of the eighteenth century, taking form as a political entity.[70]

This dispute regarding the expression of justice created an unprecedented situation. The nation, naturalized and politicized by the actions of absolutist power, finally opposed that same absolutist power, declaring it artificial. The breach between sovereignty and government remained, but the respective terms were altered. The monarchy was now placed on the side of convention (a "political" principle, which now was seen as the opposite of a "natural" principle), while the seat of sovereignty was occupied by a new "natural" entity: the nation. More importantly, it had found its own organ of expression in the margins of the state apparatus, and eventually in opposition to it, thereby bringing to a close the circle initiated in the seventeenth century.

The absolutist state then collapsed under a series of antinomies that, in the attempt to establish its authority on an indisputable basis, it had itself created. This power, which had detached itself from society and placed itself in a situation of transcendence with respect to it, estranged from the conflicts that tore it apart (since only in this way would monarchy be able to give society consistency and perform its function as the articulating agent of social totality), now came to be considered by this nation as a foreign, and even hostile, entity. It was here that the absolutist discourse folded in upon itself, only to find within itself the logic of the emancipation that would destroy it.

THE EMERGENCE OF DEMOCRACY AS A PROBLEM

Recent "revisionist" works about revolutions for independence point out the existence of fundamental continuities between the colonial and independent periods. The established (rather static) view of the colonial regime as an undifferentiated whole that remained essentially immutable throughout three centuries also projected itself onto the postindependence period. Latin America appears as a region with no history, condemned to be eternally preserved in its feudal, Catholic condition. This rather homogeneous and simplistic view of Latin American history ignores the profound political changes that the rupture of the colonial link brought with it.

The break in the monarchical regime located the Latin American political system within a democratic horizon. Certainly, the governmental regimes that were established at that time cannot, by any definition of the term, be considered "democratic." In fact, the ruling elites of the period rejected democracy almost unanimously. But this is not what matters in a conceptual history of the political. The fact that, after independence, democracy became the horizon within which all political action unfolded does not mean that democratic states were established or that their establishment would progressively materialize, as historians of ideas assume. This means that democracy arose as the site where the traumatic core of the political came to be located, the signifier that named it, the figure through which it made itself present in political discourse.

To understand this, we must go back to the seventeenth century. The split between the sacred and mundane, the universal and particular, and the consequent introduction of the need for mediation by a third factor that could reestablish the unity between the two, made democracy unthinkable, insofar as it represented the idea (now seemingly absurd) of the immediate (nonmediated) unity of society with itself. This can be clearly observed in Suárez's writings. Democracy occupied the same place in his political philosophy that monarchy occupied in Aristotle's: it was a concept that was at the core of political theory but that was, nevertheless, impossible to define.

In *Defensio fidei*, as we have seen, Suárez endorsed the Aristotelian idea that monarchy is neither the only legitimate nor the only natural form of government. But when it came to defining democracy, his argument became more complicated, clearly distancing itself from its source, Aristotle. In a first instance, he stated:

> You will say: if this reasoning were effective, it would also prove that God had not directly given to the whole community this political power, because otherwise democracy would be directly in consequence of divine institution, just as we were inferring about monarchy and aristocracy. But this no less is false and absurd in democracy than in the other

kinds of government, not only because just as natural reason does not determine monarchy or aristocracy as necessary so neither democracy; nay much less so, because it is the most imperfect of all, as Aristotle testifies, and as is evident in itself.[71]

So far, he affirmed that democracy was only one of several forms of government, like aristocracy and monarchy, and just as it was not necessary for all governments to be monarchical, neither was it necessary for them to be democratic or aristocratic. None of them was predetermined by nature but, rather, by a matter of convention, which was dependent on a subjective intervention—namely, a decision by the community. According to Suárez, this is as valid for aristocracy and monarchy as it is for democracy. Yet he immediately adds:

> But also because if any institution were divine, it could not be changed by men. Response is made by denying the first concession, for rather from the fact that power has not been given by God instituting monarchy or aristocracy, it is necessarily concluded that it has been given to the whole community, because there is no other human subject left, so to speak, to whom it could have been given. But as to the second point, namely, that hence it follows that democracy is of divine institution, we answer, that if this is to be understood of a positive institution, the consequence must be denied; but if it is understood of a quasi-natural institution it can be and ought to be admitted without any inconvenience.[72]

As we can see, here Suárez states what he denied in the previous passage: that democracy is divinely instituted, directly instituted by God. Thus, it can no longer be considered just another form of government like the rest. He then clarifies:

> For a difference is to be very much noted between these types of political government, for monarchy and aristocracy could not have been introduced without positive institution, divine or human, because human reason taken alone does not determine any one of the said kinds as necessary, as I have said; hence since in human nature, viewed in itself apart from faith or divine revelation, positive institution has no place, about these types it is necessarily concluded that they are not directly of

God. But democracy could be without positive institution, by purely natural institution or emanation, with only the negation of new or positive institution, because natural reason itself dictates that the supreme political power naturally follows from a perfect human community, and by force of the same reason pertains to the community as a whole, unless through a new institution it is transferred to another, because by force of reason neither does another determination have place nor is a more immutable one demanded.

Therefore this power, as far as it is given directly by God to the community, according to the manner of speaking of the law experts, can be said to be of natural law negatively, not positively, or rather of concessive not of absolutely prescriptive natural law.[73]

Democracy appears in this way as having a dual entity. On the one hand, it is ("positively") just one form of government, aligned with the other forms. At the same time, he goes on to identify it ("negatively") with the initial state of nature that occurred immediately after the Fall. That is to say, he associates democracy with the state before the establishment of any type of authority, before human beings had divided themselves into nations, and in which equality ruled among men.

The two definitions of democracy will now overlap, making its concept ambiguous and problematic. Democracy appears simultaneously as a form of government and a kind of nongovernment, a state in which there are no established relationships of command and obedience. In any case, once this original state disappeared, it was no longer feasible to reestablish it. After the constitutive incongruence of the community had become manifest, democracy turned into an impossible concept, always elusive. Even so, its inherent ambiguity was not yet considered a problem. It was only after the fall of the monarchy that this became manifest.

Insofar as it was understood as the index of popular sovereignty, democracy then became the basis on which all governments would be founded. After independence, it would form the content of every posttraditional regime. As Juan Bautista Alberdi said, "Democracy resides in popular sovereignty, *which is a principle compatible with all forms of government*" (my emphasis).[74] Once deprived of any transcendent guarantees, the new governments, born out of a revolution, could only base their legitimacy on the will of their subjects. However, this generic democratic content accepted, by virtue of itself, diverse translations on the institutional field, which also explains the ambiguous consideration that the concept then enjoyed.[75] We can understand now why the coexistence of both vindication and criticism of democracy was only apparently contradictory, because each referred back to two different fields: the political foundations of the state (its generic content, the ultimate principle from which the political system gains legitimacy) and the means of its articulation in the institutional realm (the forms of government). The truth is that the two definitions (of democracy as a form of government and as an index of popular sovereignty) would never become confused in the language of the times. The two semantic threads coexisted in it. Hence the intrinsic ambiguity of the concept, which rendered "democracy" ultimately undefinable.

Nevertheless, the problematic nature of democracy did not reside in the ambiguity of the modes of its expression (the variety of forms it could adopt) but, rather, in the fact that its generic character, which made it open to diverse possible translations in the institutional realm, *also impeded its complete coincidence with any of them*. Ultimately, the institution of an order, regardless of which, involved ending, or at least temporarily suspending, democracy as the expression of popular sovereignty. Conversely, its manifestation entailed the dislocation of all authority. "This is why," states revolutionary leader Mariano Moreno, "every time a people manages to make manifest its general will, all power that previously ruled them has been brought to a halt."[76] As the expression of popular sovereignty, democracy would refer to a state prior to any institutional form of government; it would identify itself with the constituent power whose emergence would mean the disintegration of the existing legal order.

Thus understood, the presence of a conceptual (definitional) incompatibility between democracy and government became clear. All governmental institutions implied the end of equality, entailed the introduction of a split at the heart of society by means of which the governors and the governed could become disaggregated. The dual nature of the concept of democracy thus hid an even more fundamental paradox: if democracy was the generic essence of all postraditional government, so was aristocracy. As Cornelio Saavedra pointed out in his *Memoria*, "At the bosom of the [democratic] system there are citizens that, due to their right conduct adhered to the principles of morality and the laws, have become worthy of the appreciation and consideration of the citizens." He continued, "Those distinctions, considerations, and rewards for their services" are the basis upon which governments rest, "regardless of which system dominates society."[77] Thus, after independence, democracy becomes at once a destiny and a problem; something always invoked and always elusive, ungraspable, by definition. In short, what the revolution will leave as its legacy to the nineteenth century was not simply a series of principles (the liberal ideals of the Enlightenment), which demanded to become progressively materialized, but a more complex and difficult problem: how to produce the partitioning of society without dislocating the egalitarian substrate that now constituted its very foundation.

The natural solution to this aporia was the idea of representative government. As Bernard Manin observed, representative government was not considered a form of democracy but a mixture of democracy and aristocracy.[78] It was based on the premise that the constitution of the general will of the nation was not exclusively a matter of will but that it always involved some *knowledge*. It entailed the accession to a truth that objectively imposed itself upon the subjects, allowing the establishment of a voluntarily assumed agreement (that is, one that was not simply the result of the imposition of a given particular will over the will of the others). In any case, representative government appeared to be the only acceptable form of government in a postraditional context. Its opposite, direct democracy, was, in truth, self-contradictory, because it could not overcome its condition as a mere sum of individual wills. In other words, it could not solve the ancient problems of articulation: how to manage the process of reducing a multitude of subjects into a unity; how to produce a community out of the diversity of individual wills, needs, and opinions present in every society.

Producing this reduction demanded a certain *work* on society: the labor of representation. Here we find the principle established by Abbé Siéyès, which led to the abandonment of the imperative mandates of the ancien régime: the general will of the nation does not predate its own representation.[79] What predates it is merely a series of particular wills, which lack any principle that unites them and reduces them to a single voice. The general will of the nation only constitutes itself as such in the representative organs; it is there that it can become articulated.

Parliament thus assumed the role of the king as the third factor that articulated the community as one. But this did not mean that the representative link had lost the problematic nature that it got from the moment God (justice) became absent from the world. All representation assumed the absence of that which was represented.[80] If there were not a certain distance between the representative and the represented, representation would not be necessary—the people could express themselves as such.[81] In fact, the general will of the nation could only constitute itself as long as there was some distance between the representatives and the will of those he or she represented; otherwise, we would still have merely a plurality of particular wills. This meant that, paradoxically, the work of representation displays itself from the very edge in which the representative link becomes broken.

In any case, the truth was that the revolutionary fantasy of a direct (democratic) expression of the people, which avoided all institutional mediation, could not resolve the problem of articulation. That difficulty would only be transposed onto another level, where it would inevitably resurface. In effect, it still does not explain the constitution of that general will that allegedly seeks to express itself at the margins of the institutional system. To put it another way: How was it that that very constituent power was constituted?

After the end of the ancien régime, the problem of mediation would move from the transcendent to the immanent realms, opening a fissure at its very core. The ambiguity present in the concept of democracy would be replicated in its cognate concept of "the people." From then on, the mystical body of the nation (the people as a political principle, as the supposedly true and last bearer of sovereignty) would inevitably find itself in a relationship of excess with respect to its material body. Its mystical body could never be completely congruent with its material body (the distinction made by Rousseau between *volonté générale* and *volonté des tous* is its best expression). In the end, this explains the perception regarding the existence of an insurmountable gap between the people as a political principle (the bearer of sovereignty) and the "actually existing" people, which would lead to the series of measures restricting suffrage and so on. Far from being merely the empirical corroboration of an actual situation, a matter of fact, it was a kind of "effect of structure," the superficial and symptomatic expression of a political problem that was both profound and fundamental: the constitutive scission of the community and its inevitable incongruence with respect to itself.

Even so, the people as a political principle would never be able to become manifest as such, save through the people as it actually is. In other words, the general will of the nation would never be able to express itself without turning itself into a matter of controversy.[82] The traumatic core of the political, for which the word *democracy* serves as a designation, should then be reformulated in a fundamental way with respect to the seventeenth century. The problem that now emerged did not derive from the transcendental nature of power with respect to society but, on the contrary, from its immanence. The paradoxical coincidence between the figure of the subject and that of the sovereign (the fact that both refer to one and the same persona, the citizen) impeded the unfolding by which the subject could project his or her constitutive contradiction outside and expel it from within. The question that had now become an issue was how a nation could represent itself. More precisely, how could the community produce, by itself, a *political* effect, to generate that excess with respect to itself that will constitute it as such, without recreating, in the process, the ghost of transcendence (power relations)? In other words, how could a subjectively generated power impose itself objectively upon its own creators? This did not necessarily mean eliminating all mediation, but it did involve relocating it, realigning it on the same plane of reality as society itself (that is, through the paradox of an *immanent mediation*). Upon reaching this point, however, the type of political discourse born in the seventeenth century with the baroque no longer had any answer to offer. The solution to this dilemma entailed the radical reformulation of political language, through which all the relevant categories would gain a new meaning. The coordinates that guided political debate would, once again, become dislocated.

The breakdown of the transcendent notion of power entailed a new regime of political discourse. Once the opposition between the dual condition of political subject (a vassal of the king) and moral subject (a Christian), between civil obligation and moral inner conscience, faded away, the figure of the citizen would internalize this contradiction. The sovereign subject that then emerged would always live a split life, due to its dual nature as subject and sovereign at once, the two being one and the same thing. There is no longer any means to detach these two natures from each other, since one entails the other. Thus, although the contradiction would not disappear, it would no longer give way to the kind of folding logic that was characteristic of the baroque. The dualistic logic ceased to be operative and there emerged a different (and in a sense an opposite) one, by means of which that scission would seek to be closed: a logic of undifferentiation–identification. This is a version of what Dick Howard has described as a more general trend in Western thinking, which he calls "antipolitics."[83] The goal now was no longer mutually detaching the contradictory dimensions and projecting each one on separate instances, but, instead, combining and reconciling them on a different plane.[84]

In political terms, the issue at stake became how to make sure that everything that was represented actually became present on the very same level of representation, how to make the political order replicate the social order and achieve an existential identity between both, thus eliminating the constitutive excess of the social with respect to the political. In sum, it was necessary to make certain that everything present in society had an expression in the institutional system, particularly that which defined its very substance, its bottom line: its sovereign potency. Here we reach the end of the age of representation and the beginning of the age of history.[85]

THE IDEAL OF OVERCOMING THE DUALISM BETWEEN POLITICS AND SOCIETY

Contrary to what is normally accepted by the historians of ideas, the organicist concept of the social that emerged in the nineteenth century did not contradict the idea of the social contract. Rather, the organicist concept placed itself on the level of the implicit assumptions of the social contract doctrine—that which it entailed but which was unthinkable for it. The fundamental question that the social contract concept raised was, What leads some people to join with some other people and not with the rest? To put it otherwise: Which social groups can claim to be legitimate possessors of sovereign rights, to constitute a *nation* (the members of the old viceroyalties, of the provinces, or, indeed, of every single city)? It is clear that not any social group can do so. Thus, the social contract ideal entailed a delimitation criterion but was unable to provide one, given the generic nature of the subject involved in it. Providing an answer to this question entailed the reformulation of that concept. Now the task of the constitution of a nation (the problem of articulation) would be taken out of the political field (sovereignty) and entrusted to *history*. History emerged as the new master signifier around which the entire political discourse would become rearticulated. The configuration of a community (the conformation of the people) no longer resulted from a single, original, institutive act but was thought of as the result of a long evolutionary process operating behind the backs of the subjects and determining the character of their normative orientations. It meant, in short, the temporalization of the institutive act.[86]

Behind the antinomy between political power and civil society was thus discovered the presence of a common generative force that bound them together, a certain evolutionary logic from which both were derived, being then only diverse manifestations of it. History thus came to occupy the place then formerly occupied by the Parliament (and, before that, by the king) as that third factor that articulates the social totality, from which we get the expression "the labor of history." The work of mediation is transposed from the subjective plane to that of objective, material processes. History emerges as what Foucault considered the key conceptual device on which this regime of knowledge rested: the paradox of an *objective transcendental*.[87] The conditions of the possibility of the phenomenal world became immanent in it and turned objective, independent of the will of the subjects.

This conceptual shift brought about the redefinition of the meaning of the concept of political representation. That a political system was representative now signified not only that it was instituted by popular will but also that it expressed society in a substantive way. To be truly effective, the representative link should not exhaust itself in the formal mechanism of legitimization, the representation mandate—after all, a system could be perfectly legitimate and yet not very representative of the society it governs. The goal became finding an existential type of identity between the governing and the governed, a link that overcame the strictly political–legal relationship and could bring it into being.

However, in order for this substantive new concept of representation to find its expression in the field of political-institutional debate, it was first necessary that the romantic notion of the people as a homogenous and unified totality be discarded. Here the labor of history encountered its limit point, which called for a subjective supplement. At this juncture, the problem of mediation reemerged.

This reformulation was produced in the second half of the nineteenth century, when the idea of "the people" came to be seen as purely chimerical. Such an entity, it was thought, did not really exist. Rather, there existed a plurality of singular social actors, each with his or her own mutually incompatible interests, wishes, needs, opinions, and rationales. This caused the problematic of representation to reemerge, giving way to the explosion of debates over electoral systems. The half century that preceded the centennial of independence (1910) was thus a period of intense political experimentation, marked by a series of electoral reforms.

The logic of identification at work here raised the question of how to make it possible for a complex reality, composed of heterogeneous interests and opinions, to find expression in the political-institutional field without losing, in the process of representation, any of the elements it comprises. Only in this way could democracy and representation cease to be contradictory terms, allowing the idea of a representative democracy (which would replace the idea of representative *government*) to emerge.

This required, in turn, the revision of the arithmetic principle of representation. In 1868, in his review of the different projects of reform, the Brazilian writer José de Alencar corroborated it. "All these mitigations," he said, "reveal that a universal conscience has been achieved: if not the conviction then at least the suspicion of the falsity of the principle upon which the political organism rests."[88] All the proposals of electoral reform converged toward the disaggregation of representation. The common goal was to identify with precision the diverse elements of which society was composed, in order to give them representative autonomy, their own expression, so as not to suppress their particular identities under the undifferentiated principle of numeric majority.

It was clear then that the opinion of the majority would never be the opinion of all the people but, rather, inevitably, only of a part of it. Consecrating the sovereignty of the majority would thus amount to the establishment of a tyranny of some (the many) over others (the few). "From the moment in which the majority dictates the law," Alencar said, "it is clear that it is the majority that governs, and it is of little importance whether it speaks only in its own name or in the name of all. This is but a mere metaphysical subtlety."[89] In reality, there was no such thing as a popular opinion but only a set of diverse opinions. And this made it necessary to supplement the system of representation-expression, making it much more complex. As Leopoldo Maupas wrote in *Revista Argentina de Ciencias Políticas*: "Our political problem is not only electoral but also, and fundamentally, social, because of the problem caused by the need to give representation and expression in the government to the special interests in society."[90]

Thus, it was no longer about making the diverse opinions converge around a single, shared truth. Establishing a system of functional representation opened up a new field for the work of the political articulation of the social, which would not pass through the mechanisms of collective deliberation. The social totality was no longer seen as a result of a single institutive and primitive act, nor as a spontaneous process, a product that historical development produced by itself. Rather, it was regarded as a continuously renewed task of mutual harmonization and the making compatible of heterogeneous elements. This was now the actual work of politics. "Representation," concluded Rodolfo Rivarola, in "Crónicas y documentos," "will cease to be of the people of the nation, as an undefined homogenous entity, to become the representation of society, that is to say, of the heterogeneity of social interests that must find concordance or reconcilement in the Parliament."[91]

The model of social representation sought to establish an existential link between the representative and the represented that closed the breach between the two. This link would allow the representatives to follow their own conscience and still end up always deciding in a way similar to the way those whom they represented would have done. Thus, the paradox of representation could be overcome, and the ghost of transcendence could be done away with. Ideally, this could lead to the achievement of a perfect coincidence between society and the political system, in which the latter would minutely replicate the former in a condensed way.

This attempt at undifferentiation-identification between the political and the social expressed the ideal of a radical immanence. The political order was no longer a realm outside of society but a function of it, one within a system of functions, the means of its own self-constitution. Ultimately, the ideal that then became dominant was a regime in which the political was reduced to a mere art of government, from which its counterpart, the realm of sovereignty, was erased. However, the problematic point was that, unlike the bodies of the colonial regime, these functional groups were no longer conceived of as natural. And this complicated their identification, because doing so entailed a certain "labor" of discernment.

At this point, the idea of a founding knowledge of the social became reintroduced on a different level, as defining how society was composed and determining which functional groups should find themselves represented in the political system. This would be the purview of a certain type of specialized knowledge, a "social science." The Chilean writer José Victorino Lastarria, one of the principle proponents of social representation, expressed this concept as early as 1846. At that time he stated:

> The government not only must know the wealth and resources of the nation but must also distribute and direct them . . . It should know its strengths and possess, in summary, all the knowledge encompassed by the vast circle of the social sciences. It is easy to conceive that these conditions of capacity are not found in all individuals of a . . . society.[92]

The ideal of absolute immanence in the field of representation-expression thus found its counterpart in the radical transcendence in the field of representation-figuration (the manners of definition of the social space, the identification of the elements that constitute it). Those in charge of it now spoke in the name of an objective, impersonal knowledge that transcended opinions. Ultimately, it is here that the traditional idea of the arcane reemerges, transposed to a different plane and reformulated. The *intelligentsia* then become the locus of truth, previously held by history. It thus comes back to be placed on the subjective side. This means that the bearers of that knowledge now possess a double nature, a part that is not a part but is at the same time particular and universal. They represent merely one more function in the whole system of social functions, but one in which that whole system finds its point of condensation.

The truth is that the task of identification of the diverse components that form society cannot be trusted, without contradiction, to the social groups themselves, because any decision, any election, already entails a definition with regards to it. A congress, for example, cannot decide the mode of representation, because the convocation of it already entails the definition of who should be represented in it. This definition is ultimately the properly political instance. However, it is also true that, to be effective, it could no longer admit itself as such; it must obliterate its political nature.

In fact, the logic of undifferentiation/identification was nothing but the very form of the denial of the political ("antipolitics," in Howard's terms). The ultimate goal was to suppress any decisionist instance, to eliminate the vestiges of any subjective factor, which always would be contestable, by definition. The political history of the nineteenth century is actually a history of the elaboration of different mechanisms for the erasure of the sovereign agency and its eradication from political discourse. The logic of undifferentiation/identification demands that a set of devices be mobilized to render power invisible. Whereas in the ancien régime the sovereign searched endlessly to make his authority manifest through the symbols that expressed it, in the nineteenth century an attempt was made to have all vestiges of power disappear and to dissolve its brutal opacity. This gave way to the development of modern political engineering. The best example of this is the mechanism of the division of powers. Behind the system of "checks and balances" lies the imperative of the suppression of sovereignty: It is evident that, if the people transferred sovereignty to a determined agent, this agent, not the people, would be the sovereign. The mechanism of the division of powers allows the dilution and disembodiment of sovereignty after its transference, turning it in something vague and elusive. It can no longer find a home in the executive, the legislative, or the judicial branch. It would be placed in all of them and in none of them at the same time; its errant circulation through each would make it unassailable.

In the search for the realization of the ideal of a complete immanence, of the undifferentiation-identification of the political and the social, a whole set of new devices of knowledge were instrumented, which did not form part of the system of representation itself. The reduction of representation to a mere transposition entailed the obfuscation of the political (contingent) nature of the operation, which produced that reduction under the veil of scientific objectivity and neutrality. Supposedly, it did not imply an option among different possible alternatives. The constitution of a given society, the manner of its conformation, would be an objective fact, not a matter of opinion. In this context, it was not possible for the political to appear as such; because the conditions for its visibility did not exist; no discourse regarding it could be elaborated. It was necessary that the age of history be concluded, that the logic of undifferentiation/identification between politics and society, and the contrived invisibility of power that organized that regime of knowledge, come to an end before the concept of the political could become articulable on the level of discourse. But, for this to happen, we will have to wait for the coming of the twentieth century, when the age of history gives way to the age of forms.

4

THE REBIRTH OF THE TRAGIC SCENE AND THE EMERGENCE OF THE POLITICAL AS A CONCEPTUAL PROBLEM

> *Far from leading us to conclude that the fabric of history is continuous, does not a reconstruction of the genealogy of democratic representations reveal the extent of the break within it? And so, rather than seeing democracy as a new episode in the transfer of the religious into the political, should we not conclude that the old transfers from one register to the other were intended to ensure the preservation of a form which has since been abolished, that the theological and the political became divorced, that a new experience of the institution of the social began to take shape, that the religious is reactivated at the weak points of the social, that its efficacy is no longer symbolical but imaginary and that, ultimately, it is an expression of the unavoidable—and no doubt ontological—difficulty democracy has in reading its own story—and the difficulty political or philosophical thought has in assuming, without making it travesty, the tragedy of the modern condition?*
>
> —CLAUDE LEFORT, "THE PERMANENCE OF THE THEOLOGICO-POLITICAL?"

The twentieth century is certainly a challenging period in political-conceptual history. The sudden outburst, all over the world, of a long series of dramatic and bloody events seems to challenge comprehension. In *The Century*, Alain Badiou questions the commonly held view of the 1900s as a time when mankind was prey to a kind of collective madness.[1] Such a position, he says, reveals historians' perplexity about the epoch but provides little or no help in understanding it. Trying to make sense of the rationale underlying those seemingly irrational events, Badiou focuses on the conditions that made possible the upsurges of massive violence, in general, and of revolutionary violence, in particular. Actually, the emergence of revolutionary subjectivity is, for him, the most characteristic, or symptomatic, phenomenon of the times, and the transition from classical Marxism to Marxism–Leninism is the expression of it.

It is not that previously there had not been activists, but they did not have in their immediate horizon the expectation of a revolutionary seizure of power. Nor was that the goal around which their practical action was organized. According to Badiou, the assumption that a fundamental inflection in the course of history was imminent, the certainty of being at the doors of a decisive event, marked the starting point for this new epoch in political-conceptual history. Badiou calls it "the century of the passion for the Real."

The nineteenth century, he claims, was a time dominated by the belief in the spontaneous movement of history; that is, the belief that, by following its own inherent tendencies, history would eventually realize the ends that were supposedly attached to its very concept. But that goal was always projected onto a vague, indefinite, future horizon. With the coming of the twentieth century, the arrival of that ideal would become, instead, both more immediate and more uncertain. It was thought that the moment in which the utopian projections should prove their reality had finally arrived. As Badiou states, "It is the century of the act, of the effective, of the absolute present, and not of the portent, of the future."[2] However, the realization of these ends could no longer be trusted exclusively to the march of history itself; it would demand subjective intervention, which would now come to occupy the center of political reflection.

> Between 1850 and 1920 we go from historical progressivism to politico-historical heroism. That is because, in what concerns spontaneous historical development, we pass from trust to distrust. The project of a new

man imposes the idea that history will be compelled, that it will be forced. The twentieth century is a voluntaristic century. We could even say that it is the paradoxical century of a voluntaristic historicism.³

Once deprived of the teleological certainties provided by the evolutionary views of the nineteenth century, the revolutionary enterprise becomes one of subjective self-affirmation. It is the subject, it is now thought, who builds history, provides a sense and a goal, and leads to it. This is what Badiou means by "the passion for the Real," and it ultimately explains the hitherto unseen, and seemingly irrational, degree of violence that was then displayed: "The project is so radical that, in the course of its realization, the singularity of human lives is not taken into account; there is nothing there but a *material*."⁴ As André Malraux said, the twentieth century is the one in which destiny was replaced by politics, and politics turned into tragedy.

The disclosure of the political as a subject matter, its visibility as an object of reality that demands thematization, is inextricably tied to the emergence of this new view of subjectivity as deprived of objective grounds, which is necessarily in an excess relationship with respect to all objectivity (reason, history). Actually, the subjective realm, which in due course would become identified with the political field, would keep a conflictual relation with the phenomenal-objective realm: the former at the same time presupposes and denies the latter. Hence, Badiou speaks of "the paradoxical century of a voluntaristic historicism."

In any case, although the idea of a logic of History (with uppercase *H*) is still a working assumption, it now becomes clear that History itself does not speak, that it must be forced to say its truth. And this opens the field for that excess in which subjectivity emerges. The problematic point now becomes accounting for that excess, providing an insight into its nature and the conditions in which it makes itself present in the political arena.

This represents a drastic reversal vis-à-vis the nineteenth century. The subject operation would no longer hide itself under the veil of neutrality or objectivity (either reason or history) but, rather, is reaffirmed as such. This is what renders the political thinkable as a distinct field. The condition for it was the break in the idea of history as a teleological, evolutionary course. In actual fact, the twentieth century would witness the break of all that the previous century had united: reason and history, truth and knowledge, politics and society. This marks, in turn, the end of the logic of undifferentiation-identification that presided over the thinking of politics throughout that period. Somehow, we are suddenly sent back to the dualisms of the baroque. Justice becomes separated from law, meaning from history, and phenomenal world from sense horizon. Lastly, the realm of foundations is detached from immanence and placed again on the side of transcendence, which would nevertheless become radically redefined regarding the seventeenth century: *it is no longer the home of the universal, of the one, but, on the contrary, is the source of contingency, that which erupts, dislocating the immanent logic of systems and preventing their self-reproduction.* We will analyze the nature of the change in the following pages, but let us see here one consequence of this redefinition process.

If the reestablishment of the dualism between justice and law renders them incompatible, their mutual antagonism would now also be regarded as unacceptable. It is here that the "logic of leap" emerges, displacing the former logic of undifferentiation/identification. The closure of the breach between justice and law demands mediation, but it entails a leap not covered by any normativity, an abyssal operation, the leaning on the verge of radical undecidability, in which all certainties and foundations become broken—in sum, the immersion into the field that would now be designated as the political. The subject then becomes the signifier that names that operation detached from legality, thus covering under its aegis the whole terrain of the political. "The subject" and "the political" thus would become identified with each other.

SERIAL MUSIC AND THE BASIC MATRIX: HOW DETERMINISM TURNS INTO VOLUNTARISM

One strange phenomenon of the twentieth century that Badiou remarks on is the intimate link that was established between politics and art. "The most significant thesis, mainly propounded in the West, and especially by the most innovative and creative currents, is that of art's political value and impact. The avant-garde even went to the extreme of saying that there is more politics to be found in the formal mutations of art than in politics 'strictly speaking.'"[5] However, that connection between politics and art deserves an explanation; it is not self-evident. Badiou asks,

"Today, when it seems so remote, how are we to think that intimate link that bound art and politics throughout the century?" According to him, what unified art and politics was their will of rupture with the past ("Every avant-garde declares a formal break with the preceding artistic schemata"), and this explains the proliferation of manifestos as well as the permanent divisions and exclusions among avant-garde groups. In the end, avant-garde art and revolutionary politics were both expression of the same "passion for the Real" that permeated the entire "short" twentieth century. "It is still incumbent upon us," Badiou concludes, "to identify, within the art of the century, the sacrificial and iconoclastic forms of the passion for the Real."[6] More precisely, he asks: "Is there or is there not within the century a will aimed at forcing art to extract from the mines of reality, by means of willful artifice, a real mineral, hard as diamond? Can we observe, within the century, a deployment of a critique of semblance, a critique of representation, mimesis, and the 'natural'"?[7]

Music—particularly Anton Webern's serialism—was, for Badiou, the best expression of artistic avant-gardism. Yet its relationship with the musical tradition was rather more complex than he claimed. In fact, atonalism was seen by its proponents not as being in opposition to the principles of harmony but, rather, as an expansion of them. A brief analysis of *Structures*, a piece for two pianos, composed by Pierre Boulez in 1952, may help to illustrate the complex ways in which this rupture proceeded, as well as the nature of the link between art and politics. Ultimately, it lets us observe the broader conceptual conditions that made it possible for the political to emerge as a topic on the level of discourse.

For the composition of *Structures*, Boulez began with a theme from a study for piano by Olivier Messiaen. He gave a number to each of the notes in the theme and then transposed it according to the consecutive grades of it (see figure 4.1).

The entire procedure results in a grid, which will be the matrix for the first piano (S). In turn, the inverted series results in a second grid, which will be the matrix for the second piano (I) (see table 4.1).

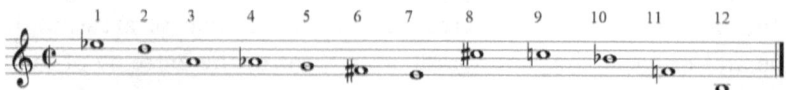

FIGURE 4.1 Pierre Boulez's original series, from a study for piano by Olivier Messiaen.

TABLE 4.1A Matrix for First Piano (S)

1	2	3	4	5	6	7	8	9	10	11	12
2	8	4	5	6	11	1	9	12	3	7	10
3	4	1	2	8	9	10	5	6	7	12	11
4	5	2	8	9	12	3	6	11	1	10	7
5	6	8	9	12	10	4	11	7	2	3	1
6	11	9	12	10	3	5	7	1	8	4	2
7	1	10	3	4	5	11	2	8	12	6	9
8	9	5	6	11	7	2	12	10	4	1	3
9	12	6	11	7	1	8	10	3	5	2	4
10	3	7	1	2	8	12	4	5	11	9	6
11	7	12	10	3	4	6	1	2	9	5	8
12	10	11	7	1	2	9	3	4	6	8	5

TABLE 4.1B Matrix for Second Piano (I)

1	7	3	10	12	9	2	11	6	4	8	5
7	11	10	12	9	8	1	6	5	3	2	4
3	10	1	7	11	6	4	12	9	2	5	8
10	12	7	11	6	5	3	9	8	1	4	2
12	9	11	6	5	4	10	8	2	7	3	1
9	8	6	5	4	3	12	2	1	11	10	7
2	1	4	3	10	12	8	7	11	5	9	6
11	6	12	9	8	2	7	5	4	10	1	3
6	5	9	8	2	1	11	4	3	12	7	10
4	3	2	1	7	11	5	10	12	8	6	9
8	2	5	4	3	10	9	1	7	6	12	11
5	4	8	2	1	7	6	3	10	9	11	12

The fundamental aspect of Messiaen's study, the one that attracted Boulez's attention, was that he expanded the idea of the series to include all parameters. That is, the series ordered the succession not only of the notes but also of the durations (semifuse, fuse, and so on), the pitches or forms of attack (staccato, normal, and so on), and the levels of intensity (from pianissimo to fortissimo) (see figure 4.2).

Boulez then took these grids and drew on them a different trajectory for each parameter—horizontal and vertical lines for tone and duration; diagonal lines for intensity and pitch (see table 4.2 and table 4.3).

The total effect is that, while the elements remain constant, they become permanently displaced and transposed, producing ever-new sound constellations (see figure 4.3).[8]

The arbitrary character of the trajectories produced by the series (in the series, any note may assume the role of the tonic or *Grundton*) underlines the formalism of the composition. They are axiomatic systems. Serialism, shall we say, is musical composition in a non-Euclidean world. It draws attention to *forms*. What matters here is not the content, or the result, but the very procedure. The series is a music machine; today, it would be perfectly possible to design a computer program that could read, translate, and play Boulez's piece. Ultimately, musical formalism replicates and illustrates a more general drive in the art and the thinking of the time, the distinguishing feature of what Friedrich Kittler calls the "discourse network of 1900," which separates it from the "discourse network of 1800": "In the discourse network of 1900, discourse is produced

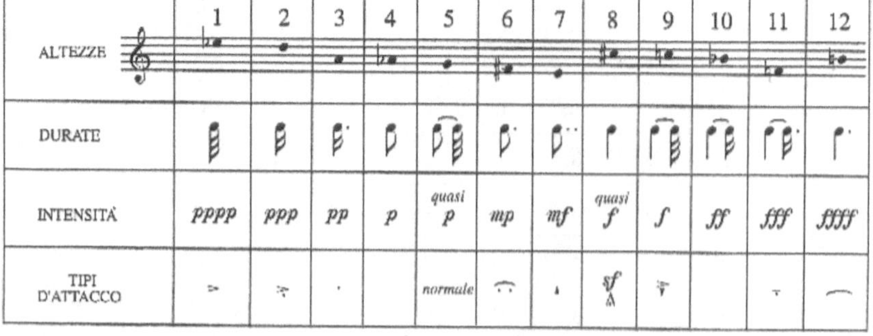

FIGURE 4.2 The Matrix for the series of the four parameters.

TABLE 4.2A Illustration of the Paths Used for Composition (*Intensitá*)

```
S
                              7                        12
                                 9                  7
                                    6    7
                                       11    1
                                    11           3
|                                5                     2
7                             5
      9              11
          6     11
             7    1
          7        3
12                      2
```

TABLE 4.2B Illustration of the Paths Used for Composition (*Intensitá*)

```
I
                              2                        5
                                 6                  2
                                    9    2
                                       8    1
                                    8           3
                                 12                    7
2                             12
      6              8
          9     8
             2    1
          2        3
5                       7
```

by RANDOM GENERATORS. Psychophysics constructed such sources of noise; the new technological media stored their output."[9] The application of technology to musical composition thus contains an inherent ambiguity. The creation of the Institute for Research and Coordination Acoustic/Music (IRCAM) was the crystallization of a rationalistic drive implicit in it. It carried out Boulez's project of giving musical composition a scientific basis. He wrote: "The musician must assimilate a certain scientific knowledge, making it an integral part of his creative imagination . . . At educational meetings scientists and musicians will become familiar with one another's points of view and approach. In this way, we hope to forge a kind of common language that scarcely exists at present."[10]

The *Traité des objets musicaux*, written by Pierre Schaeffer, systematized the concept implicit in the composition of *Structures*, setting up the premises for a scientific approach to the fundamental element in music: sound object. Schaeffer, an engineer, analyzed the structure of the sound object, making possible the manipulation and composition of it. Electroacoustic music, which Schaeffer cofounded with Pierre Henry, was a direct result of it.

Acoustic material would allegedly provide a natural basis for avant-garde musical theory, which could be approached in a methodical, scientific fashion. And it would explain the progression followed in the history of music. For Arnold Schoenberg, the entire trajectory from Bach to

FIGURE 4.3 Detail of the first three lines of matrix S.

TABLE 4.3A Illustration of the Paths Used for Composition (*Tipi d'attaco*)

S								
1				6				
	8		6					
		1	2					
		2	8					
	6		12					
6				3				
				11				9
					12		1	
					3	5		
					5	11		
					1		5	
					9			5

TABLE 4.3B Illustration of the Paths Used for Composition (*Tipi d'attaco*)

I								
1				9				
	11		9					
		1	7					
		7	11					
	9		5					
9				3				
				8				6
					5		1	
					3	12		
					12	8		
					1		12	
					6			12

atonalism was the result of the progressive unfolding of the physical properties of the sound; the introduction of dissonances was a natural outcome of the successive incorporation in composition of further harmonics.[11] Unlike Badiou, Schoenberg did not see avant-garde composition as standing in contradiction with past developments in the history of music. Quite the contrary. He regarded it as continuous with what had preceded it. Now, in the same way that Schoenberg postulated chromaticism as merely the prolongation of diatonicism, Schaeffer saw electroacoustic music as the expansion of the principles of composition of tonality to the other parameters that constitute the sound (timbre and pitch). Whereas the system of tonality limited itself to the composition of two parameters (tone and intensity), the disclosure of the inner structure of the sound object (an achievement comparable, for Schaeffer, to the revolution produced in the natural sciences by the development of the microscope) allowed the new music, and its composition, to also comprise the two other variables that are intrinsic to it. Sound itself thus became only a series. Figure 4.4 condenses his findings.

		Durée demesurée (macro-objets) pas d'unité temporelle		Durée mesurée unité temporelne / durée réduite \ (micro-objets)			Durée demesurée (macro-objets) pas d'unité temporelle		
		facture imprévisible	facture nulle	tenue formée	impulsion	itération formée	facture nulle	facture imprevisible	
hateur masse définie fixe	ENCHATILLONS	(En)	Hn	N	N'	N"	Zn	(An)	ACCUMULATIONS
hateur complexe		(Ex)	Hx	X	X'	X"	Zx	(Ax)	
masse peu variable		(Ev)	Tx Tn trames particulières	Y	Y'	Y"	Zy pédales particulières	(Ay)	
variation de masse imprévisible		unité causale					causes mulitples mais semblables		
		E cas générale	T cas générale	W	φ	K	P cas générale	A cas générale	
		←——— sons tenues				sons itératifs ———→			

FIGURE 4.4 Recapitulative table of the typology of sounds.

In this fashion, Schaeffer somehow carried to completion Boulez's (and, before him, Schoenberg's) ideal of rationalizing music.[12] Yet, paradoxically, it is also at this point that the radical arbitrariness of the principles of tonality and musical composition, in general, is revealed: "We find in the musical object an objective ground in relation with the physical world, but we also must choose among infinitely larger latitude than what it hitherto seemed. Thus the symbols of *solfeo* are no longer representations of physical sounds but relatively arbitrary signs, musical 'ideas.' "[13] The diatonic scales were only some of the possible series, and so were the sounds of the orchestra with respect to the sound object. Schaeffer relates his musical concept to the contemporary findings in the field of linguistics; sounds, like signs in language, are the basic unit.[14] In both, too, we find the same paradoxical alliance between radical determinism and radical arbitrariness.[15] Yet, as we will see, the explanation of this paradox demands the introduction of a third element, which is both things (deterministic yet arbitrary) at the same time, although in a very different sense.

Let us go back to serialism. The series, as we saw, is an impersonal, mechanical device to produce music, but the mechanism does not exhaust itself in its own function. It is an artifice, but it is not yet art. What turns the artifice into a piece of art is the gesture of the artist, the one who sets the music machine into motion and who delineates the arbitrary trajectories in the series. Composition thus acquires a performative nature, becomes a two-dimensional act. Sounds and series are—like Marcel Duchamp's urinal or Karlheinz Stockhausen's helicopters, in his *Helicopter String Quartet*—ready-mades, materials that only become "works of art" through the subjective decision of the artist who designates them as such. And, conversely, the artist constitutes himself as an artist in the very act of designating the pieces "works of art." Musical composition is thus at once a deterministic process resting on a natural (physical) ground and an act of subjective self-affirmation of the artist, which transforms that acoustic matter into an artistic piece. How does the procedure by which historicism turns into avant-gardism, and radical determinism into radical voluntarism, operate? How is the field structured in such a way that the opposite extremes of physical objectivity and disembodied subjectivity become inextricably linked? The answer to these questions demands the introduction of a third factor.

At this point, we must go back in history. In actual fact, musical formalism was a discovery of the baroque and is, thus, at the very origin of Western (modern) music. Baroque music was pure architecture. The formalism of baroque architecture entailed the break with any extramusical substance. Its expression is the disappearance of the ancient modes (Dorian, Phrygian, Lydian, Ionian, and Myxolydian), which were associated with "states of the soul" or "humors" (the Dorian was phlegmatic, the Phrygian was choleric, and so on), and the reduction of them to only two modes: major and minor. The only modes that survived were those fitting the rigors of artifice. The subordination of melody to harmony meant not only the reduction of the modes but also a break with the substantive principle on which they were founded, to give the primacy to the formal requirements of musical composition. But formalism rested on a foundation of natural relations, the principles of harmony. It was nature that then placed itself on the plane of forms. Nature itself became a system.

Yet, between baroque architecture and serial formalism lies a deep abyss. Serial formalism did not abandon the idea of a natural substratum for musical composition; rather, it reinforced that concept. But that natural substratum was no longer the system of harmony but noise—more precisely, white noise. White noise, similar to the blowing of the wind, is the sound that contains all the harmonics. It is the original material out of which all sounds are created. A synthesizer produces the sound of a flute or a piano, for example, by applying a system of filters to white noise and then providing it with a particular pitch. Just as diatonic scales are only series—the result of a particular, arbitrary *mise en forme* of sounds—the sounds themselves are also series—the result of a particular, arbitrary *mise en forme* of the acoustic material, of noise. Thus, beyond forms, the series, the music-making machines, lies the undifferentiated acoustic mass of the noise, which, like Henri Bergson's vegetative plasma of life, only gains consistency through the arbitrary process of its *mise en forme*. Forms, in turn, demand their permanent transposition to produce new musical arrangements. The series are discrete, irreducible, untranslatable. There is nothing behind them, no common principle that allows for mutual correlations to be established among them.[16] But the elements that constitute them are infinitely transposable, thus generating ever-new sound constellations, like Bergson's blows of kaleidoscope in the forms of life.

The transposition of forms thus rests on a natural basis, finds its ground in the physical properties of acoustic matter. Noise is the natural basis of composition, but this natural basis, unlike the natural basis of the baroque (the principles of harmony), has no substance, consistency, or inner structure. It is like the guttural noise of God that precedes his fiat—the amorphous, meaningless substratum out of which forms and meaning emerges. "Circa 1900 noise was everywhere," observes Kittler.[17] We can see now what was the basic matrix of the "discourse network" of the twentieth century, and the way it worked. The transformation of historicism into avant-gardism, and of determinism into voluntarism, demanded the desubstantialization of the natural substratum. White noise, unlike harmony, does not set any limits on subjective arrangements or provide any orientation to produce them. Here we see the central aspect behind the musical formalism of the twentieth century: the oscillation between form and subject that structured the entire regime of knowledge of the twentieth century proceeded through the traversing of the medium of the noise. Noise (the expression of a desubstantialized concept of nature) thus works as the "shifter," which operates the paradoxical alliance between historicism and avant-gardism, between radical determinism and radical voluntarism.

This must be understood not merely as indicating the overlapping of randomness and necessity in musical composition. Both series and noise are like a Markov chain: composite mixtures of determinism and arbitrariness. They are arbitrary and deterministic at the same time, albeit in very different ways. The deployment of the series is deterministic, but the series itself is arbitrary (the result of purely subjective decision). Conversely, white noise is an objective element, whose ground is nature itself; yet it contains no direction or structure. Thus, the deployment of what it contains is inevitably arbitrary; the provision of a form to the acoustical matter is structurally indeterminate.

In any case, noise always comes first in the series, not only in the sense that the formless precedes the formed (the provision of the form is always a subsequent event) but also in the sense that it indicates an "outside" to musical composition itself. Noise is a kind of denied premise of musical expression. Noise is itself inexpressible; in order to become expressible in musical terms, it must be invested with a form. Thus, if the transposition from one series to another entails the reversion to the natural substratum of white noise, it also means sinking into the swamp of uncertainty, where forms become shattered and intelligibility fades away. As Derrida says, after Kierkegaard, "The moment of decision is the moment of madness."

Here we get the new concept of the subject. It designates the impossible operation of traversing the inexpressible, that which cannot be experienced or represented, the intrusion into the morass of the formless, prior to meaning itself. After the desubstantialization of nature, the subject would simply indicate that the creation-of-meaning operation is it itself meaningless. Yet, in this way, the (artistic) subject, once displaced from the realm of the music-producing machine (the series), reemerges, in a reinforced fashion, on the prediscursive level of the institutive act of the machine itself. By enhancing the creative power of the agent, the desubstantialization of nature would have as its counterpart the ontologization/substantialization of the subject. As we saw, the deployment of the content of the natural substratum is structurally indeterminate; the acoustic material does not provide any direction or orientation, depending for its articulation exclusively on a decision of the subject, lacking any objective ground. The subject operation works here as the unthought premise on which this basic matrix rests, at once always assumed and never thematizable.[18]

We enter here the realm of pure arbitrariness, which escapes rationality. In sum, it represents the limit notion of this entire system of knowledge, the twentieth-century "discourse network." And, as we saw, its underlying premise—the hidden premise that allowed it to emerge—was the process of undermining of the concept of nature, the desubstantialization of it. This is expressive, in turn, of a broader historical-conceptual phenomenon and represents the basic mold for a general process of desubstantialization of political and social concepts. All those concepts that hitherto functioned as master signifiers, which were elaborated in the course of the nineteenth century as a response to the crisis produced by the baroque, which came to occupy the vacant place left by "the death of God," would now undergo a similar process. Particularly relevant in this regard is the dislocation of concept of History (with uppercase *H*) which it produced. Eventually, this moment in conceptual history will represent a reversal of Reinhart Koselleck's *Sattelzeit* (a phenomenon that Koselleck himself overlooked). We may now understand the nature of the inflection that allowed the political to emerge as an object on the level of discourse.

THE BREAK OF THE EVOLUTIONARY CONCEPT OF "HISTORY" AND THE EMERGENCE OF THE AGE OF FORMS

The basic matrix we observe in contemporary music underlies the thinking of the political, although, contrary to the postulates of Theodor Adorno, this does not mean that we could derive from it any concrete political program.[19] Rather, it illustrates the structure of the new terrain on which the different political programs will be displayed and will eventually contend with one another. That basic matrix should not be understood as a set of concepts or principles but as a particular mode of *production* of concepts. And it permeates the entire thinking of the twentieth century, even crossing through the great divide between the humanities and the natural sciences. As a matter of fact, the dislocation of the evolutionary concept of history produced at the end of the nineteenth century was intimately associated with the redefinition of the concept of "organism" in biology, which then lost its teleological connotations, thus paving the way for the emergence of a new, "stronger" notion of temporal irreversibility, of the radical *constructability* of historical processes, a concept of temporality that also was the basis of the artistic avant-garde.[20]

In the field of biology, this process culminated in 1900, when Hugo de Vries delivered the final blow to the holistic-functionalist concept of the organism. To de Vries, evolutionary phenomena at a phylogenetic level resulted from sudden transformations or random global mutations. This way, mutations (that is, change) became reduced to unpredictable happenings, which were internally generated but had no perceptible aim or purpose. As early as the beginning of the twentieth century, Ernst Cassirer remarked, "One of the most important developments" is that "biology has learnt to rigorously apply the point of view of totality, without being thereby pushed on the path of teleological considerations or accepting final causes."[21]

Again, we are witnessing the end of the age of history and the emergence of the age of forms. The distinct mark of this age is the overcoming of the evolutionary model and the emphasis on discontinuity. It is the same pattern we observed in the series in music, where the emergence of each new form entails a global reconfiguration of the system according to a unique and singular arrangement of its constituent elements. This "revolution in thought," as Cassirer called it, had its starting point, in the field of natural sciences, in the turn from a physics of elements to a physics of fields.

> The first fundamental turning point in this shift in orientations can be found in the concept of the electromagnetic field established by Faraday and Maxwell. In his study *What Is Matter?* Hermann Weyl exposes in detail the twist from the old "theory of substance" to the new "theory of field." According to him, the true difference between these two theories, the only one which matters from the point of view of knowledge, lies in the fact that a "field" cannot be conceived of as merely an aggregated whole or a conglomerate of parts. The concept of "field" is not the concept of things but of relations; it is not formed by fragments, but is a system, a totality of lines of force.[22]

This also meant the desubstantialization of physical concepts: they no longer referred to objects or elements but to the relations among them. For Cassirer, the general theory of relativity represented the culmination, in physics, of this process of conceptual reconstitution, insofar as "it collects all particular systematic principles into the unity of a supreme postulate, in the postulate not of the constancy of things, but of the invariance of certain magnitudes and laws with regard to all transformations of the system of reference."[23] As Cassirer remarks, it provides the basis for an entirely new conceptual system, gives rise to a new symbolic form, which would completely rearticulate the order of knowledge, in both the natural and the human sciences.

> The recognition of the concepts of totality and structure has not deleted the difference between cultural and natural sciences. Yet, it has pulled down the barrier that used to separate these two kinds of science. Now culture can focus on the study of *its* forms, *its* structures and manifestations more freely and impartially than before, insofar as the other fields of knowledge have also focused on their own particular problems of form.[24]

Gestalt psychology was an example of a new symbolic form. "With it," Cassirer wrote, "the old psychology of elements becomes structural psychology." The form thus becomes the tie keeping together words and things. Empirical objects are downgraded as merely phenomenal realities in order to discover, behind them, not the principle of their formation but the system of their relationships. This will bring about, in turn, the rebirth of metaphysics.

As Michel Foucault maintained, the nineteenth century untiringly proclaimed the end of metaphysics. The return to metaphysics proceeds by means of a double movement: while it reintroduces the idea of a gap between the empirical and the transcendental orders, it also, at the same time, reduplicates the regime of representation, folding it back on its own constructive mechanisms.[25] This produces the bifurcation in the concept of subjectivity, which now becomes tainted by radical ambiguity.

On the one hand, this transformation implies the destruction and dispersion of the notion of the subject, which becomes contingent on the plurality of games of systematic relationships within which it will be eventually articulated. A new paradigm of temporality then emerges. Time becomes diversified, but—and this is the main point—it is no longer a function of a determined kind of being, a subject, but of an element in a particular configuration of the place-time. As Cassirer points out, in connection with the theory of relativity:

> Is there not found in this last expression the characteristic and decisive opposition between the theory of space and time of critical idealism and the theory of relativity? Is not the essential result of this theory precisely

the destruction of the unity of space and time demanded by Kant? If all measurement of time is dependent on the state of motion of the system from which it is made, there seem to result only infinitely many and infinitely diverse "place-times," which, however, never combine into the unity of "the" time . . . "The boldness and the high philosophical significance of Einstein's doctrine consists," we read, e.g., in the work of Laue, "in that it clears away the traditional prejudice of one time valid for all systems."[26]

If the subject is still, as in the age of history, *function*, this function does not plunge its roots into natural objects but refers, like language, to the very representative configuration in which it becomes defined: "The theory of relativity shows with especial distinctness how, in particular, the thought of function is effective as a necessary motive in each spatial-temporal determination."[27]

The development of the non-Euclidean geometry put an end to the idea that there is only one possible way of conceiving of physical space. It is no longer always presupposed in knowledge (one of the a priori of intuition) without becoming an object constructed by a subject, insofar as the two of them—the object and the subject—are now placed in the interior of a particular form. These contingently articulated forms are, in addition, radically discontinuous with each other; they do not respond to any genetic pattern of successive formation. "None of these forms can be simply reduced to, or derived from, the others; each of them designates a particular approach, in which and through which it constitutes its own aspect of 'reality,'" Cassirer stated, long before structuralism arose (although contemporaneously with Ferdinand de Saussure).[28] This shatters the premises on which the age of history rested.

> What constantly comes to obstruct and delay the recognition of the polydimensionality of knowledge is the circumstance that it seems to be destructive of the principle of evolution. Actually, an "evolution" does not exist which, in a continuous succession, leads from one dimension to another. We must accept the existence, at any given point, of a generic difference, which can be established but not explained. It is also obvious that today this problem has lost much of its gravity. Nor in biology do we understand evolution in the sense that every new form

comes up from the former one by the simple accumulation of a series of accidental changes ... This has introduced a very essential limitation to the principle *Natura non facit saltus*. The problematic aspect of this principle has been shown, in the field of physics, by the theory of *quanta* and, in the field of organic nature, by the theory of mutation. Also in the circle of organic life would "evolution" be at last a vain word if we understand it as the "unfolding" of something already given and preexistent.[29]

The notion of "totality" (structure) thus became detached from that of "finality" (function), dissociating, at the same time, necessity from contingency. The category of totality (necessity) referred now to self-integrated systems, whose immanent dynamics tended to the preservation of their inner balance (homeostasis) and their own self-reproduction. "Historicity," therefore, could only come to systems from outside them; it indicated the action of an intentional agent, one that is transcendent to structures. We find here the second conceptual turn upon which the regression to metaphysics will hinge.

Once the notion of the subject was dislocated from the phenomenal field in which it appears, in a desubstantialized fashion, as merely a function within a given, particular field or form, it reemerges with a reinforced (ontological) power on another level. In this second sense, it refers to a previous instance of form (to the ontic realm). While the notion of form becomes the principle that articulates the entire field of ideal objectivities, including that of the determinate (ontic) subject, beyond or below this field there is still the primary (ontological) act of institution by which that given form took its particular, contingent configuration.[30]

This institutive act, which Edmund Husserl designated as the egological field (a process of subject formation previous to the constitution of it), the field of articulation of primitive senses of reality (immediately given to intentional consciousness), which in his later writings, he redefined in terms of "lifeworld" (*Lebenswelt*),[31] will traverse the entire philosophical thinking of the period under the label of the generic category of "life." This is the radical metaphor encompassing the idea of a reality beyond the realm of forms, which would shelter the creative potential, the source of the contingency that disrupts systems and from which a new form would emerge. The title of the text that the "young" Georg

Lukács dedicated to Kierkegaard (included in *Soul and Form*) illustrates this: "Form breaks up when crashing against life." As he explains:

> Among the things you have found to be different you must choose one, you must not seek "middle ways" or "higher unities" which might resolve the "merely apparent" contradictions. And so there is no system anywhere, for it is not possible to live in a system . . . There is never any room for life in a logical system of thought; seen in this way, the starting point for such a system is always arbitrary and, from the perspective of life, only relative—a mere possibility. There is no system in life. In life there is only the separate, the individual, the concrete. To exist is to be different.[32]

Life operates by leaps, like Bergson's blows of kaleidoscopes. The entire field of knowledge, including both the natural sciences and the human disciplines, would be reconfigured according to this "logic of leap," which, as we said earlier, would now displace the logic of undifferentiation/identification that presided over thinking in the nineteenth century. The dislocation of a given form and the articulation of another do not follow a progressive, evolutionary course but involve the incursion into that transcendental realm in which (as in white noise) distinctions blur, intelligence fades away, and all senses of reality become dissolved. The "subject," in this second (ontological) sense (the nonthetic subject), would simply be the name for that unthinkable operation. At any rate, with the idea of a dynamics inherent in systems having become broken, with systems now lacking any teleological impulse by which they could transcend themselves (since they tend only to their self-reproduction), change in history, the emergence of contingency (the implicit premise of this model, given the relativity of forms), could not be explained except by assuming the presence of some instance placed outside those systems, which disturbs them from without forcing their reconfiguration. In sum, this is a metaphysical field in which the primitive senses of reality—on the basis of which systems became articulated—are constituted and eventually dislocated to make room for the emergence of a new sense horizon. Hence, the permanent oscillation between structuralism and phenomenology, between determinism and voluntarism. Beyond their apparent opposition, they presuppose and permanently refer back to each other, since they are integral parts of, and together articulate, a shared archaeological ground.

In due course, this new kind of cosmological split, very different from that produced in the seventeenth century with the baroque, would allow the political to become conceivable as a concept. The debate between Hans Kelsen and Carl Schmitt illustrates this—specifically, how the opposition between form and life, structure and subject results in the "disclosure" of a new system of relationships between politics and society.[33]

THE POLITICAL BETWEEN FORM AND SUBJECT (KELSEN VERSUS SCHMITT)

Hans Kelsen's criticism of the idea of social representation is illustrative of how, during the twentieth century, political language mutated vis-à-vis the preceding century. As we saw, the second half of the nineteenth century witnessed the process of the dissolution of the romantic idea of "the people," as a single, unified whole, and its disaggregation into a number of singular, heterogeneous groups constituting a "civil society." This paved the way for the emergence of the ideal of social representation, which was intended to close the breach between society and the political system. Yet this ideal would raise a "technical" problem: how to identify the groups that are homogenous enough so that their representatives could legitimately claim to represent all of their members and not merely a majority of them. This technical problem soon revealed that the ideal of a perfect identity between society and the political system was unattainable and, as a consequence, that there was no means of overcoming power relations. Ultimately, what it revealed is the inevitability of the action of mediation, the intercession of a mediating agent, which is necessarily transcendent to society itself.

According to Kelsen, if the late nineteenth-century criticism of the romantic notion of people or nation (and the discovery of its illusory nature) led to another, counter idea—such as the notion of a "social group," whose unity and homogeneity were no less illusory than that of the nation—it was because that criticism did not manage to penetrate the conceptual core behind those illusions, that which generated those illusions as its surface effect.

That technical problem ultimately makes manifest a feature intrinsic to social dynamics. Society is, by definition, the realm of division and conflict. It does not, by itself, produce homogeneity. Producing it demands a supplement. Unity can only be achieved on the political field, which now becomes distinguished tout court from the social field. The notions of nation and the people become restored, but they are no longer thought of as objective realities, the result of historical process. They are merely the illusory projections of the only entity that truly exists and that generates those illusions: the state. And the state, in turn, is a juridical concept. It is not an object itself but the expression of the unity of the normative formal order.

> But what is this "people"? It seems to be a basic condition of democracy that a *multitude of human beings* becomes a *unity* in it. For democracy, the "people" as a unity is even more essential, as it is not only, or not so much, the *object* as the ruling *subject*—or should be, according to the idea. And yet, the unity that appears under the name "people" creates the greatest problems for a study of reality. Split by national, religious, and economic conflicts, that unity is—according to sociological findings—more a bundle of groups than a coherent mass of one and the same aggregate state. Only in a *normative* sense can one speak of a unity. For the unity of the people as a concord of thought, feeling, and desire, as solidarity of interests, is an ethical-political *postulate* declared to be real by the national or state ideology by means of a fiction that is generally used and therefore no longer thought about. Fundamentally, only a *legal* element can be conceived more or less precisely as the unity of the people: the *unity* of the *state's legal order*, which rules the behavior of the human beings subject to its norms. In this unity and through the content of its norms, the unity of the variety of human action is constituted, which the "people" as an element of the state, as a specific social order, represents. As that unity, the "people" is by no means—as is naively believed—an embodiment, a conglomerate, as it were, of human beings, but merely a system of the acts of single human beings determined by the state's legal order.[34]

This meant the disembodiment of the articulating instance. It no longer refers to any subject or institution, but to a *procedure*. And it is specific to that given field (the political). Ultimately, the idea of social representation, the desire for the complete congruence between society and the political system (the elimination of every vestige of transcendence and, along with it, power relations) entails the illegitimate transposition of spheres, obliterating the fact that the social and political spheres obey two very different logics. They are two different forms, two different relational systems, following principles of articulation that are specific to each: causality and imputation, respectively.[35]

Kelsen thus proceeds to desubstantialize political concepts. For him, they do not designate objects but, rather, the play of the systematic relations among them.[36] We can perceive how this new mode of production of concepts (the basic matrix) operates in the political field. What we just said about the concept of state could also be applied to its cognate concept: the "citizen." It is a political concept, not a sociological one. It has no actual entity but takes its sense only from the very juridical-formal system in the interior of which it is defined. The citizen is merely the imputation point in the given normative order, a node in a particular web. Implicit in this is a criticism of the idea of natural rights. There would not be such things as rights predating the legal system that establishes them. For Kelsen, all rights are political rights. The idea of natural rights, as well as the idea of the citizen, is only a juridical fiction, an illusion generated by the very legal order that establishes those rights. In sum, for Kelsen, there is no freedom (life) beyond forms. And the idea of form is inextricably associated, in his political theory, with the question of relativism.

As we have seen, Kelsen, whose position is normally conceived as representing the epitome of twentieth-century liberalism, runs against the entire nineteenth-century liberal tradition in his rejection of the idea of natural rights. He claims that this notion is at the root of all forms of totalitarianism, because it leads to positing a particular normative horizon as an absolute value that must be imposed on subjects, even against their will. For him, the best expression of this is Rousseau's distinction between *volonté générale* and *volonté de tous*. The general will of the people, which is supposedly in tune with these transcendent values (natural rights), turns out to be merely a metaphysical entity, which necessarily stands in opposition to the actual wishes of the subjects, which are, by definition, multiple and singular.

> Here we see clearly the insoluble conflict between the idea of individual freedom and the idea of a social order that, in its truest essence, is possible only through objective validity—that is, through a validity independent of the will of those subject to its norms . . .
> In an individualist understanding of society the subject is the isolated individual; in a universalist understanding of society the citizen is only part of a greater organic whole, of a collective that, from an entirely individualist, freedom-based starting point, has a transcendent, metaphysical character.[37]

Beyond the ideological contention that underlies Kelsen's criticism of the idea of natural rights, his view reveals a characteristic feature of the political language of the time, which is based on the assumption of the irreducibility of the political to the social. The result of this is the sharp distinction between "matters of value" and "matters of fact." Max Weber exposed it in the most systematic way.[38] According to Weber, rational thinking, science, can tell us the means we can use to achieve an end, but it has nothing to say about the ends themselves. Science cannot tell us what ends we must pursue, because it is not a technical determination; it demands an ethical option. Following this logic, in his reply to Eric Voegelin, Kelsen asserts:

> A positivistic social science is not in a position to justify an established social order as the realization of absolute values. For it can evaluate a social institution only as a means appropriate to achieve a presupposed end, but inappropriate if another end is presupposed. That is to say, it can evaluate a social institution only conditionally, or, what amounts to the same, it can attribute to it only a relative value—"value" positive or negative—meaning the relationship of a means to an end.[39]

The idea of a radical discontinuity between the realm of facts and the realm of values is the concrete expression, on the political level, of the more general split that occurred at the turn of the twentieth century between systems and finality, structures and subject (the ontic and the ontological). Only structures, systems, were supposed to respond to the logic of reason and could thus be turned into legitimate objects of scientific inquiry. Yet, beyond systems, there lies life (otherwise referred to as the realm of ethics, freedom, and so on, back and forth),[40] which cannot be reduced to reason without inflicting violence on it. In sum, it participates in the phenomenon that Husserl designated "the return of metaphysics," the idea of the presence of a realm of intentional subjectivity that lies beyond the phenomenal world, which is characteristic of the age of forms. Yet, Kelsen's view is particularly radical in this regard. He alone takes this opposition in the realm of political and social thinking to its last logical conclusion, which is also the point where that opposition becomes suppressed.

Forms, as we know, are contingent, relative, discrete, mutually irreducible. They are not universal, since they are not founded on reason or nature. Nor can they be considered historical. This results from the former postulate of the radical discontinuity between the realms of norms and facts. Norms (right) do not derive from facts (history). To think otherwise would mean committing a naturalistic or a psychologistic fallacy. The twentieth-century revolt against History (with uppercase *H*) thus unfolds itself into a struggle against natural-psychological explanations for political-juridical realities. History may eventually explain subjective inclinations—why a given society opted for a particular system of norms rather than the other possible ones. That is, it can explain its empirical *origins*, but it cannot account for its *foundations*. The production of the justice effect, unlike natural phenomena, follows the logic of imputation, not of causality. The dimension of ideality, which is intrinsic to every normative order, is an immanent dimension in the realm of right and politics; it is born at the interior of a given form, and can only be so.

Thus, even though Kelsen endorses the postulate that values are not the object of science because they refer to an extraconceptual realm beyond the reach of rational knowledge, he also rejects the existence of values different from those generated in the interior of a given normative system. He denounces all kinds of normative considerations that follow a logic different from that of imputation as metaphysical, illusory, and ultimately dangerous, because they contain within them the seeds of totalitarianism. The best examples of this, for him, were the communist and fascist regimes, which, at the time Kelsen was elaborating his concept, were rapidly spreading over Europe and seemed on the verge of dominating the entire continent.

In Kelsen's view, the formal-juridical encompasses the entire field of the political, exhausts all of its substance. Yet, as we have seen, it has an implicit tension, because the relativity of forms demands an option among competing normative frameworks and, thus, the assumption of the presence of an ethical realm located beyond systems. The conception of this extrasystemic realm soon reveals itself as the problematic core in Kelsen's theory, something at once implicit in it and yet unthinkable. It would lead, in turn, to the emergence of an opposite approach, which would radicalize the transcendent nature of the value-formation realm.

Carl Schmitt, the best representative of this opposite approach, makes Kelsen's operation of reducing the political to the juridical the central target of his contention. His theory of sovereignty is, in fact, the exact opposite of Kelsen's positivistic doctrine of right. Yet, although they are mutually incompatible, the former follows from the very premises of the latter.[41] If, as Kelsen states, every normative order is a relative and contingently articulated form, if it is not grounded in pure reason or nature or history, then that order entailed an original disorder, out of which it emerged and from which it took the basis on which it was constructed. To put it a different way: the realm of ground-foundation is itself ungrounded (like noise, in music).

This is what Schmitt means when he states that the "sovereign is he who decides on the [state of] exception."[42] Kelsen desubstantializes concepts but substantializes Forms, thus committing a fallacy.[43] The juridical system is not, and can never be, self-contained. "The decisive argument," says Schmitt, "remains the same: the basis for the validity of a norm can only be a norm; in juristic terms, the state is identical with its constitution, with the uniform, basic norm." Now, once this order has been deprived of natural or rational foundations, the question that immediately arises is, "How can it be possible to trace a host of positive attributes to a unity with the same point of ascription if what is meant is not the unity of a system of natural law or of a general theory of the law, but the unity of a positive-valid order?" To put it another way: "On what does the intellectual necessity and objectivity of the various ascriptions with the various points of ascription rest, if it does not rest on a positive determination, on a command?"[44]

The decisional (sovereign) instance constitutes the uniformity of the legal order, and also dislocates it, preventing the iterability of history, the pure reproduction of systems, opening them to contingency, temporality. "In every transformation," Schmitt says, "there is an *auctoritatis interpositio*."[45] Following the premises on which the entire thinking of the period rests, including Kelsen's theory, against form, Schmitt opposes the life that underlies it at its hidden substance: "In the exception, the power of real life breaks through the crust of a mechanism that has become torpid by repetition" (this is a phrase that recalls the title of Lukács's article, quoted earlier).[46] This displacement of the focus from forms to life finally opens the horizon for the thinking of the political.

"The concept of the state presupposes that of 'the political,'" are the opening words of Schmitt's book *The Concept of the Political*.[47] For him, the political is not the realm in which contending normative systems struggle for imposition. If we understand it in that sense, we remain within the natural or empirical-historical field. "This has nothing to do with the causal and psychological origins of that decision."[48] The struggle among antagonistic axiologies already presupposes their existence without explaining how they were generated. That struggle always has a concrete form and takes place within a given, particular field. As Kelsen states, values, whatever they are, only become articulated within the interior of a normative system. The political, however, sends us back to the articulatory instance of the normative systems themselves. It thus leads us beyond the realm of ethics and the opposition among contending axiologies, because it emerges at the point at which every normative horizon shatters.

This allows Schmitt to observe the basic problem in Kelsen's doctrine. Behind his operation of juridical reduction of the political lies a second operation, much more fundamental, because it makes the former possible, giving consistency to it: the ethical reduction of antagonism. Only by ignoring antagonism can Kelsen remain blind to the political dimension implicit in his own theory of right and erase the decisionist (subjective) foundations on which systems rest. Schmitt is precise when showing the contradiction present in Kelsen's theory:

> Kelsen contradicted himself when, on the one hand, he took such a critically derived subjectivist concept of form as the starting point and also conceived the unity of the legal order as an independent act of juristic perception, but then, on the other hand, when he professed his world

view, demanded objectivity, and accused even Hegelian collectivism of a subjectivism of the state. The objectivity that he claimed for himself amounted to no more than avoiding everything personalistic and tracing the legal order back to the impersonal validity of an impersonal norm.[49]

This results in the substantialization of the democratic form. Although Kelsen proclaims the relativity of forms, he cannot conceive of any legitimate form other than the democratic one. As an alternative, we would only have a radical illegitimacy: autocracy. His worldview thus turns narrowly dualistic; he reduces the old tripartite theory of forms of government to a twofold one.

> It is possible for the idea of freedom to enter into the calculus of the social and even political ideas only through a transformation of meaning, which turns an absolute negation of social links in general, and therefore of the state in particular, into a special form of the same [the democratic] that, in conjunction with its dialectic opposite, represents all possible forms of the state and even society in general: *democracy* and *autocracy*.[50]

It is clear that this opposition is not neutral, that it is ethically loaded. Democracy and autocracy thereby become asymmetric counterconcepts, defined by their mutual opposition, being that the latter (in this case, autocracy) gathers all the negative attributes that have been detached from the former (in this case, democracy).[51] Only democracy is ethically admissible. Kelsen's denial of the political instance ultimately implies acceptance of democracy as a quasi-natural entity, as the only rational one. In this way, affirms Schmitt, the ethical reduction of the political turns the liberal ideal of democracy into the worse form of exclusion; those who do not accept it are denied their very human condition, are excluded from humankind itself.[52]

The ethical reduction of antagonism and the consequent disavowal of the political places Kelsen's theory in the ontic field, remaining blind to the ontological dimension. Ultimately, Kelsen's argument reveals that the thinking of politics (unlike that of the political) always takes place within a given form, presupposes a given form, which, therefore, assumes the appearance of a natural premise. That is, the thinking of politics entails reproducing the illusions that are constitutive of that given form within which it becomes articulated. In contrast, the thinking of the *political* would require breaking with these illusions; it would pose the challenge of being able to observe forms from without any of them. Yet, this can be done only by ontologizing the extrasystemic realm. If Schmitt, with his theory of sovereignty, lays bare that blind spot in Kelsen's juridical doctrine, and is somehow able to work out its intrinsic contradiction, he can do it only at the price of developing his own theoretical blind spots, of positing a number of premises that radically refuse their thematization from within his own system, which become axiomatic in the context of it and only become rendered thinkable when, conversely, we approach them from the perspective of Kelsen's theory.

In effect, while Kelsen substantializes forms, and Schmitt can clearly observe it, Kelsen reveals the hidden mechanism by which Schmitt substantializes the decisional instance, the subject. Schmitt's concept of sovereignty has theological roots in a much deeper sense than he himself thought. As Kelsen shows, the idea of a *subjectum superaneum* is a "senseless monster," a metaphysical concept, an imaginary projection.[53] There is no such thing as a subject, placed outside forms, who could decide. His unity is illusory. What we find beyond forms is a plurality of social agents. Only in the political realm do they constitute themselves as a single subject.[54]

Schmitt's fallacy lies in the fact that, from systems' need for a decisional instance, given their discrete, contingent nature, we cannot conclude the actual existence of a subject who decides. In order to devise his concept of sovereignty, Schmitt must create a metaphysical entity (the sovereign subject). Yet the assumption of the existence of such a sovereign subject is not sufficient to make his concept consistent. That first operation calls for a second one, which Schmitt refuses to produce, at the price of leaving unexplained the problem that centrally concerns Kelsen: the transition from facts to norms. Even if we were to accept the existence of such a thing as a sovereign subject, this still cannot explain how a subjectively made decision can claim objective validity. In the best of cases, we would remain on the naturalistic historical field. As we saw in connection with the concept of history in Kelsen, that (illusory) subject can eventually account for the *origin* of a norm but not for its *founda-*

tions. This second operation, which is implicit but omitted in Schmitt's theory (and it is this omission that makes his theory "scandalous"), would consist in associating this metaphysical figure of the subject with a transcendental value, identifying it with reason or nature, or imagining it as in secret complicity with history (the incarnation of a historical *telos*). We get here the basic paradox of this system of knowledge, which Badiou referred to in *The Century* as the simultaneous opposition-presupposition between voluntarism and historicism. Subjective voluntarism both excludes and presupposes the idea of history; it contradicts and entails a teleological view of it.

The point that matters here is that, while the focus on the subjective-decisionist instance (the ungrounded ground of value formation) finally allows the concept of the political to become articulated in public discourse, this can be done only at the price of the resubstantialization of political concepts. Its thematization, detached from all theological-metaphysical vestiges, would involve the radical reformulation of political languages. Only a new historical-conceptual turn, produced at the last quarter of the twentieth century (coinciding with the end of what Eric Hobsbawm called "the age of extremes"), would finally open the doors for it. This would mark the end of the age of forms. The point now will be how to desubstantialize the political concepts, referring not only to those elements within the forms but also to that reality placed beyond them (the properly political realm, according to Schmitt). Yet, at that moment, the concept of the political would reveal itself as a problem, something ungraspable.

THE CONTEMPORARY SCENE: THE EMERGENCE OF THE POLITICAL AS A PROBLEM

As we have seen, the idea of subject was only the counterpart of that of form. The two are mutually opposite, yet they presuppose each other. Insofar as forms are seen as conventional, that they are not grounded in nature or a universal reason, they entail a founding instance. Forms necessarily change over time, but the transition from one form to a different one can only be produced by an external agent, by a subject. The prospect of desubstantializing the categories of the extrasystemic realm thus previously demanded the dislocation of that opposition, the overcoming of that antinomy between form and subject, between self-regulated systems and intentional action (structuralism and phenomenology), which entailed a radical reformulation of the issue of temporality, the ideas regarding the historicity of systems, the source of change.

Once the assumption of the presence of an instance transcendent to systems, which comes to dislocate them from without, is seen as revealing the persistence in political philosophy of the vestiges of the theological-metaphysical universe out of which it emerged, the very idea of form must be twisted upon itself to find within that which taints it with the stain of contingency. That is, the change of forms would be conceivable only if we think that they are never completely self-enclosed and self-regulated systems; that in their center lies a void, which determines their permanent disjunction with respect to themselves and their opening to an exterior, which is not just an exterior but also inhabits and founds them. As Jacques Derrida states:

> If totalization no longer has any meaning, it is not because the infiniteness of a field cannot be covered by a finite glance or a finite discourse, but because the nature of the field—that is, language and a finite language—excludes totalization. This field is in effect that of play, that is to say, a field of infinite substitutions only because it is finite, that is to say, because of being an inexhaustible field, as in the classical hypothesis, instead of being too large, there is something missing from it: a center which arrests and grounds the play of substitutions. One could say—rigorously using that word whose scandalous signification is always obliterated in French—that this movement of play, permitted by the lack or absence of a center or origin, is the movement of *supplementarity*. One cannot determine the center and exhaust totalization because the sign which replaces the center, which supplements it, taking the center's place in its absence—this sign is added, occurs as a surplus, as a *supplement*.[55]

As Hans Blumenberg remarks, Schmitt's concept of the subject is nothing but the result of the rhetorical operation intended to symbolically fill the void inherent in forms.[56] The epistemic regime springing from the dislocation of the age of forms would no longer invoke a primitive founding instance but would aim at confronting these horizons of sense with their inherent void, that which founds them but cannot be objectified within the frameworks of their inner logic without dislocating it (their condition of possibility-impossibility).[57] The concept of the subject becomes then radically reformulated. It is not conceived of as something prior to structures (their institutive act), nor is it seen as a mere effect of structure, as structuralism stated, but rather as *an effect of dis-structure*.[58] It is simply the index pointing, not to outside systems (transcendence), but to their inner, ontological void. More precisely, it is the means of naming that void, of giving to this latter a linguistic presence in order to symbolically control it. Yet, in this fashion, the concept of it (the subject) would become detached from any positive attribute. It would turn into a generic, formless concept; ungraspable, inapprehensible, inexpressible; merely a name for a void; an empty signifier. We find here the premise for the process of the desubstantialization of the elements belonging to the extrasystemic sphere.

That constitutive void at the heart of every instituted order that the figure of the subject now comes to incarnate is what Derrida named *khōra*: the empty place, prior to the formation of the world, where, according to Plato, the demiurge inscribed things.[59] And this again translates reflection to a new phenomenological terrain. The thinking of the period would then move beyond the realm of forms, not to recover their primitive sense (the act of their primitive institution) but to penetrate the instance previous to sense where (as in white noise) sense and nonsense are merged.

Here we face a new paradigm of temporality—in Heidegger's terms, a "temporalization of time" (*die Zeitigung der Zeit*). It raises the question about a type of historicity inherent on forms. More than an *Urgrund*, the *khōra* would indicate a point of fissure; it would work as an index to the instance where a given order is intrinsically dislocated. Temporality is no longer something that is given to forms from their exterior but is something they shelter in their interior, in their very simultaneous necessity-impossibility to become instituted as objective orders, as completely self-enclosed and self-regulated systems. In turn, this would reconfigure the ways of conceiving the political. Claude Lefort's idea of democracy and the concept of sovereignty as an "empty place" (a definition that, not incidentally, recalls Derrida's idea of the Platonic *khōra*) is the best expression of this process of reformulation, of the changes in political languages in the last quarter of the twentieth century.

Actually, Lefort is the one who somehow reintroduced in contemporary philosophical debates the distinction between politics (*la politique*) and the political (*le politique*). For him, the political does not really indicate a field but is a relational concept. It designates the fact that the community is constituted with reference to an "outside." The point of reference from which the community takes its consistency is external to the community itself. It is not necessarily an entity, yet it contains the premises on which communal life rests, that which articulates its normative horizon. It is also the proper place of power. As Lefort writes:

> The fact that this [social] space is organized as *one* despite (or because of) its multiple divisions and that it is organized as *the same* in all its multiple dimensions implies a reference to a place from which it can be seen, read, and named. Even before we examine it in its empirical determinations, this symbolic pole proves to be power; it manifests society's self-externality, and ensures that society can achieve a quasi-representation of itself. We must, of course, be careful not to project this externality to the real; if we did so it would no longer have any meaning for society. It would be more accurate to say that power makes a gesture towards something *outside*, and that it defines itself in terms of that outside. Whatever its form, it always refers to the same enigma: that of an internal-external articulation, of a division which institutes a common space, of a break which establishes relations, of a movement of the externalization of the social which goes hand in hand with its internalization.[60]

The political, as we have seen, is a play of immanence/transcendence, and the different regimes of exercise of power we have been analyzing are diverse modes of production of the transcendence effect out of immanence, a justice effect. It is this that Lefort alludes to when he speaks of society's self-externalization. According to him, this reference to an outside ultimately has theological roots and reveals the permanence of the theological in the political. Yet this does not entail linear continuity. The shifting point that catalyzes the transition to modernity is the new dynamics that assumes this relation after the disembodiment of that outside.⁶¹ The outside no longer designates an Other. At that point, the founding (transcendent) instance gets a generic character. Lefort's revision of Marx's criticism of the notion of "human right" illustrates this.

In his text titled "On the Jewish Question," Marx takes on Max Stirner's critique of the notion of "man," of his "spectral" and fictitious character, to reveal the inconsistencies inherent in the Declaration of the Rights of Man and of the Citizen, which, for Marx, were symptomatic of the contradictions of the formal political-judicial emancipation produced by the bourgeois state.⁶² In contrast, Lefort discovers its coherence precisely in the abstract (generic) character of the "man" qua the bearer of the so-called human rights. His indetermination expresses the anonymity that confers on him his eminently political nature. As Lefort points out:

> Now the idea of man without determination cannot be dissociated from the idea of the *indeterminable*. The rights of man reduce right to a basis which, despite its name, is without shape, is given as interior to itself and, for this reason, eludes all power which would claim to take hold of it, whether religious or mythical, monarchical or popular. Consequently, these rights go beyond any particular formulation which has been given of them.⁶³

If the political order has a natural basis, if it demands one, that natural basis always remains indefinable, conceptually ungraspable. Like the Lacanian Real, it is irreducible to its institutionalization, marks a point of excess vis-à-vis the very order it founds. From this point of view, democracy is defined as an "atopology" of values; their nature as pure excess impedes identifying them with any particular social place or political subject. The democratic subject is always out of place, inevitably errant and erratic. The abstract and generic nature of the subject of human rights determines that human rights can always be invoked to call into question a given positive order, even the so-called democratic. These rights, he says, "elude all power which would claim to take hold of [them], whether religious or mythical, monarchical or popular."

Therefore, for Lefort, the essence of totalitarianism does not reside in the denial of human rights, as is normally assumed, or in the very concept of human rights, as Kelsen stated, but in the appropriation of them by a particular subject or institution that identifies itself as *the* place in which the given right or value would become incarnated. This means that democracy itself can eventually turn into a form of authoritarianism as long as it becomes a value and someone (some subject or instance of power) intends to identify himself with it.[64] The totalitarian logic is, then, indifferent to its content. It does not depend on what values are appropriated but on the very act of appropriating them. It is aimed at dissolving the democratic uncertainty regarding the foundations of the political order by identifying a given social place as the one where essence and appearance are congruent.

We can see here how the deontologization of the subject is produced. The bifurcation in the regime of knowledge in the age of forms, between self-contained systems and transcendental subjectivity (structuralism and phenomenology), expresses itself in a parallel bifurcation of the modes of production of concepts. Whereas the desubstantialization of the categories belonging to the intrasystemic realm is produced by means of converting them into relational concepts (points of imputation within a field), the desubstantialization of the categories belonging to the extrasystemic realm is produced *by turning them into generic concepts,* whose content is indeterminate and whose definition cannot be fixed without destroying them as generic concepts.

This indeterminate nature of political concepts is precisely what opens up the horizon to democracy. For Lefort, the term *democracy* does not refer to any given form of government. It is, rather, a translation of Derrida's concept of "justice." Like justice, the premise of democracy resides "in the irreducibility of the awareness of right to all legal objectification."[65] It simply indicates the existence of a beyond-the-given, which is always unattainable, which resists its reduction or appropriation by any institutional order. Democracy is thus simply another name for the political itself. In the end, to Lefort, it is situated at the edge of its own impossibility; it can never become actualized in the political realm without ipso facto destroying itself. It is only the expression of the fact that society is inevitably disjointed with respect to itself.

Yet it is also the point at which all political thinking meets its ultimate limit, insofar as it is destructive of any political discourse, including the so-called postfoundational. The radical undeterminability of political categories makes any discourse on it impossible. The articulation of any thinking of the political necessarily demands the reintroduction of a metaphysical element, the substantialization of a given instance, and the consequent dissolution of the generic nature of political concepts. They must be reduced in their singularity to make them expressible in political discourse. Slavoj Žižek observes this in connection with Jacques Lacan's contention against the desubstantialization of the subject produced by Deleuze. "This 'anti-Oedipal' radicalization of psychoanalysis," he states, "is the very model of the trap to be avoided at any cost: the model of false subversive radicalization that fits the existing power constellation perfectly." In the face of it, Žižek expresses his reservations: "What if there is a need for *a minimal ontological support of the very dimension of spectrality*, some inert *peu de réel* that sustains the spectral opening?"[66] In effect, insofar as he wants to articulate a political discourse and posit a political project, Lefort cannot ignore this demand for "a minimal ontological support," a *peu de réel*. He thus proceeds to undermine his own premises and to dissolve the generic nature of his concept of democracy, introducing in it a distinction:

> Democracy combines these two apparently contradictory principles: on the one hand, power emanates from the people; on the other, it is the power of nobody. And democracy thrives on this contradiction. Whenever the latter risks being resolved or is resolved, democracy is either close to destruction or already destroyed. If the place of power appears, no longer as symbolically, but as *really* empty, then those who exercise it are perceived as mere ordinary individuals, as forming a faction at the service of private interests and, by the same token, legitimacy collapses throughout society. The privatization of groups, of individuals and of each sector of activity increases: each strives to make its individual or corporatist interests prevail. Carried to an extreme, there is no longer a *civil* society.[67]

As seen previously, the distinction between people and democracy that Lefort establishes only leads to its ultimate logical consequence: the idea of the indeterminacy of the generic human principles. Now, however, Lefort shows that the institution of a democratic order entails a certain identification/appropriation by political power of certain generic principles; otherwise, all notion of legitimacy would fade away, that order could not be established, and, as a consequence, the social would become dissolved as well:

> If, in effect, the mode of the establishment of power and the nature of its exercise or, more generally, political competition, prove incapable of giving form and meaning to social division, a *de facto* conflict will appear throughout society. The distinction between power as symbolic agent and power as real organ disappears. The reference to an empty place gives way to the unbearable image of a real vacuum.[68]

In the end, without the determinacy of human rights, without the actualization of power, there would be no politics proper. The erasure of the state as the place of realization of values; the dissolution of its dual nature, transcendent and immanent at the same time; and its reduction to a crudely mundane, empirical reality inevitably leads to totalitarianism.

> If conflict is exasperated, if it no longer finds its symbolic solution in the political sphere, if the governors and the parties can no longer sustain that internal social transcendence that constitutes the character of the democratic system, power becomes reduced to the plane of mundane facticity, as something *particular* at the service of the ambitious interests and appetites—if the power shows itself *within* society and at the same time indicates or points to the image of it as a fragmentation—then the ghost of the one-people, of its substantial identity, the rejection of division, the reactivation of the search of a soldier's body for its head, of an incarnating power, gives way to the emergence of totalitarianisms . . . There, where the loss of foundations of the political order and the world order are experienced, where the institution of the social gives rise to the sense of an ultimate indetermination, the desire for liberty brings with it the potentiality of its inversion in the desire of servitude.[69]

Yet the process of desubstantialization of political concepts makes it, at the same time, unfeasible. Actually, the status of this statement is not clear in the context of Lefort's political theory. It seems to replicate Leo Strauss's distinction between the "esoteric" and the "exoteric," the "philosophical" and the "political" discourses.[70] As Strauss remarks in

Natural Rights and History, we must postulate the existence of natural rights, even though we know they do not exist; otherwise moral judgments would be unfeasible.[71] For him, the awareness of the lack of foundations of the political order is a privilege of the philosophers (a kind of aristocracy of knowledge); society must ignore it. Lefort certainly rejects that concept, as well as the conservative consequence it entails. He terms it merely a hoax (*un leurre*) and claims that no legitimacy could be based on pure deception.[72] But what he says in the preceding citation seems not so dissimilar from Strauss's statement.

In any case, following Lefort's own logic, that postulate could and should be inverted. What is denied but still implicit in his proposal is that, in the same fashion, without an opposite identification/appropriation of rights by a part of the people, all ideas of legitimacy would also be dissolved. If the determinacy of rights were unilateral on the part of power, deprived of the possibility of the actualization of the people—that some inevitably particular subject could eventually say, like the East Germans, "*Wir sind das Volk*" (We are *the* people)—that is, without a "one people," there would also be no proper place for politics, either, but only for the dictates emanating from power. In sum, democracy would become reduced to the narrowly political-juridical. And the complete elimination of all vestiges of political ontology does not solve it, either. The only way to avoid totalitarianism would not be to avoid the ontologization of the subject but the reduplication of it.

The best example of the attempt to erase all vestige of ontology, of the radical deontologization of political power, is the concept of "empire," by Antonio Negri and Michael Hart, which somehow represents the negative counterpart of Lefort's idea of "democracy." The idea of a power without a center and lacking any identifiable positive attributes would also prevent thinking of any challenge to it, would not leave room for the articulation of a counter-power that could oppose it (although, as will be discussed, Negri and Hart are not willing to admit this). The democratic dream of Lefort (the erasure of every metaphysical vestige) reveals itself here as the worst totalitarian nightmare.[73] To avoid that, we should be able to think of a form of transcendence opposite from that of power, that is, to counter it by producing a parallel ontologization, not of the values that found the political order but of those that eventually permit its contestation (actually, it is this second *peu de réel* that Žižek demands). To put it in Walter Benjamin's words, to the "mythical violence" that founds and sustains the legal order, we must oppose the "divine violence" that destroys that order.[74]

The true paradox, however, is that, either way (whether by substantializing power or counterpower), what Lefort calls the "totalitarian logic" (the attempt to suture the ontological fissure of the social and postulate a system of representation that would deny itself as such, in which the social totality would become transparent to itself) would remain untouched as the working assumption on which political discourse would rest. To be operative, every emancipatory project must invoke a value; therefore, it must dissolve its generic nature, provide itself with a definite content, and identify itself with that value, which, for Lefort, is precisely the quintessence of totalitarianism. In sum, every emancipatory project would contain a totalitarian impulse that is intrinsic to it, since this constitutes its condition of possibility. (Žižek himself does not ignore this negative side contained in his demand for a minimum of ontology.) Totalitarianism and democracy, far from being opposite terms, would be inseparable, because the former would be at the basis of the latter; oppression and emancipation would be inextricably associated. "What is the imaginary realm of autonomy," asked Lefort, "if not a realm governed by a despotic thought?"[75]

This means the dissolution of the entire set of antinomies on which the thinking of the political has rested so far. The project of desubstantializing political concepts thus would prove ultimately unattainable. To be operative, the outside in relation with which a sense of community is produced must be invoked, localized, reintroduced within the webs of discourse and, as a consequence, its singularity undermined and its generic nature dissolved. Yet it has become at the same time impossible: once the presence of an agent placed outside the system reveals its metaphysical foundations, the attempt to resubstantialize the subject has lost its ground.

All the thinking of the last quarter of the twentieth century would revolve around this simultaneous necessity and impossibility of resubstantialization of political concepts. Ultimately, the project of desubstantialization of political concepts would end up dislocating the very concept of the political, making the set of oppositions that articulated its horizon collapse. Some recent elaborations on the democratic problem allow us to better observe the type of aporia intrinsic to that very endeavor.

THE "RETURN OF THE POLITICAL" AND THE PROBLEM OF THE AGENT

Jacques Rancière's recent book *Hatred of Democracy* illustrates the shift in political language that has taken place in the past quarter century, particularly the way in which the mechanism of desubstantialization of power that demands the substantialization of the agent (in order to avoid ending up ontologizing power) at the same time makes it impossible. But it also shows that, although the substantialization of the agent is no longer feasible, it is no less necessary for the conception of the political. In sum, it enables us to observe the deeply aporetic nature of the problem that philosophical discourse currently faces in its attempt to think of the political as a concept, and not only of its contents.

Rancière starts by discussing what he defines as the "scandal" of democracy, its heterotopic character vis-à-vis the political field. At this point, he refers this concept back to its historical origins. The practice in the ancient world of randomly distributing offices is, for him, the best expression of the distinct, original, and "scandalous" nature of democracy. In opposition to all other forms, democracy was conceived as government by those who have no title to govern. Democracy was not really government by the totality of the people, as we now conceive of it, but government by the "no ones," the "nobodies." "It is the scandal of a superiority based on no other title than the very absence of superiority."[76] Hence the necessary intervention of chance, which was the only way to introduce difference into the undifferentiated mass of the common people (the demos), and without which no government is possible.

In the end, the idea of a government by those who have no title whatsoever to govern expresses a paradox that is intrinsic to the political and that represents its ultimate limit. In principle, insofar as ruling entails preeminence, the right to rule must be conferred on those who excel by virtue of their superior knowledge or moral capacity. Thus, every form of government is, by definition, aristocratic. Far from being obvious, as we now tend to assume, the idea that a "nobody" could eventually rule is strange. But, for Rancière, it is also symptomatic. Actually, those who demand for themselves the legitimate right to govern can only do so insofar as the rest understand the reasons that support their demand; thereby, the two parties (the ruler and the ruled) become equalized in their common participation in the Logos.

> There is no service that is carried out, no knowledge that is imparted, no authority that is established without a master having, however little, to speak "equal to equal" with the one he commands or instructs. Inegalitarian society can only function thanks to a multitude of egalitarian relations. It is this imbrication of equality in inequality that the democratic scandal makes manifest in order to make it the basis of a public power.[77]

Inequality, Rancière contends, necessarily rests on a soil of equality. In the moment of the foundational instance of political power, in the establishment of the ancillary difference that constitutes the community, the "unequals" must be treated as equals. Democracy, for Rancière, is thus not a form of government (actually, there would not be something like a democratic regime of government; what we take for it, representative democracy, is an oxymoron, a contradiction in terms) but merely the vestige of the foundational moment of political power, the residue of equality present in the heart of inequality. It is the permanent reminder that what founds the political order is in a "heterotopic" relation with it; what provides the ground for the play of differences that constitute political order is also what dislocates it (equality). In sum, "democracy" simply designates an "an-archic" principle.

> There is, strictly speaking, no such thing as democratic government. Government is always exercised by the minority over the majority. The "power of the people" is therefore necessarily also heterotopic to inegalitarian society and to oligarchic government . . .
>
> Political government, then, has a foundation. But this foundation is also in fact a contradiction: politics is the foundation of a power to govern

in the absence of foundation. State government is only legitimate insofar as it is political. It is political only insofar as it reposes merely on an absence of foundation. This is what democracy means when accurately understood as "the law of chance" . . . Democracy is neither a society to be governed nor a government of society, it is specifically this ungovernable on which every government must ultimately find out its basis.[78]

Rancière thus transfers the idea of equality or natural right from the subjective to the objective realms: equality does not have to do with the nature of the subject but with the nature of the political realm, of its structural incongruence. The subject, he explains, is simply the mark of that constitutive gap in the social space.

Here he takes on a line of reasoning already developed in a previous book, *Disagreement* (1995), in which he elaborates on Marx's concept of the proletarian. As he points out, the term *proletarian* (the member of the demos) does not indicate any substance; it refers to none of the social actors within a determined structural situation, nothing that could be identified in it. *Proletarian* simply refers to that instance that makes a hole in the ruled system of social relations. It marks the existence within it of a (spectral) sector that forms a constitutive part of that system but that does not count within it, "a part that is not a part."

The proletarian that Marx spoke of is simultaneously immanent in and transcendent of that order. In classic capitalistic conditions, as a part of the working class, he integrates himself into the structural field. But its inclusion also includes an excess that no longer belongs to that field, which cannot be spoken of in the available language within it. As Marx showed, the type of injustice (*tort*) that the worker suffers (the extraction of plus value) is not articulable according to the categories belonging to the system of capitalist production; as a member of the workforce, the worker receives a "just" salary. That the worker is something more than the workforce is both the basis of the capitalist mode of production and, at the same time, that which it cannot contemplate, the revelation of which would be destructive to it, produces the torsion (*tort*) of its immanent logic.

Nevertheless, Rancière's interpretation of the concept of the proletarian departs from Marx's in a fundamental aspect, in which the consequences of the more general process of desubstantialization/deontologization of the political concepts are made manifest. The "subject" that arises here does not have any project assigned to its structural condition; it is not distinguished by any particular capacity or faculty; it simply designates "a litigation operator, a name to count the uncounted, a manner of subjectivization superimposed over the reality of social groups," which is irreducible to the ruled field of the social space and that interrupts the repetitiveness of history (the mere reproduction of existing structures).[79]

However, once the concept of proletarian has been stripped of all positive attributes, it also loses the quality of determinate negation of the capitalistic system that it possessed in Marx—the identification of the proletariat as the social place in which the given order finds its hidden truth, the locus of universalizing effects. Like the concept of democracy to Lefort, it becomes a generic concept, indistinguishable from other generic forms of political exclusion, as those designated today by the appellation "minority." The clearest expression of this process of desubstantialization/deontologization of political concepts currently in process is, once more, Negri and Hart's notion of "multitude."

The multitude, to these authors, does not designate more than an insubstantial potency from which no defined political project can be drawn. It is merely a pure impulse for its own manifestation, standing in opposition to another, no less generic and indeterminate category: the "empire." This is something that the critics of Negri and Hart have already extensively shown and that these authors have actually ended up admitting.[80] The truth is that a politics based on the call for the inclusion of an insubstantial subject, defined exclusively by its situation of finding itself excluded from the system (the uncounted in the situation, according to Rancière), can only give way to a project of expanding the given order, making it more socially comprehensive, without ever managing to call into question its very foundations. In this way, politics becomes indistinguishable from its opposite, what Rancière called the "police," a mere displacement within the system's own inherent logic.

This leads us back to Badiou and his definition of the twentieth century as a paradoxical century of a "voluntaristic historicism." Although the political is opposed to all historicism, it presupposes the idea of a sense in history. Restoring politics as different from the police requires the possibility of identifying a social place as the point of reference of the transcendent, that in which the given order exceeds itself, where it finds its denied truth. In other words, we should be able to attribute to a particular subject the capacity to produce universalizing effects, to dislocate the logic articulating that order (a part that has ceased to be a part and has become the expression of the social whole), and thus to give it a *historical* mission to realize.

In sum, the thinking of the political demands the desubstantialization of the subject, but once it is deprived of an identity, of any positive valence or attribute and is turned into a generic notion, merely the name of a problem, then the very concept of the political starts dissolving, becomes something vague, indefinable, and ultimately indistinguishable from its opposite term, Rancière's *police*. Hence, even a project of radical desubstantialization of the subject, like Negri and Hart's, inevitably relapses into some form of ontologization at the moment of attributing political effectiveness to it. As Alberto Moreiras remarks, the proposal of the redemptive nature that the multitude is imagined to possess simply assumes the existence of it without accounting for the process of its configuration: "Empire does not offer a theory of subjectivization. It limits itself that the subject, always already seemingly formed, can go about assuming its rightful or chiliastic position."[81] Negri and Hart refuse to figure out how the multitude articulates itself in a practical-political arena and realizes its supposedly emancipatory potential. But the counterpart of this is that the process of the constitution of the multitude as a subject can no longer be considered the result of political action. In the end, the multitude would not be a political construction but a historical one, in the nineteenth-century sense of the word, the result of an objective, material process. Negri and Hart thus attribute to History (with an uppercase *H*) the mission of constituting the subject that allegedly will put an end to the maladies of the present state. Ultimately, this view implies the existence of a sort of complicity between the spontaneous, objective unfolding of History and the sphere of values (some version of the idea of "the cunning of history"). In sum, it entails a philosophy of history of an idealistic (metaphysical) matrix. As Chantal Mouffe points out:

> All the crucial questions for a political analysis are avoided, for instance those concerning the way in which the multitude can become a revolu-

tionary subject. We are told that this depends on its facing empire politically, but this is precisely the question that, given their theoretical framework, they are unable to address. Their belief that the desire of the multitude is bound to bring about the end of empire evokes the determinism of the Second International with its prediction that the economic contradictions of capitalism were bound to lead to the collapse of capitalism. Of course, in this case, it is not the proletariat, but the "multitude" which is the revolutionary subject. But despite this new vocabulary, it is the same old deterministic framework which leaves no space for effective political intervention.[82]

This radical subjective indetermination, which postulates as a historical agent an entity that has been divested of all positive attributes, necessarily has as its counterpart the reinforcing of historicist determinism. In any case, this is symptomatic, revealing a problem that goes beyond the thinking of Negri and Hart. The fact that all the different "postfoundational" authors cannot help reintroducing, surreptitiously, an ontological assumption—either on the side of a philosophy of history or on the side of the substantialization of the agent (objective or subjective teleologism, respectively)—reveals that, once detached from every form of ontology, the political becomes unthinkable, that it is impossible to elaborate any discourse about it. Nevertheless, that this relapse into the metaphysical realm becomes manifest today in political thinking only symptomatically also reveals up to what point teleological projections no longer find any symbolic ground on which to sustain themselves. The current political vocabulary contains no categories that allow authors to discursively articulate these assumptions. "The intriguing thing," asserts Badiou, "is that today these categories are dead and buried."[83] And this leads us back to our initial point, which Badiou remarked as the distinguishing expression of the emergence of the twentieth century as the time when politics became tragedy, and also the point at which the traumatic core of the political came to be condensed: the issue of violence and, particularly, of revolutionary violence.

REVOLUTIONARY VIOLENCE AND THE PROBLEM OF THE AGENT

Certainly, violence is not just one more issue like any other, since it represents the bottom line of politics, its ground zero. The singularity of violence lies in the fact that it marks an exception point. In fact, after condemning it, no author can refrain from stating that, nonetheless, violence must be accepted under some circumstances. It lives in the exception.[84] It plays a fundamental role in history but cannot be a part of the regular march of it. Violence participates in history and at the same time dislocates its very concept.

Early in the twentieth century, in *Reflections on Violence* (1907), Georges Sorel elaborated on this. In opposition to the social democratic leaders of the Second International and their socialist-evolutionary concept, he underlined how violence did not participate in a political economy, and even less in any "revolutionary economy"—a phrase that, for him, represented a terminological contradiction. From the point of view of a political economy, the Second International's trade unionism was rational. By peaceable, legal means, the working class could get much more than by violence. Yet, to Sorel, this would mean the seclusion of the revolutionary horizon within the ambit of bourgeois rationality. The resort to violence by the working class (which was the meaning of the general strike) gave rise to another logic, the logic of subjective self-affirmation, which Sorel put under the rubric of "myth." It broke all political rationality, rebelled against all "revolutionary economy." It represented a bet on the infinite. It meant an "assault on the heavens." In short, it confirmed the working class as the revolutionary subject.[85] The working class thus became inhabited by two souls: the trade unionist and the revolutionary. The split in the body of the proletariat is another expression of the phenomenon that defined the twentieth century as a moment in political-conceptual history, namely, "the return of metaphysics." Sorel quoted Bergson to illustrate this:

> Bergson asks us ... to consider the inner depths of the mind and what happens there during a creative moment. "There are," he says, "two different selves, one of which is, as it were, the external projection of the

other, its spatial and, so to speak, social representation. We reach the former by deep introspection, which leads us to grasp our inner states as living things, constantly becoming, as states not amenable to measure . . . But the moments at which we thus grasp ourselves are rare, and that is just why we are rarely free. The greater part of our time we live outside ourselves, hardly perceiving anything of ourselves but our own ghost, a colourless shadow . . . Hence we live for the external world rather than for ourselves; we speak rather than think; we are acted rather than act ourselves. To act freely is to recover possession of oneself, and to get back into pure duration" (Bergson, *Time and Free Will*).[86]

The split between the systemic subject and the transcendental subject had its counterpart, for Sorel, in the split in the working class between trade unionism and revolutionary militancy. Revolutionary militancy is the expression in politics of what Emmanuel Levinas would later call the "preontological self."[87] It marks the point at which the symbolic order breaks down, and also the instance that institutes that order. In the end, this is also the realm in which Schmitt's sovereign is lodged, the point, at last, where the political might emerge as a concept. Yet, in the course of the twentieth century, the issue of violence would end up rendering problematic that idea of the transcendental subject and, along with it, the very concept of the political. Maurice Merleau-Ponty's reflection on the revolutionary experience in the Soviet Union illustrates how this was produced.

In 1940, immediately after the Moscow Trials, Arthur Koestler published his novel *Darkness at Noon*, in which he depicts the violence imposed in the Soviet Union in the name of revolutionary principles and, particularly, the dilemmas this posed to leftist thinking. In Koestler's novel, the inquisitor Ivanov states that, every year, nature kills millions of people. Now, he asked, if the Communist Party killed some hundred thousand Russians for the "most promising experimentation in history, why the moral outrage?" Nature, he says, has "plenty of unconscious experimentations with mankind, why does mankind have no right to experiment with itself?"[88] The accused in Koestler's novel, Nicholas Rubashov, an opponent of Stalin's policies, would end up, as Nikolai Bukharin actually did—confessing his treason and his betrayal of the revolution.

Seven years later, as a response to Koestler's novel, Merleau-Ponty published his essay "Humanism and Terror." In it, he intends to tackle the dilemmas the novel raised for leftist thinking. As he says, the kind of liberal humanism that Koestler proposes, insofar as it lacks the dialectical spirit of revolutionary humanism, is radically unable to understand that "cunning, deception, bloodshed and dictatorship are justified if they bring the proletariat into power, and to that extent alone."[89]

The humanism of the "beautiful souls," that folds itself upon inner being and refuses to intervene in history, preserves its good conscience at the price of keeping a passive attitude in the presence of evil and violence in history. Refusing to appeal to revolutionary violence entails the sacralization or naturalization of the existing order, which, far from annulling violence, helps to preserve it (the "violence from above"). And this leads us back to the paradox highlighted by Merleau-Ponty: "Once humanism intends to fulfill itself with any consistency, it becomes transformed into its opposite, namely, into violence." In the end, violence is not something we can dispense with. There is no way of avoiding it. "An anti-Communist," he writes, "refuses to see that violence is universal." And this is precisely what confers the tragic mood on politics. Those who condemn the massacres in the Soviet Union "are trying to forget a problem which had troubled Europe since the Greeks, that the human condition may be such that it has no happy solutions."[90] Thus, the revolutionary militant, if he really wants to be so, cannot avoid appealing to those very same methods he intends to abolish.

For Merleau-Ponty, the crucial point consists in neatly distinguishing between legitimate and illegitimate forms of violence. This is the point at which things become complicated. The criterion for making this distinction cannot be abstract morality, which is radically unable to discern the specificity of the contexts and situations in which violence takes place. Ultimately, the point cannot be addressed independently of a given vision of the future and of the ends to which it will be oriented. "For the moment, the question is not to know whether one accepts or rejects violence," he states, "but whether the violence [with] which one is allied is 'progressive' and tends towards its own suppression or towards self-perpetuation."[91]

Yet Merleau-Ponty is aware of the problems this principle poses. In fact, it is also the one to which the "traitor" Rubashov appeals, in Koestler's novel, to justify his actions. For Merleau-Ponty, the appeal to history is nothing more than an excuse for Rubashov to ignore his responsibility for his deeds, to transfer to history the burden of it (a statement that, Merleau-Ponty knows, could also be applied to the officials of the Soviet regime). This leads Merleau-Ponty to introduce nuances into the concept of history, making it relative. Actually, only the presence of a gap in the rational course of it could pave the way for the thinking about subjective responsibility.

For Merleau-Ponty, the error of Rubashov and the counterrevolutionaries resides in a mistaken concept of history, a "mechanistic" view of it, which leaves no room for subjective decision and action:

> The solidarity of the individual with history which Rubashov and his comrades experienced in the revolutionary struggle gets translated into a mechanistic philosophy which disfigures it and is the source of the inhuman alternatives with which Rubashov finishes. To them, man is simply the reflection of his surroundings; the great man is the one whose ideas reflect most exactly the objective conditions of action; and history at least in principle is a rigorous science . . .
>
> Here Rubashov and his comrades are following a sort of sociological scientism rather than anything in Marx. Political man is an engineer who employs means useful to achieving a given end. The logic which Rubashov follows is not the existential logic of history described by Marx and expressed in the inseparability of objective necessity and *the spontaneous movement of the masses*; it is the summary logic of the technician who deals only with inert objects which he manipulates as he pleases.[92]

Certainly, Merleau-Ponty is attributing to Marx a concept that belongs to his own time, to the age of forms, and that was inconceivable for Marx. The concept of the subject to which he adheres connotes the presence of a residue that is not covered by historical laws, an excess point at which history does not speak by itself, at which it must be forced to deliver its truth. It is there that teleological certainties fade away. This indeterminacy of history is, according to Merleau-Ponty, what Rubashov pretends to ignore, making his argument inconsistent:

> Evidently, Rubashov knows very well that no one can know anything but fragments of such a thoroughly deterministic History, that for everyone there are lacunae in this objectified History and no one can possess more than a "subjective image" of it which he is in no position to compare with an objectified History conceived as something far transcending humanity.[93]

That uncertainty regarding the ends of history is, eventually, what opens the field for politics, makes acts of violence "political actions and not operations of knowledge."[94] However, this does not deny the assumption that history is the ultimate yardstick to assess the legitimacy of political action and, particularly, of violent actions. To the mystification of history cannot be opposed the mystification of private ethics, which is its counterpart. As Merleau-Pontu asserts:

> The Marxist has recognized the mystification involved in the inner life; he lives in the world and in history. As he sees it, decision is not a private matter, it is not the spontaneous affirmation of those values we favor; rather, it consists in questioning our situation in the world, inserting ourselves in the course of events, in properly understanding and expressing the movement of history outside of which values remain empty words and have no other chance of realization.[95]

The truth of history is not accessible, but it is always presupposed: "Despite everything, we have to work without certainty and in confusion to uncover a truth."[96]

Nevertheless, although Merleau-Ponty's statement about violence does not deny the idea of history as the final judge of the progressive nature of subjective actions, it does transfer the question to another terrain. He knows that, with regard to the ends of history, there never is only one opinion. As he says, after Weber, there is "polytheism" and "struggle of the gods."[97] It is here that we find the roots of the indeterminacy that makes room for the emergence of the subject, and also the operation that cancels that breach. The problem here is not really how to establish in what circumstances violence is legitimate but, rather, to determine who can dictate it, who is entitled to decide when a violent act is legitimate. This means that for the subject to emerge, history must become indeterminate; however, we must be able to establish the social place where the truth of history becomes visible. Otherwise, no subject and no history could be possible. As he says:

> The Marxist revolution is not irrational because it is the extrapolation and conclusion of the logic of the present. However, the latter, according to Marxism, is only fully perceptible in a certain social situation and for the proletarians who are the only ones to live the revolution because they are the only ones who experience oppression . . . The critique of the subject reflecting in terms of generalities, the resort to the proletariat as the agency which is not only revolutionary in thought but in action as well, the idea that the revolution is not just an affair of reason and will, but a matter of existence, or that "universal" reason is class reason and that inversely proletarian *praxis* is the vehicle of an effective universality—in a word, the least element of Marxism shows (in the sense the word has in chemistry) man's creative force in history.[98]

We get here a more precise formulation of Schmitt's concept of sovereignty: the *subject is the one who decides when violence is legitimate or not*. This conceptual tripod (sovereignty–subject–violence) is the vector that organizes the field of the political during the "short twentieth century" and the basis on which it would emerge as a concept.

We also get here the ultimate limit to the process of desubstantialization of political concepts. The indeterminacy of history demands the determinacy of the subject. It is expressed in the asymmetry present in Merleau-Ponty's discourse. While the affirmation by a subject of the ends of history has a performative nature—it seeks to impose those ends on history—, the determination of the subject gets a constative character—it seeks merely to recognize a given reality. There is no room for uncertainty at this level.

Again, the desubstantialization of history has as its counterpart the substantialization of the subject. However, it is clear that, in this fashion, Merleau-Ponty simply moves the problem to a different plane without solving it. Calling on the working class rather than history does not make things better. Why would we be unqualified to determine *what* the ends of history are or *how* to achieve them but be qualified to identify the subject *who* would lead us to those ends? In fact, the latter already presupposes the former: if we do not know what the ends of history are, we cannot know, either, who should lead us to them. The answer to both questions demands an insight into the assumed logic in the march of history, its prospective development. Even more radically, why was the determinacy of the ends of history allegedly perverse whereas the determinacy of the subject of it was not?

Merleau-Ponty actually perceives the ambiguous position of the subject. The subject is at once internal and external to history, simultaneously its creator and its product: "The act of revolution presents itself both as the creation of history and as the truth of history in relation to its total meaning."[99] He also is aware of the paradox implicit in this statement, without, however, being able to avoid it. Just as history does not speak on its own behalf, neither does the subject. This latter must be named as such. And this raises the question, Who is that subject behind the subject who may designate this latter as such, who can determine what is the locus where social universality finds concrete expression, that agent whose action would be in a secret complicity with history? If disagreements about this issue are inevitable, they cannot be accepted except as expressions of an incorrect comprehension of reality.

In the end, it is here, in the act of naming the subject, that the invocation of history becomes unavoidable. The one who designates that locus of truth as such cannot come to terms with the evidence of the subjectivity of that very act without finding himself locked in a vicious cycle. In the last instance, should disagreements arise, the determination of the truth or falsehood of the designation of the historical subject should be trusted to history itself. We should let it say its truth, to pronounce its final sentence. In this fashion, Merleau-Ponty ends up doing the very thing he criticized in Koestler's character, Rubashov:

> He simply projects it into the future and in the expectation of that happy day when we shall have knowledge of the whole of history, though a rigorous science abandons us to our disagreements and conflicts. It is only in a far-off future that science will be in a position to eliminate the subjective elements in our forecasts and to construct a thoroughly objective model of our relations with history.[100]

His argument thus traces a complete circle; it is suddenly sent back to the same point from which it initially wanted to depart: the "metaphysical" idea of a hidden logic in history and his possession of an unequivocal perspective on it. Ultimately, as he stated, such an appeal to history would be merely an excuse to elude subjective responsibility, transferring to history the burden for our misdeeds. Yet, as we saw, he cannot avoid it. Actually, assuming responsibility for our actions can only mean being able to justify them in historical terms; that is, to do so, to become responsible for our deeds, we must resort to that very appeal to history that, as he shows, empties the idea of subjective responsibility of meaning.

In any case, this problem transcends Merleau-Ponty's theorizing. It only expresses and makes manifest a wider issue: the paradoxical relation between voluntarism and historicism that Badiou indicates is characteristic of political thinking in the twentieth century, the simultaneously contradictory and inseparable relationship that was then established between those two terms. The typical solution, as we have seen, consisted in unfolding the planes, dissociating the objective and subjective planes. That is, history must be dislocated at the level of political discourse, to free the subject of teleological certainties, which are then projected to a second-order political discourse (the subjective plane), where they work as the implicit and, at the same time, denied foundation of the first-order political discourse.

The fact is, once the idea of history has been displaced from the level of political discourse, once the assumption of its objectivity has been undermined, the idea of subject also becomes untenable. Translating the problem from one level to a different one does not solve it—yet. The breach produced by the uncertainty regarding the ends of history could no longer be closed, and sooner or later it would appear again on that other level of the subject. Here we get to the truly problematic aspect of the issue of violence, which was implicit in Merleau-Ponty's argument but was unthinkable by him: the radical undecidability of the issue of its legitimacy, the fact that there is no way to distinguish revolutionary violence from totalitarianism. There is neither an objective criterion to decide it nor a subjective agent entitled to dictate it.

In effect, what Merleau-Ponty could not manage to express, and what locked his argument within a vicious circle, was, as Lefort remarks, what constitutes the true core of totalitarianism (and of Stalinism, in particular). The founding operation of it, which Merleau-Ponty replicates in his own argument, is not, as he states, invoking the objectivity of history (Rubashov's "sin," to him) but, rather, referring to a social subject as the locus of truth. The traumatic core of politics would already be contained in the very act of nomination of the subject as such. The identification/appropriation of a value that is implicit in this action, the assumption that there may be someone who would be entitled to dictate when violence would be legitimate, not only would be the source of all sort of atrocities but also would be the atrocity itself.

Yet it is still true that, without the possibility of designating a given social actor as a subject, it is not possible to think of politics, either. We cannot avoid it, if we intend to counter the atrocities of power, even though we know that doing this is no longer possible, that any admonition, any attribution, would lack a foundation, would entail the institution of a transcendent instance that would reveal its theological origins. In sum, doing so would mean restoring an idea of history that has already laid bare its metaphysical nature—and something even more serious: that it is perverse in political terms; that, as Lefort shows, it is the basis of "the totalitarian logic."

In any case, it is clear that the same kind of undecidability that Merleau-Ponty observes with regard to the determination of the legitimacy of violence would inevitably reemerge with regard to the question of agency, of *who* can do it. There would be no way of delimiting the "we" (the ethical subjects) who could decide the issue. As Badiou remarks, "What the crisis of the political reveals is that all the groups are inexistent, that there is no French or proletariat, and because of that, the face of representation and also its inverse, the face of spontaneity, are themselves inconsistent."[101]

We can now thus complete the initial hypothesis formulated by Badiou in *The Century*. As he said, the transition from classical Marxism to Marxism–Leninism was a local expression of a broader phenomenon. It accompanied the dissolution of the nineteenth-century teleological concept of history. At that moment, the impossible determination of the ends of history was no longer merely a practical, material impossibility but a conceptual one. These ends were no longer seen as preestablished, already inscribed in the very concept of history. This opened the field to the effectiveness of subjective agency, not merely in the realization but in the very determination of these ends. All the thinking of the first half of the twentieth century was founded on this premise, and that marked an epochal transformation in political-conceptual history.

Yet the second half of the twentieth century witnessed a new shift in political-intellectual history. More precisely, there was a deepening of the process of dissolution of the teleological concept of History (with uppercase *H*), which was associated, this time, with the dissolution of the very concept of the subject as the agent of it (subjective teleologism). Again, the impossible determination of it is not merely material, practical—due to empirical circumstances, as the topic of the absorption of the working class by capitalist logic suggests—but conceptual. The true paradox here is that the dissolution of the teleological view of history, which opened up the field for subjective agency, which conferred upon subjective action a new relevance in the very definition of the ends of history, would also eventually render it untenable. Just as Nietzsche said that, without God, the idea of truth becomes untenable, so too, without history, the idea of subject would also become untenable. At this point, we get into a postragic universe.

As we have seen, the turn to the twentieth century was also that moment in Western history in which politics turned into tragedy, in the words of André Malraux. Once the certainties regarding the ends of history fade away, the invocation of it takes the form of a Pascalian bet. We do not know if there is an end in history, and that is why we must bet on it. The tragic scene has the form of a bet on the Absolute, deprived of any objective guarantee. Yet the idea of a bet on the Absolute implies the assumption of the presence of a subject of that bet. The uncertainty about that premise, in turn, makes discourse fold in upon itself. The posttragic scene has the form, then, of a second-order bet. It is no longer a bet that there is an Absolute but a bet that there is a bet—a subject of the bet. The aim of discourse is no longer to create an illusion of transcendent meaning but to create the very subject of that illusion, to construct ourselves as the illusory subjects of our own illusions of meaning.

This leads us back to the issue of violence. As we saw earlier, for Georges Sorel, the resort to violence institutes a different logic, which is not that of means and ends but of subjective self-affirmation. Once that logic is detached of any end, however, once it is no longer inscribed within a temporal horizon, a teleological framework, a given view of historical becoming, the subject becomes locked into the circle of its own self-generation.[102] And this marks the term of the play of transcendence/immanence that hitherto articulated the horizon of the political. The whole set of oppositions that have articulated this field will then fade away. "The political" Badiou then discovers, "has never been anything more than a fiction."[103] The long cycle initiated four centuries ago with the baroque thus comes to its conclusion. It represents a "second disenchantment of the world."

CONCLUSION

The End of a Long Cycle—
the Second Disenchantment of the World

> *Ten million things were as yet uncovered to Pierre. The old mummy lies buried in cloth on cloth; it takes time to unwrap this Egyptian king. Yet now, forsooth, because Pierre began to see through the first superficiality of the world, he fondly weens he has come to the unlayered substance. But, far as any geologist has yet gone down into the world, it is found to consist of nothing but surface stratified on surface. To its axis, the world being nothing but superinduced superficies. By vast pains we mine into the pyramid; by horrible groupings we come to the central room; with joy we espy the sarcophagus; but we lift the lid—and no body is there!—appallingly vacant as vast is the soul of a man!"*
>
> —HERMAN MELVILLE, *PIERRE; OR, THE AMBIGUITIES*

The emergence, in the twentieth century, of the political as an object that could be thematized is the expression of a crucial shift in political-conceptual history, which marked a radical rupture with respect to the nineteenth century. The nineteenth-century ideal was the identification between a political system and civil society, the erasure of any vestige of transcendence of the political vis-à-vis the social sphere. It entailed a specific mode of production of a transcendence effect out of immanence, in which the political lacked the conditions for its visibility. The issue then was how to conceive of the society's self-transcendence.

Political action was thus seen as nothing more than the work of the constitution of society by itself, merely one function among a system of social functions.

The ideal of undifferentiation/identification of the social and the political represented, in turn, an attempt to close the cosmological breach that had opened two centuries earlier, during the baroque period—as illustrated in El Greco's *The Burial of the Count of Orgaz*—and ultimately was aimed at fusing the two levels depicted in that painting, the sacred and the mundane. Yet, after the emergence of the political, the problem of mediation would always resurface at some given level. The idea of the constitutive disjunction of society with respect to itself necessarily posed a tension between expression and transformation. Although the goal of the political system was to replicate society in a concise fashion, that very society was not thought complete in its own terms; it had to be constituted as a community of free agents, and this was, precisely, the task of the political system.

Overcoming scission demanded mediation, the intervention of an agency that, like the priest in El Greco's painting with respect the cortege, should be placed outside of society itself. The paradox of an immanent mediation demanded a mechanism of social articulation (the reduction of the plurality of subjects to the unity of the community) that did not entail any decisional instance, to translate it from the subjective to the objective realms. Here we get the concept of History that then emerged—a singular, collective noun that, according to Reinhart Koselleck's definition, displays a temporality from itself. History then came to fill that gap, to occupy the place of the mediating agent, becoming the third term that would produce the fusion and reinstitute unity in a split universe. But if the role it assumed was not new, the introduction of the term brought about the crucial reformulation of the ideas about its modes of operation.

The translation of that mediating action from the subjective to the objective planes presupposed some kind of secret complicity between the sphere of values and factual reality, and only then could the constitution of society be entrusted to the spontaneous development of history. In this fashion, that process became deprived of its political substance, of the quintessentially political character of the agent and its action, which was replaced by an impersonal force, historical automatism. The positing of a decisional instance would have implied the reintroduction of a transcendent agent, whose presence would stigmatize the existence of power relations. It would make visible that unbearable residue of facticity intrinsic in every instituted order.

The nineteenth century could not accept this. It could not come to terms with the factual existence of asymmetries of power, inherent in every social system. It needed to preclude the decisionist ground, and the ultimately arbitrary nature of every instituted order. Yet the disjunction of society was not merely a circumstantial happening that could eventually be overcome; it was a condition intrinsic to it, a constitutive factor of it. The reformulation produced by the introduction of the concept of history was tantamount to the erasure of sovereignty, to making it invisible, but this was doomed to failure. Sooner or later, the problem of transcendence would inevitably reemerge.

The political-conceptual history of the nineteenth century is thus the history of the different attempts to produce that erasure, and of the ultimate impossibility of achieving it. As Carl Schmitt said of liberalism, it represented the political denial of the political. In turn, the emergence of the political as an issue in the twentieth century expressed a drastic reversal in the modes of thinking and practicing power. It actually set an irreversible turn, entailed the crossing of a boundary beyond which there was no return. The rendering problematic of the topic of the legitimacy of violence is the best expression of it. The simultaneous necessity-impossibility of distinguishing between the legitimate and the illegitimate uses of violence is not a new thing; it is at the basis of, and confers a tragic sense on, the political. But this aporia got a radically new meaning in the twentieth century. Far from disappearing, the antagonism between justice and law was taken to an extreme in which it became perceived as unbearable, unacceptable. Eventually, the radical undecidability of the issue of violence turned into the urgent demand for a subject who took charge of it, who was responsible for deciding the issue, thereby closing the secular breach between law and justice. The eminently political nature of that action (violent, alien, and impervious to legal or ethical norms), far from being erased, was now placed at the center of political reflection and practice.

This, in turn, was the result of the break in the evolutionary idea of history, which would pave the way for the new, "stronger" view of subjective agency. The subject would no longer be seen as merely a bearer (*Träger*) of a historical project but as the demiurge of it. The problematic issue here would emerge at the moment when, as a reaction to the totalitarian experiences during the second half of the twentieth century, the same kind of undecidability about the ends of history would repeat itself in connection with the subject. The generic nature that then received all subject projections (the best expression of which is the concept of "multitude") would render it radically unable to assume or devise any historical role. More precisely, what was then revealed was the nonexistence of such a thing as a subject who could decide the issue, a "we" who would be entitled to exercise legitimate violence or determine who could do so. It revealed itself as merely a metaphysical illusion, and indeed a perverse one. Unlike mere indecisiveness, radical undecidability, which defines the nature of the political field, has to do not with the need to adopt a decision deprived of any ground but rather with the dissolution of the very deciding subject, the revelation of its illusory nature. However, this was only the external symptom of a deeper problem.

The dissolution of the subject is actually the surface expression of a crucial structural transformation of the field of the political, the result of the collusion of the oppositions that articulated it. At that point, although deciding between legitimate and illegitimate violence remains necessary, it becomes, rather than undecidable, meaningless. Ultimately, the pretension to it becomes definitively perverse, the source of totalitarianism. From the moment that the idea of an end in history collapses—and, as a consequence, there is no longer any way of distinguishing between "reactionary" violence (which would historically tend to its own self-perpetuation) and "progressive" violence (which would tend to its own cancellation), or, to put it in Benjamin's terms, between "mythical" (empirical, mundane) violence and "divine" (meaningful) violence—the decisional action also becomes stripped of its tragic sense.[1] Although it is still necessary to decide, that choice, whatever it is, would make no difference because nothing substantial is at stake, no historical destiny whose realization depends of the content of that decision. The very decisional action then absorbs all of its substance, debasing it of any meaning. Thus, the same thing that provided latitude for subjective agency (the break of the teleological certainties of historicism) would end up making it meaningless.

In the last instance, what is at stake behind the problem of the undecidability of violence is the very concept of the political, and the play of immanence and transcendence that hitherto had articulated its field. As we have seen, the postulate of a transcendent subject functioned simply as an index pointing out to a beyond-the-given. Only this invocation could sustain the emancipatory expectations without which we would be condemned to remain trapped within the cage of systemic determinations. Yet, at the very moment that this premise is established, we also discover that the attempt to actualize that supposedly emancipatory potential has a potentially destructive messianic drive. Here we see the other way in which the logic of indiscernibility operates in political discourse: in the collusion of the opposite terms, insofar as both of them derive from the same totalitarian logic, thereby reproducing it. Here we get to the point where all political philosophies collapse, including the so-called postfoundational versions of them.[2]

In effect, for the neo-Schmittean thinkers, political philosophy is born out of the denial of conflict as constitutive of the political. As Roberto Esposito points out:

> Naturally, there exists a reason for why philosophical representation denies conflict, a "life-or-death" reason, one could say, and the reason is that it is originally conflict that denies representation, in the sense that it cannot be represented—save in the form of its own dissolution—within the categorical marquee of political philosophy. Regardless of this, conflict, in its full range of expressions, is nothing more than the *reality* of politics, its *factum*, its factualness—and also . . . its "finiteness." Such real factualness, such factual reality, does not fit within the schemes representative of political philosophy and is not pronounceable in conceptual language.[3]

Certainly, all political philosophy entails the symbolic domestication of antagonism, its sublimation under the decompressed form of *agonism*.[4] According to Esposito, it could be expressed in political discourse only under the form of the prospect of its own suppression. In this way, in their different versions, the "postfoundational" contemporary perspectives propose to refound political philosophy upon other bases—bases that, instead of denying conflict, locate it at their center of reflection as the basic datum of politics. Yet the characteristic illusion of this postfoundational thinking of the political consists in believing that it is possible to neatly distinguish the philosophies of order from the philosophies of conflict, the politics of subjection from the politics of emancipation. In fact, the singularity of conflict that robs itself of its possible thematization is nothing more than the superficial manifestation of an even more radical singularity: the "scandal" of the indiscernibility of emancipation and subjection ("emancipation" is actually the signifier for the prospect of violence's self-suppression, a device for its symbolic domestication, undermining its brutal factualness, dissolving its singularity) as a consequence of the break of the play of immanence–transcendence that articulated the horizon of the political. Here we get the "second disenchantment of the world."

NEO-AVANT-GARDE, THE THOUGHT OF THE OUTSIDE, AND THE BREAK OF THE HORIZON OF THE POLITICAL

The first disenchantment of the world, which occurred during the period we call *Schwellenzeit* (1550–1650), when God abandoned the world, showed the sphere of values as already radically absent from the world. It got a transcendent character, inexpressible in our conventional language, unable to be incarnated in any terrestrial power. Justice then divorced itself from law and became ethereal, inapprehensible. Even so, it would always be presupposed. If positive law can never identify itself with justice, neither can it cease to invoke it constantly as its foundation.

This opened the field of the political, which underwent a number of successive reconfigurations, from its inception to the present. But, as Lefort remarks, the idea of an "outside" (the reference to it) remained as its constitutive premise. The different regimes of exercise of power analyzed in the preceding chapters expressed different ways of articulating the relation with that outside that Lefort speaks about—they expressed different modes of production of the transcendence effect out of immanence. Each epoch in the archaeology of the political (the age of representation, the age of history, and the age of forms) entailed a particular mechanism for the generation of a sense of justice, of meaning. Each worked according to a specific logic of functioning: the logic of folding, for the age of representation; the logic of indifferentiation/identification, for the age of history; and the logic of leap, for the age of forms. The desubstantialization of this outside, produced in the twentieth century, did not break the dualism between the transcendent and the immanent. Rather, it radicalized the opposition between the two terms to the point of rendering them unacceptable, and the logic of leap (the paradoxical combination of historicism and voluntarism) was the expression of it. However, it represented the last stage in this game of immanence–transcendence.

In effect, the process of desubstantialization of that outside, in connection with which society is defined, soon turned it into a formless substance, getting a generic character, devoid of any positive content. And this would pave the way for its dissolution, producing the folding of discourse upon itself to thematize the conditions for that very appellation, the mechanisms operating behind this projection of sense. At that point, the categories of "democracy" in Lefort, or "justice" in Derrida, come to appear simply as operators for the remission to transcendence; that is, they have the function, after the dissolution of both objective and subjective teleologisms, of performatively establishing the connection between the given and the beyond-the-given, thus making manifest the inherent disjunction of the established order. "Outside" thus comes to appear as merely an effect of discourse, which does not assume the actual presence of a transcendent sphere. It would be only the product of the outer projection of the inner void intrinsic to every instituted order. And this revelation marks the end of the founding antinomies that had hitherto articulated the field of the political, and the game of immanence–transcendence that was proper to it. The transformations in the arts from avant-garde to the neo-avant-garde forms of expression, in the second half of the twentieth century, enlightens us as to how this conceptual displacement was produced.

White on White (figure C.1), painted by the Ukrainian suprematist Kazimir Malevich just one year after the Russian Revolution, illustrates this mutation in the nature of the dualism, between transcendence and immanence, after the desubstantialization of that outside during the first decades of the twentieth century. Just as serialism sought to reduce musical composition to its acoustic primary element, the sound, Malevich intended to reduce plastic expression to its essential attribute: color. Actually,

FIGURE C.1 Kazimir Malevich, *Suprematist Composition: White on White* (1918). New York, Museum of Modern Art (MoMA). © 2015. Digital image, The Museum of Modern Art, New York / Scala, Florence.

a colorless color. Although the white, like white noise in harmonics, contains all colors, it itself is no color, just as white noise is no sound. It represents the absence of color resulting from its own plenitude—the fact of encompassing the entire tonal spectrum makes it also inexpressive. Such a desubstantialization of the natural substratum of art amounted to a reversal of the system of representation. *White on White* can actually be seen as the twentieth-century counterpoint to El Greco's *The Burial of the Count of Orgaz*.

In Malevich's picture, the dualistic universe remains as the basis of the composition, expressed by the play of differences in the undifferentiated mass of the white color, but the contours of the opposite figures now fade away. The rich texture of characters, motifs, and allegories in El Greco's paintings is replaced by an insubstantial geometry, lacking any expression, the boundaries of which are diffuse, slippery.

The depth of the baroque scene that accompanied its tragic sense becomes here a flat surface with no content. And this makes more noticeable the only perceptible element on that surface: the brushstrokes of the painter. These are the only things that differentiate the figure of the background. In this way, as in El Greco's painting, the artist makes himself present in the system of representation, revealing its conventional nature.

But the radicalization of this revelation, to the point of emptying representation of any substance, is at the same time a cry of rebellion against it. In El Greco's painting, the opposition of the planes of the sacred and the profane looked perfectly encircled by the frame, depicting a closed, self-contained universe, despite its inner fissure. In Malevich's picture, the superposition of the geometrical figures and the imprecise contours of the asymmetrical square (with the background in white no longer placed above it, as in El Greco, but around it) suggests an infinite space. It produces the impression of projecting itself beyond its frame, creates the feeling that it intends to break the boundaries that encircle it and embrace the life that surrounds it, as if it were impelled by the force of the outside that irresistibly attracts it. The traces of the artist (the strokes of the brush) appear here as the inner vestiges of that life lying beyond the picture, that which at once sustains representation, creates it, and also makes violence upon it, demanding it to break out of its inherent boundaries and to fuse with itself. (Let us recall that the picture was painted in the aftermath of the Russian Revolution.)

Malevich simply wished to let the painting "swim in the white free abyss." The fact is that this desire would end up, in the course of the second half of the century, dissolving the entire dualistic universe, which even in its desubstantialized way still articulated the avant-garde composition. The proliferation in the 1960s of monochrome art is an expression of this. In Robert Rauschenberg's *Erased de Kooning Drawing* (1953), commonly considered the postmodern counterpart of Malevich's work, even the subtle distinction between figure and background has disappeared (figure C.2). The strokes of the brush (the artist's subjectivity) would eventually remain, but now, emptied of their former expressiveness, they are no longer vestiges of any surrounding life. The only highlighting element in this picture has become the gilded frame and the understated inscription, the manifestation of the art's institution that constitutes the

FIGURE C.2 Robert Rauschenberg, *Erased de Kooning Drawing* (1953). © 2015 Robert Rauschenberg / VAGA, New York / SAVA, Buenos Aires.

artist, the underlying mechanisms of its consecration as such. Without the title, we would have no idea what is within the frame, hidden under the strokes of the painter's brush: de Kooning's actual erased drawing.[5] The piece would be indecipherable. As in the case of violence, undecidability expands itself and encompasses the decisional instance, and not only the products of it.

Ultimately, what the neo-avant-garde calls into question is the founding premise of the avant-garde, the idea of an outside representation, of a life lying beyond art, to which this latter should seek to rejoin itself, which is the (impossible) operation that the name of the subject designates.[6] In Rauschenberg's picture, the outside disappears. It becomes internalized and erased, like de Kooning's drawing, under the white abyss of the painting. The painting is like the Platonic *khōra* referred to by Derrida. That which founds expression is within it, but it can never appear in it except "under erasure" (*sur rature*). This means the final break of the system of representation, whether figurative or nonfigurative. What then emerges as a problem is what Foucault called, in connection with Maurice Blanchot's writings, "the thought of the outside."

Like Malevich with painting, Blanchot intends to let language swim in the white free abyss, or, as Foucault puts it, "Not a word, just a rumination, a shivering, less than silence, less than the abyss of void, the plenitude of void." Blanchot's operation is to revert language to the formless substance of white noise, "to regress to the equivocal void of the outcome and the origin," to find there the potency that makes room to express what is itself inexpressible. We can call it "Blanchot's linguistic atonalism." Foucault continues:

> It demands of language a symmetrical conversion. It must cease to be the power that untiringly produces images and makes them shine, and turn, to the contrary, into the potency that unbinds them, frees them of all their ballasts, and impels them with the inner transparency that little by little throws light on them to make them explode and disperse into the weightlessness of the imaginable ... Thus, fiction does not consist of making us see the invisible but of making us see to what point the invisibility of the visible is invisible.[7]

Blanchot's writing is impelled, as is Malevich's play of white figures, by the force of the outside. It is irresistibly attracted by that which does not lend itself to representation and can be expressed in the interior of discourse only as its inner void. "Attraction has nothing to offer but the void," says Foucault. Yet, like the siren's song, "fascination does not spring from its present song, but in ... the promise that that song will be."[8] What is the promise that the song of the outside contains? It is the same one that Adorno, in *Philosophy of New Music*, believed to find in atonalism: the liberation from the cage of forms (and, furthermore, from the frameworks of the capitalist market, the commoditization of artistic goods). The freedom from the constraints of the law—or the rules of harmony, in musical composition—would open our horizon to the indeterminate, would make us experience the plenitude of life.[9]

The outside is thus seen as that which founds systems and at once contains the emancipatory potential of them. In short, it is nothing other than that which, at that moment, philosophy designates as the political realm. The emergence of the avant-garde and the concept of the political are strictly contemporary, and the two share the same archaeological ground. Furthermore, the two are regarded as similarly inexpressible in ordinary language. In connection with Blanchot's writing, Foucault says that the attempt to capture it makes room for the emergence of a "second language," beyond discourse.[10]

As Lefort tells us, such a reference to an outside, which defines the very concept of the political, "manifests society's self-externality." Yet, he also advises us, "not to project this externality to the real . . . It would be more accurate to say that power makes a gesture towards something *outside* and that it defines itself in terms of that outside." And he continues, "Whatever its form, it always refers to the same enigma: that of an internal-external articulation, of a division which institutes a common space, of a break which establishes relations, of a movement of the externalization of the social which goes hand in hand with its internalization."[11]

We get here Rauschenberg's painting ideal, the concept of art's internalization of the outside, the project of an inner self-externality. The idea of an inexpressible outside is reintroduced within the frameworks of representation itself. In the end, the representation of that outside as radically inexpressible is itself nothing more than a form of representation. As Rauschenberg shows in his painting, the hiatus is not really beyond the picture, is not a breach that separates the representation from something outside it (life), but rather is the manifestation of that fissure which is intrinsic to it. It is the erased drawing that is *inside the picture itself*, the artistic (inexpressible) ideal that is hidden under expression as its implicit substance and is only perceivable in the very designation of it (the inscription underneath). There is nothing here beyond its gilded frame. The outside, and the thought of a gap in relation to it, is just the outer projection of that inner fissure, which is inscribed at the heart of the system of representation.

Now, what do we get, once we discover that there is nothing outside, that it is just an illusory projection or, more precisely, a symptomatic manifestation of the inner, constitutive void of the systems? It is the "thought of the outside." The break in the system of representation inevitably makes it fold in upon itself. As the conceptual artist Joseph Kosuth claimed, the only role for an artist after the end of art was "to investigate the nature of art itself."[12]

The dissolution of the concept of art is indicative of a broader phenomenon, namely, the arrival of the "second disenchantment of the world." This is the moment when all the concepts forged in the nineteenth century, which hitherto worked as articulators of collectively shared horizons of life in a secular world (nation, history, revolution, and so on), lost their former efficacy. All projections of transcendent meaning were then revealed as not only inapprehensible but also, more radically, as nonexistent, illusory, purely mythical, and, lastly, potentially perverse. In sum, it marks the end of the game of immanence and transcendence. At this point, we would discover that the political, as Badiou pointed out (like nations, to Hobsbawm, or history, to Koselleck), is not an eternal category but a contingent reality, that its emergence is, in fact, a relatively recent phenomenon, merely a kind of accident resulting from a bifurcation within the theological universe of thought. And this revelation would be destructive of it. As Lefort remarked, with regard to the theological categories, although they remained after secularization, they now belonged to the order of the imaginary, but have lost their symbolic efficacy.

In any case, like the process of the secularization of the world, the dissolution of the horizon of the political (the second disenchantment of the world) is also an objective phenomenon, something that we cannot alter at will. We cannot produce a "reenchantment" of the world the way we can, for example, change our religious beliefs or our political persuasions.[13] The contemporary dissolution of these nineteenth-century categories heralds a rupture no less irreversible than the rupture that took place during the seventeenth century. However, at that point we also discover that, having broken all illusion of meaning, we cannot do without it, we still require it, we cannot cease to search for it, even without believing in it. And this creates a completely new setting for political thinking.

The question this raises is, How can a sense of community be articulated, once it is deprived of every reference to an outside? Or, to put it another way, What type of symbolic universe can emerge in a context in which not only God but also all his secular transpositions have revealed their mythical source? This question unfolds itself into a number of other, correlative ones: What sort of political practice is possible after it is deprived not only of all objective guarantee but also of subjective sustenance? And finally, what is the structure of the political field that opens up beyond the game of immanence–transcendence that articulated it? In short, what kind of political practice might take place beyond the field of the political?

These questions are both absolutely critical and completely unsolvable today. And this is not a merely factual impossibility. The very nature of the questions prevents it; they do not lend themselves to answers, which would necessarily entail their reelaboration according to other conceptual coordinates, and the consequent redefinition of the kinds of issues to which the fading of the horizon of the political gives rise. In any case, though we are not currently in a condition to answer these questions, we can nonetheless trace the trajectory that has led us to them, reencountering that historical-conceptual inflection from which the horizon of the political emerged and tracing the series of displacements it historically underwent, attempting to penetrate the particular type of logic that articulated it in the different courses it traversed. And, finally, we could identify the conditions that ended up dislocating the field of the political, turning its concept into a "problem," something symbolically elusive and materially indiscernible.

NOTES

SERIES EDITOR'S FOREWORD

1. This more Hegelian approach is suggested in Warren Breckman, *Adventures of the Symbolic: Post-Marxism and Radical Democracy* (New York: Columbia University Press, 2013), part of the Columbia Studies in Political Thought / Political History series. Like Palti's, Breckman's study belongs to the domain of conceptual history, and the books share many themes and analyzed authors. Breckman, however, stresses the import of the romantic project.
2. David William Bates, *States of War: Enlightenment Origins of the Political* (New York: Columbia University Press, 2012), published as part of Columbia's Political Thought / Political History series. An earlier volume in the series, Paul Kahn, *Political Theology: Four New Chapters on the Concept of Sovereignty*, trans. George Schwab (New York: Columbia University Press, 2011), reflected an American constitutional theorist's attempt to read Schmitt creatively. A more recent book in the same series analyzes the place of German antiliberal constitutional theory. See Dieter Grimm, *Sovereignty: The Origin and Future of a Political and Legal Concept*, trans. Belinda Cooper (New York: Columbia University Press, 2015).
3. I have illustrated this distinction by comparing the American republican democracy with the French quest for a democratic republic. In the American case, the republican constitutional framework protects the autonomy of an individualist (implicitly Protestant) society; in the French case, the action of the state on the individual is supposed to produce an identity of state and society (a sort of secular Catholic vision). See Dick Howard, *The Primacy of the Political: A History of Political Thought from the Greeks to the French and American Revolutions* (New York: Columbia University Press, 2010), which also appeared in the Political Thought / Political History series.

4. The English translation appeared Claude Lefort, *Complications: Communism and the Dilemmas of Democracy*, trans. Julien Bourg (New York: Columbia University Press, 2007). Another possible direction for a "political practice . . . beyond the field of the political" is suggested by Martin Breaugh, *The Plebeian Experience: A Discontinuous History of Political Freedom*, trans. Lazer Lederhendler (New York: Columbia University Press, 2013). Both volumes are part of the Columbia Studies in Political Thought / Political History series.

INTRODUCTION

1. Carl Schmitt, *Political Theology: Four Chapters on the Concept of Sovereignty* (Chicago: University of Chicago Press, 2005), 5.
2. The title of Julien Freund's book, *L'essence du politique* (1965), is the best example of this tendency.

1. THE THEOLOGICAL GENESIS OF THE POLITICAL

1. Quentin Skinner, "Meaning and Understanding in the History of Ideas," in *Vision of Politics*, vol. 1, *Regarding Method* (Cambridge: Cambridge University Press, 2002), 57–89 (esp. 59–65).
2. Behind this method lies a normative drive. A good example of this is Hwa-Yong Lee's *Political Representation in the Later Middle Ages* (New York: Peter Lang, 2008), in which the author discusses what we can draw from Marsilius of Padua for our own theories of political representation. In this fashion, the book goes back and forth from the fourteenth to the twenty-first centuries, as if seven hundred years in conceptual and political history were not a relevant factor but, rather, a disposable element.
3. As Quentin Skinner writes, "The mythology of doctrines can similarly be illustrated from 'histories of ideas' in the strictest sense. Here the aim (in the work of Arthur Lovejoy, pioneer in this approach) is to trace the morphology of some given doctrine 'through all the provinces of history in which it appears.' The characteristic point of departure is to set out an ideal type of the given doctrine—whether that is that of equality, progress, reason of state, the social contract, the great chain of being, the separation of powers, and so on." Skinner, "Meaning and Understanding," 62.
4. Despite Skinner's sharp criticism of that procedure, he himself succumbs to it. The very title of his major work, *The Foundations of Modern Political Thought*, is already a concise expression of what he denounces as the mythology of doctrines: he "sets out the morphology of a given doctrine" (in this case, that of the modern state) and then "trace(s) the morphology of (it) 'through all the provinces of history in which it appears.'" Skinner, *The Foundations of Modern Political Thought* (Cambridge: Cambridge University Press, 1988), xx. A good short example of the regrettable conse-

quences of this method can be seen in his "Political Philosophy," in *The Cambridge History of Renaissance Philosophy*, ed. Quentin Skinner (Cambridge: Cambridge University Press, 1988), 389–452. Skinner begins by stating that Italian republicanism was something of an anomaly in the sixteenth century. However, he devotes his chapter about Renaissance political thinking almost exclusively to this subject. This clearly suggests that Skinner was less interested in understanding the political thinking of the epoch under study, in historical terms, than in recovering what he considered a tradition worthy of attention for contemporary politics. The subjectivism of this approach is undeniable. In any case, it is evident that Skinner's focus remains on the level of "ideas." The selectivity of his procedure ultimately reveals that his intention is not to understand the structure of the political thinking of the period in the light of its underlying language, that is, to recreate the mental structure of the Renaissance worldview, what Edwin Panofsky called its characteristic "habitus," and see how this expressed itself in the realm of political thinking. This would have been a fundamental contribution, as one would have expected from a work befitting the so-called new intellectual history. Skinner does not even profit from the other works included in that very volume, many of which analyze the Neoplatonist—more specifically the Florentine Neoplatonist—system of knowledge, and the natural philosophy, astrological theories, rhetorical techniques, and so forth that were proper to it. All of this might have helped him explain how Machiavelli and his contemporaries could say what they eventually said—as he claims, in his theoretical works, he intends to do. Lacking this explanation, the essay presents a rather traditional account of the political ideas of the time. For an excellent review of Skinner's intellectual trajectory and of the criticism his work received, see Kari Palonen, *Quentin Skinner: History, Politics, Rhetoric* (Cambridge: Polity, 2003).

5. Lucien Febvre, *The Problem of Unbelief in the Sixteenth Century: The Religion of Rabelais*, trans. Beatrice Gottlieb (Cambridge: Harvard University Press, 1982), 460.
6. See Reinhart Koselleck, *Futures Past: On the Semantics of Historical Time*, trans. K. Tribe (Cambridge, MA: MIT Press, 1985). Koselleck identifies two factors that would explain the conceptual shift that gave birth to our modern worldview: the scientific developments of the eighteenth century, which gave rise to the idea of progress, and the French Revolution, which provided the European mind with a new sense of men's and women's agency in history. However, he does not explain the emergence of these two factors or the conditions that made them possible. It is certain that neither the scientific developments of the eighteenth century nor the French Revolution would have occurred if some conceptual changes had not preceded them. As Husserl remarks in the writings gathered in *The Crisis of European Sciences*, it is not true that scientific discoveries gave rise to our secular world; it was the other way around. It was necessary for the world to detach itself from its mysteries so that the technical attitude to it could emerge. Similarly, if kings were considered gods, they could not be executed. So how could the phenomena that he invoked happen? To explain this we must trace the series of preceding conceptual changes that made such developments possible.

184　1. THE THEOLOGICAL GENESIS OF THE POLITICAL

7. Lucien Febvre's concluding remarks clarify his point: "All in all, the deep religiosity of the majority of those who created the modern world, a phrase that applies to someone like Descartes, was, I hope I have shown, applicable to a century earlier to Rabelais, and to those whose deep faith he knew how to express superbly." Febvre, *The Problem of Unbelief in the Sixteenth Century: The Religion of Rabelais*, trans. Beatrice Gottlieb (Cambridge: Harvard University Press, 1982), 464.

8. As Febvre stated, "Not to believe. Would you say the problem was simple? Was it so easy for a man, as nonconformist as he could conceivably be in other respects, to break with the habits, the customs, even the laws of the social groups of which he was a part?" (Febvre, *The Problem of Unbelief*, 455).

9. According to Febvre, a new secular, rational "language" would be available only one century later. Only then could a nontheological worldview emerge. "Neither Rabelais, nor his contemporaries," he stated, "had the touchstone yet that could have allowed them to choose the right scale on which to weigh opinions: a strong scientific method. Let us give it both of its names: the experimental method and the critical method" (Febvre, *The Problem of Unbelief*, 462). Thus, Febvre's "solution" (which is not really so) consists of positing the development of a scientific method as the independent variable from which all the rest derive, a self-explanatory factor that would not require, it itself, explanation. Ultimately, for him, it was not a contingent conceptual development but the final discovery of an eternal truth, of the "the right scale on which to weigh opinions."

10. The present book can be read as a rebuttal to Giorgio Agamben, *The Kingdom and the Glory: For a Theological Genealogy of Economy and Government* (Stanford: Stanford University Press, 2011), which affirms a linear continuity between the theological and the political.

11. Following Skinner's methodology in *The Foundations of Modern Political Thought*, and in discussion with him, Annabel Brett intends to posit the Hispanic thinkers of the seventeenth century as the true precursors of modern republicanism. See Brett, "Scholastic Political Thought and the Modern Concept of the State," in *Rethinking the Foundations of Modern Political Thought*, ed. Annabel Brett and James Tully (Cambridge: Cambridge University Press, 2006), 130–148. Thus, her position misses the crucial point: the seventeenth-century conceptual universe was radically different from our own, and disclosing that difference is precisely what historical understanding is about. Indeed, the search for the precursors of modern political thinking (be they Hispanic or whatever) necessarily entails the anachronistic retrospective projection of our own, current ideas.

12. As Gilles Deleuze remarked in his lectures on Spinoza at Vincennes University, between November 1980 and March 1981, in philosophy, as in painting, resorting to God served to enhance creativity by freeing the mind of all kinds of constraints (the lack of constraints was supposed to be one of God's intrinsic attributes). See Deleuze, *En el medio de Spinoza* (Buenos Aires: Cactus, 2011). This is the only edited version of this lecture available in any language.

1. THE THEOLOGICAL GENESIS OF THE POLITICAL   185

13. Regarding the reintroduction of Aristotle's work in the West, see Bernard Dod, "Aristoteles latinus," in *The Cambridge History of Later Medieval Philosophy*, ed. Norman Kretzmann, Anthony Kenny, and Jean Pinborg (Cambridge: Cambridge University Press, 1988), 45–79; and C. H. Lohr, "The Medieval Interpretation of Aristotle," in *The Cambridge History*, 80–98. Regarding *Politics*, in particular, see Jean Dundbabin, "The Reception and Interpretation of Aristotle's *Politics*," in *The Cambridge History*, 723–737.
14. Aristotle, *Politics*, trans. Benjamin Jowett (Kittchener: Batoche, 1999), 3.
15. Aristotle, *Politics*, 84.
16. Aristotle, *Politics*, 83.
17. Aristotle, *Politics*, 82.
18. See Otto Hintze, *Staat und Verfassung* (Gotinga: Vandenhoeck & Ruprecht, 1962).
19. As we know, lords had vassals, but they themselves were vassals of superior lords, and so on. At the apex of this pyramid of hierarchies was the king, but his authority was a mere prolongation of this system of relations of subordination that organized the entire society.
20. These years witnessed the spread of the adage *Rex in regno suo est imperator*. Regarding this, see Walter Ullmann, *Escritos sobre teoría política medieval* (Buenos Aires: Eudeba, 2003); and Michael Wilks, *The Problem of Sovereignty in the Later Middle Ages* (Cambridge: Cambridge University Press, 1963).
21. In this context, justice is understood as giving to each individual that which corresponds to him or her according to the place he or she occupies in society. As Thomas Aquinas says, "The perfect social community comes to be when each individual keeps order due to the actions that correspond to his status." Aquinas, "Gobierno de los príncipes," in *Tratado de la ley, Tratado de la justicia: Gobierno de los príncipes*, trans. Carlos Ignacio González (Mexico: Porrúa, 1975), 509.
22. In 1240, a few years before the translation of Aristotle's *Politics*, there was a confrontation between Frederic I and Pope Gregory IX in which the emperor denounced the pope's moral depravity. Frederic I then resurrected the idea formulated long before by Pope Leo I, who had defined the pope as the *indignus heres* (unworthy heir) of Jesus Christ. This appellation was originally aimed at legitimating the pope's decisions independently of his moral condition, or lack of it. In other words, the papal sanctions were valid regardless of whether they were adopted by a saint or a villain. However, over time, this would serve to establish a distinction between the sacred body and the profane body of the supreme pontiffs. See Ullmann, *Escritos sobre teoría*, 150–155.
23. Walter Ullmann proposes this idea, though he uses it in a different sense than we do. According to him, the contribution of Aquinas and the thirteenth century to political thought is the discovery of the Natural Man, who, from then on, would be distinguished from the Christian subject. Regarding this, see Ullmann, *Individual and Society in the Middle Ages* (Baltimore, MD: Johns Hopkins University Press, 1966), chap. 3.
24. Aquinas, "Gobierno de los príncipes," 361. Aristotelian teleologism will also enable Aquinas to justify the subordination of worldly goods to sacred goods: "Every primary

186   1. THE THEOLOGICAL GENESIS OF THE POLITICAL

cause is more influential in the created being than the secondary cause; and the first cause is God. Thus, if all things move by virtue of the first cause, and everything is influenced by the first mover, then the movement of the lords will be by virtue of God, one that is a first mover" (408). The goal of a community, he states, is to reach virtue and, ultimately, acquire a vision of God (*visio cut Dei*). From this he derives the principle that earthly monarchs are no more than instruments of God and his only true representative on earth is the pope. "In the law of Christ," he concludes, "kings must be subordinated to priests" (365).

25. Aquinas, "Gobierno de los principles," 487. Actually, in *Politics*, Aristotle distinguishes a large number of constitutions beyond the three basic ones.
26. Aquinas, "Gobierno de los príncipes," 333–334. Ultimately, for Aquinas and the thinking of his era, social order entailed inequalities among men. They are the ones who weave the social fabric and keep it tight. "It is this that demonstrates," Aquinas says, "the notion of order and nature, because, quoting Saint Augustine, order is the disposition of the similar and dissimilar things, in a way so that each has what it deserves. This makes it clear that order assumes a certain inequality, and this is also true in government, as according to this principle the governing of a man over others is natural" (427).
27. "The governors of a republic are compelled to observe political laws, and cannot trespass them in the pursuit of justice, while kings and other monarchs possess the law within them and can apply it on a case-by-case basis. And it is a law that which pleases the prince, as indicated by the laws of the people; but this does not occur with political governors, because they may not introduce novelties unforeseen by laws" (Aquinas, "Gobierno de los príncipes," 460).
28. On the semantic transformation that the concept of "politics" underwent in connection with the distinction between civil government and monarchical government, see Nicolai Rubinstein, "The History of the Word *Politicus* in Early-Modern Europe," in *The Languages of Political Theory in Early-Modern Europe*, ed. Anthony Pagden (Cambridge: Cambridge University Press, 1990), 41–56. This transformation was, in turn, the basis for the distinction between *gubernaculum* and *imperium*. See Charles H. McIlwain, *Constitutionalism: Ancient and Modern* (Ithaca, NY: Cornell University Press, 1958).
29. Dante Alighieri, *The* De Monarchia *by Dante Alighieri*, trans. Aurelia Henry (Boston: Houghton, Mifflin, 1904), 4.
30. Alighieri, *De Monarchia*, 54.
31. Alighieri, *De Monarchia*, 72–73.
32. This also is the means by which God reveals to human beings the secret design of Creation: "The will of God is in itself an invisible attribute, but by means of things which are made, the invisible attributes of God become perceptible to the intellect. For, though a seal be hidden, the wax impressed therewith bears manifest evidence of the unseen signet; nor is it remarkable that the divine will must be sought in signs, for the human will, except to him who wills, is discerned no way else than in signs" (Alighieri, *De Monarchia*, 74–76).
33. Alighieri, *De Monarchia*, 23.

1. THE THEOLOGICAL GENESIS OF THE POLITICAL   187

34. Dante's conclusion is that, as long as the plurality of monarchies persists, the threat of division will remain. Following this principle, he concludes that, to realize the kingdom of God on earth, there must be but a single universal monarch, the emperor.
35. The identification of the monarch with God certainly existed long before Dante's time. What now changed was the idea of the God with which the monarch would be identified. It is now a nominalist God—a pure, unconditioned will. And it is this idea of God that is also found in the concept of law elaborated by the neoscholastics. As Francisco Suárez stated in *De legibus*, if a law is binding, it is not so because it is just; what makes a law compulsory and universal is the nature of the authority from which it emanates. Suárez, *De legibus* (Madrid: CSIC, 1971). Ultimately, for a law to be a law it must necessarily be associated with a coercive power, someone capable of sanctioning it and enforcing it.
36. The mundane nature of the actual subject who assumes the role of the mediator is emphasized by the fact that he is merely a local priest.
37. Ernst Kantorowicz, *The King's Two Bodies: A Study in Medieval Political Thought* (Princeton: Princeton University Press, 1981), 26. As Kantorowicz states, the king was traditionally considered a "mixed person," that is, one person with a dual nature. However, this is not what Kantorowicz focuses on in *The King's Two Bodies*. The key word here is *body*. "The duplication expressed in the concept of *mixed person* refers to the temporary and spiritual capacities, not natural and political bodies" (45). This change from persona to body expresses a crucial conceptual shift, as a result of which the topic will become invested with a new—hitherto unknown—political connotation.
38. Walter Benjamin, *The Origin of German Tragic Drama* (London: Verso, 2009), 69.
39. Baltasar Gracián, *El Criticón* (Buenos Aires: Losada, 2010), 55.
40. Gracián, *El Criticón*, 67.
41. "'We are now,' said the wise man to the inexperienced Critilo, 'entering into the world . . . You have seen hitherto the works of nature, admired and contemplated on them; now observe those of art, the artificial skill of men . . . Oh, what a vast distance and difference you will find between the civil and the natural world; this I thought fit to advise you, that you may not admire whatsoever it is'" (Gracián, *El Criticón*, 68). A later passage reads, "So that, if you observe well, all take advantage of the miserable man. The world deceives him, life flatters him, fortune derides him, health forsakes him, his youth passes, felicity withdraws, years fly away, and dissolves him, oblivion swallows him, and he who yesterday was a man, today is dust, and tomorrow nothing" (115).
42. It is no coincidence that the tragic century in which this novel takes place (the seventeenth) is also the century of Galileo and Descartes. It is then, when all natural links with God have been broken, that man must draw those artificial lines that let him make his way through the world of mundane phenomena and escape this labyrinth. Rational knowledge will never be able to encompass that reality, which is always infinitely more complex and richer than any knowledge. "There are more things in heaven and earth, Horatio, / Than are dreamt of in your philosophy," observed Hamlet

188 1. THE THEOLOGICAL GENESIS OF THE POLITICAL

(act I, scene 5), but at least "philosophy," or reason, offers a guide to traverse and move through it. On this topic, see Hans Blumenberg, *The Genesis of the Copernican World*, trans. Robert Wallace (Cambridge: MIT Press, 1987); and Blumenberg, *The Legitimacy of the Modern Age*, trans. Robert Wallace (Cambridge: MIT Press, 1991).

43. Gracián, *El Criticón*, 169.
44. Gilles Deleuze, *The Fold: Leibniz and the Baroque* (Minneapolis: University of Minnesota Press, 1992), 5–6.
45. Note that the handkerchief in the pocket of the boy contains El Greco's signature. Actually, there is another character in the cortege who looks at us: El Greco himself. The replication at different levels of the figure that represents representation itself is another typical technique of the baroque, a means of expressing the *mise en abyme* implicit in the very attempt of representing representation.
46. It is not by chance that, when Michel Foucault, in *Les mots et les choses*, begins describing what he calls "the age of representation" of the seventeenth century, he refers to Spain. Both of the examples he cites in the text are Spanish: *Don Quixote* and Velázquez's *Las Meninas*. See Foucault, *The Order of Things: An Archeology of the Human Sciences* (New York: Random House, 1990), an English translation of *Les mots et les choses*.
47. As Foucault remarks, "Perhaps there exists in the painting by Velázquez the representation, as it were, of Classical representation, and the definition of the space it opens up to us. And, indeed, representation undertakes to represent itself here in all its elements, with its images, the eyes of which it is offered, the faces it makes visible, the gestures that call it into being. But there, in the midst of this dispersion, which it is simultaneously grouping together and spreading before us, indicated compellingly from every side, is an essential void: the necessary disappearance of that which is its foundation—of the person it resembles and the person in whose eyes it is only a resemblance. The very subject—which is the same—has been elided. And representation, freed finally from the relation that was impeding it, can offer itself a representation in its pure form." Foucault, *The Order of Things*, 16.
48. It is interesting to observe the turn that is produced, in the course of the sixteenth century, in the concept of the relation between the sign and its reference. One example of the way in which what Foucault calls the signature system of the Renaissance operates is the case of Columbus. Tzevan Todorov shows Columbus's nearly compulsive thirst to name those things he discovers, which is linked to his intention to capture the very essence of the named things. See Todorov, *The Conquest of America* (New York: Harper & Row, 1984). A century later, this had changed radically. Having produced the ultramarine expansion, the Europeans discovered the infinite diversity of cultures and languages that existed on earth, and with that came a new sense of cultural relativity, a sense that the ways of designating and naming things would be conventional and mutable over time. For someone like Fray Luis de León (one of the great Spanish mystics at the end of the sixteenth century), names contained within themselves the true essence of things, but he believed that this would be true only in the Edenic tongue. Unlike the original prelapsarian state, in which God presented himself imme-

diately before our eyes, now He could only reveal Himself through figures. But all figures are imperfect and deficient, as none have inscribed within themselves their ultimate meaning. After the Fall, language went on to become an artificial construct, separated from all natural substance, and between the natural and the artificial there is no common measure. Due to its conventional character, the essence of the named thing never really finds itself present in the word used to name it. See de León, *De los nombres de Cristo* (Madrid: PMI, 1994). Even though this does not break with the Thomistic scheme, there would be now an insurmountable breach between the two orders, between the primary causes that immediately relate to God and the secondary causes that are the way of operation on earth of those primary causes.

49. Francisco Suárez, *Defensio fidei*, trans. José Ramón Eguillor Muniozguren (Madrid: Instituto de Estudios Politicos, 1971), book I, chap. 10, no. 4.
50. Suárez, *Defensio fidei*, book I, chap. 10, no. 7.
51. James I's complaint about the Puritans was that, by "making their owne imaginations (without any warrant of the word) the square of their conscience," they would have deprived the kingdom of any foundation for authority. James I, "Basilikon Doron," in *Political Writings: King James VI and I*, ed. Johann P. Sommerville (Cambridge: Cambridge University Press, 1994), 26–27.
52. Suárez, *Defensio fidei*, book II, chap. 4, no. 1.
53. Suárez, *Defensio fidei*, book I, chap. 9, no. 11.
54. Suárez, *Defensio fidei*, book III, chap. 2, no. 10.
55. "To argue this thesis [of the divine rights of kings]," states Jean-François Courtine in one of the best studies of Suárez's thinking, papal theorists will not stop deconstructing "the underlying analogy between the institution of pontifical sovereignty and that of political sovereignty. It is thus that the very logic of doctrinal conflict will lead them to point out the intrinsic necessity of mediations that exist between divine will (decision) and political authority." Courtine, *Nature et empire de la loi: Études suaréziennes* (Paris: J. Vrin, 1999), 22.
56. The idea of a social contract does not indicate here that the king should follow the will of the members of the community. Popular will did not have a normative force in this context (the majority's wish for something does not make it good or just). The pact works here as the reminder that power was conferred on the monarch for the sake of community and for his own sake. That is, that the king must observe the eternal principles of justice. Thus, the limits on the action of the sovereign are given not by the popular will but by the ends that are supposedly attached to the royal investiture. See Tulio Halperin Donghi, *Tradición política española e ideología revolucionaria de Mayo* (Buenos Aires: CEAL, 1965).
57. As a matter of fact, in *De rege et regis institutione* (1599), the Jesuit Juan de Mariana discusses the most properly Christian means of killing a king.
58. Suárez, *Defensio fidei*, book III, chap. 3, no. 3.
59. The very definition of the king as a tyrant already has implicit a lack of acknowledgment as such. Nor did James I reject it. At the moment of establishing the difference between a legitimate king and a tyrant, he cannot help resorting to some contractual

ideal. "Consider first," he says, "the trew difference betwixt a lawful good King, and the usurping Tyrant . . . The one acknowledgeth himself ordained for his people, hauing receiued from God a burthen of gouernment, whereof he must be countable: the other thinketh his people ordained for him, a prey to his passion and inordinate appetites" (James I, "Basilikon Doron," 20).

60. Suárez, *De legibus*, book II, chap. 3, no. 1, no. 6.
61. Suárez, *De legibus*, book I, chap. 8, no. 9. In fact, Suárez refers here to a postulate raised by James I, who, in his First Discourse to Parliament, stated, "I am the Head and it [the Commonwealth] is my Body; I am the Sheperd, and it is my flocke: I hope therefore no man will be so vnreasonable as to thinke that I am a Christian King vnder the Gospel, should be a Polygamist and husband to two wiues; that I being the Head, should haue a diuided and monstruos Body . . . Could euer the Body be counted without the Head, which was euer vnseparably ioined therunto? So that as Honour and Priuiledges of any of the Kingdomes could not be diuided from their Sovraigne. So are they confounded and ioined in my Person, who am equall and alike kindly Head to you both" (James I, "Speech of 1604," in *Political Writings*, 136).
62. See Alain Petit, "Le pastorat ou l'impossible raccourci théologique-politique," in *Figures du théologico-politique*, ed. E. Cattin, L. Jaffro, and A. Petit (Paris: J. Vrin, 1999), 9–24; and Passerin D'Entrèves, *The Notion of the State: An Introduction to Political Theory* (Oxford: Clarendon, 1969).
63. In recent historiography, the school presided over by Bartolomé Clavero has become the best representative of the former trend, which emphasizes the traditionalist nature of neoscholastic thinking (and which actually has deep roots in Hispanic historiography). Annabel Brett is one of the most vocal today in expressing the latter trend in the Anglophone world, which remarks the potentially democratic aspects of that thinking. See Clavero, *Antidora: Antropología Católica de la economía moderna* (Milán: Giuffrè, 1991); and Brett, "Scholastic Political Thought and the Modern Concept of the State," in *Rethinking the Foundations of Modern Political Thought*, ed. Annabel Brett and James Tully (Cambridge: Cambridge University Press, 2006), 130–148.
64. Deleuze, *The Fold*, 3.
65. Lucien Goldmann, *Le Dieu caché: Étude sur la visión tragique dans les* Pensées *de Pascal et dans le théâtre de Racine* (Paris: Gallimard, 1955), 219. "Tragic negation comes from the fact that one cannot live in the world but only by choosing between extremes that, despite being contrary, do not cease to be equally necessary, and present themselves with the same absolute and unavoidable demand" (422).

2. THE TRAGIC SCENE

1. Quentin Skinner, "Hobbes on Rhetoric and the Construction of Morality," in *Vision of Politics*, vol. 2, *Hobbes and Civil Science* (Cambridge: Cambridge University Press, 2002), 141.

2. An associated device is that of equivocation, which was cultivated by the Jesuits and consisted of deceiving by telling half-truths. Shakespeare included in his work many references to this device. In *Macbeth*, for example, he speaks of "the equivocation of the fiend / That lies like truth" (*Macbeth*, act V, scene 5). Regarding Shakespeare's "perspectivism," see W. R. Elton, "Shakespeare and the Thought of His Age," in *A New Companion to Shakespeare Studies*, ed. Kenneth Muir and S. Schoenbaum (Cambridge: Cambridge University Press, 1971), 180–198.
3. On the relation between politics and rhetoric in Shakespeare, see David Colclough, "Talking to the Animals: Persuasion, Counsel and Their Discontents in *Julius Caesar*," in *Shakespeare and Early Modern Political Thought*, ed. David Armitage, Conal Condren, and Andrew Fitzmaurice (Cambridge: Cambridge University Press, 2009), 217–233; Markku Peltonen, "Political Rhetoric and Citizenship in *Coriolanus*," in *Shakespeare and Early Modern Political Thought*, 234–252; and Cathy Shrank, "Counsel, Succession, and the Politics of Shakespeare's *Sonnets*," in *Shakespeare and Early Modern Political Thought*, 101–118.
4. Donna B. Hamilton provides an excellent picture of the political background of Shakespeare's plays, showing the contradictory arguments that were set at debate during the Jacobean period. Against James I's proposition of the divine right of kings, which was supported by philosophers such as Francis Bacon, who compared the king to Aristotle's prime mover and called him the *principalis agens*, the Commons in Parliament presented in 1610 the Petition of Temporal Grievances, in which they reminded the king that he must "be guided and governed by the certain rule of law" and that excessive royal power reduced the subjects to slaves. Hamilton, "Shakespeare's Romance and Jacobean Political Discourse," in *Approaches to the Teaching of Shakespeare's* The Tempest *and Other Late Romances*, ed. Maurice Hunt (New York: Modern Language Association of America, 1992, 68–69.
5. A. P. Rossiter has described the ambivalence about every major issue in Shakespeare's plays. Rossiter, "Ambivalence: The Dialectic of Histories," in *Angels with Horns: Fifteen Lectures on Shakespeare* (New York: Theatre Art Books, 1961). See also Norman Rabkin, *Shakespeare and the Problem of Meaning* (Chicago: University of Chicago Press, 1981).
6. William Empson, *Seven Types of Ambiguity* (New York: Meridian, 1955), 217.
7. Actually, a long tradition of thought associates the baroque with a tragic sense. And this is not incidental: in the nineteenth century, tragedy was in decline as a dramatic form, and the romantics were certainly aware of that fact. As we will see in chapter 3, Koselleck's *Sattelzeit* represents the simultaneous culmination and closing of the horizon opened by the baroque's *Schwellenzeit*. And it was only then that the underlying structure of its particular kind of discourse could become visible. The field of the political remained open, but what was lost was the sense of both the necessity and impossibility of choosing, which was intrinsic to the baroque and determined its tragic mood.
8. Lucien Goldmann, following the Lukács of "Metaphysics of Tragedy," poses this conflict in terms of the contradiction between Man and World (the disproportion between

the hero's inner self and the outer world, his permanent maladjustment with it), which, though not incorrect, does not thoroughly express the nature of tragic conflict. The contradiction between love and honor is both subjective and objective. The two principles are both real, intrinsic parts in the world, compelling aspects of human experience (love here cannot be taken for mere desire). At the same time, they express a subjective scission: the fact that human beings are simultaneously compelled by two opposite drives (faith and duty). Lucien Goldmann, *Le Dieu Caché: Étude sur la visión tragique dans les* Pensées *de Pascal et dans le théâtre de Racine* (Paris: Gallimard, 1955).

9. In the case of princes and kings, this is literally so. As Laertes tells his sister, Ophelia, "His greatness weigh'd, his will is not his own; / For he himself is subject to his birth: / He may not, as unvalued persons do, / Carve for himself; for on his choice depends / The safety and health of this whole state; / And therefore must his choice be circumscrib'd" (*Hamlet*, act I, scene 3).

10. See Martha C. Nussbaum, *The Fragility of Goodness: Luck and Ethics in Greek Tragedy and Philosophy* (Cambridge: Cambridge University Press, 1989).

11. "The measure of Good and Evil," Thomas Hobbes stated, "is the Civil Law: and the Judge the Legislator, who is always the Representative of the Common-wealth." Hobbes, *Leviathan* (Cambridge: Cambridge University Press, 1994), chap. 29. "Where there is no common Power, there is no Law: where no Law, no Injustice" (chap. 13).

12. In *Two Treatises of Civil Government*, Locke argued against those authors who, like Robert Filmer, rejected the right of insurrection. In doing so, Locke claimed, they ended up undermining monarchy by depriving it of its foundations: "They have denied mankind a right to natural freedom: whereby they have not only, as much as in them lies, exposed all subjects to the utmost misery of tyranny and oppression, but have also unsettled the titles, and shaken the thrones of princes (for they too, by these mean systems, except only one, are all born slaves)." Locke, *Two Treatises of Civil Government*, chap. 1.

13. See Hobbes, *Leviathan*, chap. 29; and Locke, *Two Treatises of Civil Government*, chap. 1.

14. According to Friedrich Nietzsche, this is also the function of the amphitheater: the circular shape allows the spectators to observe the play from all the different perspectives; nothing is hidden from them.

15. Friedrich Nietzsche, "The Birth of Tragedy," in *The Philosophy of Nietzsche* (New York: Random House, n.d.), 209.

16. As Michel Foucault noted, "The world of the seventeenth century is strangely hospitable to madness... Madness is here at the heart of things and men." Foucault, *Madness and Civilization* (New York: Random House, 1965), 31, 37.

17. In those years, marginal references in the scripts to stage effects multiplied. Actually, the most sophisticated mechanical devices of the time were developed for the stage, not for the manufacture of goods. See José Antonio Maravall, "The Social Role of Artifice," in *Culture of the Baroque: Analysis of a Historical Structure*, trans. Terry Cochran (Minneapolis: University of Minnesota Press, 1986), 225–250.

18. Richard II: "God save the king! Will no man say amen? /Am I both priest and clerk? well then, amen. / God save the king! although I be not he; / And yet, amen, if heaven do think him me" (Shakespeare, *Richard II*, act IV, scene 1).

19. There is an explicit reference to this in *Hamlet*, when the prince observes how turning a common man into a king is not a natural thing but the result of artifice. As he says, "It is not very strange; for mine uncle is king of Denmark, and those that would make mows at him while my father lived, give twenty, forty, fifty, an hundred ducats a-piece for his picture in little. 'Sblood, there is something in this more than natural, if philosophy could find it out" (*Hamlet*, act II, scene 2).
20. The idea of life as a fluid was a basic principle of the age. The one who would systematize this theory was Georg Ernst Stahl, who also formulated the phlogiston theory.
21. See Arturo Farinelli, *La vita è sogno, parte seconda* (Torino: Fratelli Bocca, 1916), 283–285.
22. That ideas are or may be deceitful or illusory was certainly not a new discovery. To interpret the baroque in this sense would be reductionist.
23. E. H. Gombricht, *Art and Illusion: A Study of the Psychology of Pictorial Representation* (New York: Pantheon, 1960), 5–6; quoted in Norman Rabkin, *Shakespeare and the Problem of Meaning* (Chicago: University of Chicago Press, 1981), 35.
24. The link between Richard II and James I (the supporter and protector of Shakespeare's company) is clearly expressed in the play. In several scenes, Richard describes in the most elaborate of terms James's doctrine of the divine right of kings. Even after being informed of Bolingbroke's uprising and the defection of most of his followers, he shows himself confident of the very power that emanates from his sacred investiture. As he says, "Not all the water in the rough rude sea / Can wash the balm off from an anointed king; / The breath of worldly men cannot depose / The deputy elected by the Lord: / For every man that Bolingbroke hath press'd / To lift shrewd steel against our golden crown, / God for his Richard hath in heavenly pay / A glorious angel: then, if angels fight, / Weak men must fall, for heaven still guards the right" (*Richard II*, act III, scene 2).
25. The mirror, as a symbol, had also two opposite meanings: it was both the expression of external appearances, of the illusions of representation, and a device to penetrate the soul, the inner being of things and men. When Hamlet is trying to determine whether his mother, Gertrude, was guilty in his father's death, he says, "You go not till I set you up a glass / Where you may see the inmost part of you" (*Hamlet*, act III, scene 4).
26. "Give me the glass, and therein will I read. / No deeper wrinkles yet? hath sorrow struck / So many blows upon this face of mine, / And made no deeper wounds? O flattering glass, / Like to my followers in prosperity, / Thou dost beguile me! Was this face the face / That every day under his household roof / Did keep ten thousand men? was this the face / That, like the sun, did make beholders wink? / Was this the face that faced so many follies, / And was at last out-faced by Bolingbroke? / A brittle glory shineth in this face: / As brittle as the glory is the face; / [*He dashes the glass against the ground.*] / For there it is, crack'd in a hundred shivers. / Mark, silent king, the moral of this sport, / How soon my sorrow hath destroy'd my face" (*Richard II*, act IV, scene 1).
27. In *Hamlet* (act IV, scene 2), Shakespeare returns to that motif. Hamlet says, "The body is with the king, but the king is not with the body. The king is a thing—" Guildenstern responds, "A thing, my lord!" To which Hamlet says, "Of nothing . . ."

28. Cf. Northrop Frye, *On Shakespeare* (Markham, ON: Fitzbury & Whiteside, 1986), 67–69.
29. Shakespeare, *Richard II*, act V, scene 5.
30. A more traditional interpretation sees the arrival of Fortinbras as the symbolic restoration of order to the kingdom. However, we know that he was not a legitimate king, either. Horace tells us that at the very beginning of the play. Ultimately, in that "conservative" view, tragedy appears as merely an episode within a framework of order and stability, which is a very anti-Shakespearean concept. All of Shakespeare's work remarks on the fragility and precariousness of every order, or even worse, the inescapable mixture and confusion of order and disorder: "Fair is foul, and foul is fair," repeat the witches in *Macbeth* (act I, scene 1).
31. The analogy of the king as the husband of his kingdom had a long tradition, and was one of the central motives of James's discourse. "I am the Husband, and all the whole Isle is my lawfull Wife," he stated. James I, "Speech of 1604," in *Political Writings: King James VI and I*, ed. Johann P. Sommerville (Cambridge: Cambridge University Press, 1994), 136. Yet, gender analogies are rambling. As Jonathan Goldberg shows, the king is sometimes referred to as a woman, too. Goldberg, *James I and the Politics of Literature: Jonson, Shakespeare, Donne, and Other Contemporaries* (Stanford, CA: Stanford University Press, 1999). Regarding this and similar analogies in Shakespeare's plays, see W. R. Elton, "Shakespeare and the Thought of His Age," in *A New Companion to Shakespeare Studies*, ed. Kenneth Muir and S. Schoenbaum (Cambridge: Cambridge University Press, 1971), 182–183.
32. John Hunt, "A Thing of Nothing: The Catastrophic Body in *Hamlet*," *Shakespeare Quarterly* 39, no. 2 (1988): 29. According to Molly Smith, "The intensity of Stuart fascination with the fragmented body becomes most apparent when we compare Jacobean treatments of the subject with earlier depictions that emphasize the unity rather than fragmentation between the dual bodies of the monarch." Smith, *The Darker World Within: Evil in the Tragedies of Shakespeare and His Successors* (Cranbury, NJ: Associated University Presses, 1991), 42.
33. As we will see in chapter 3, this explains why, in the same way that monarchy, as a principle, was unthinkable for Aristotle and the ancients, it is democracy, as a principle, that now would be conceptually ungraspable to seventeenth-century political philosophy (even though it would be continuously invoked).
34. Georg Friedrich Creuzer, *Symbolik und Mythologie des Altes Völker, besondres des Griechen* (1819), quoted in Walter Benjamin, *The Origin of German Tragic Drama* (London: Verso, 2009), 164–165.
35. Benjamin, *Origin of German Tragic Drama*, 178.
36. Georg Lukács, "Metaphysics of Tragedy," in *Soul and Form*, trans. Anna Bostock (Cambridge: MIT Press, 1974), 159.
37. Lukács, "Metaphysics of Tragedy," 161.
38. Lukács, "Metaphysics of Tragedy," 159. Following Lukács's concept, Benjamin asserted, "Just as in the ordinary creature the activity of life is all-embracing, so, in the tragic hero, is the process of dying, and tragic irony always arises whenever the hero—with

profound but unsuspected justification—begins to speak of the circumstances of his death as if they were the circumstances of life" (Benjamin, *Origin of German Tragic Drama*, 114).

39. On the inconclusiveness of Gertrude's guilt, see Carl Schmitt, *Hamlet or Hecuba: The Intrusion of the Time into the Play* (New York: Telos, 2009). Schmitt, however, ascribes this inconclusiveness to the (irregular) circumstances of the accession of Shakespeare's sponsor, James I, to the throne, which is, actually, only a partial aspect of the whole question. Let us note here that Schmitt wrote that book as an answer to Benjamin's criticism of his idea of sovereignty in *Origin of German Tragic Drama*. As we will see in chapter 3, Benjamin observes inconclusiveness as expression of a much more crucial and inherent aspect in monarchical power.

40. It is true, however, that the acceptance of a king who is clearly a usurper is always partial and conditional. At that juncture, to speak of *the* kingdom becomes misleading: there is no longer that thing, but only different parties holding opposite views. It would be more appropriate to say that, like Gertrude, the kingdom, as a whole, is and is not guilty, that it accepts and does not accept the usurper as a legitimate king.

41. On the connections between *Richard II* and the politics of its time, see Chris Fitter, "Historicising Shakespeare's *Richard II*: Current Events, Dating, and the Sabotage of Essex," *Early Modern Literary Studies* 11, no. 2 (2005): 1–47; Charles R. Forker, preface to *King Richard II*, by William Shakespeare (London: Bloomsbury, 2004), 1–169; and Ernest William Talbert, *The Problem of Order: Elizabethan Political Commonplaces and an Example of Shakespeare's Art* (Chapel Hill: University of North Carolina Press, 1962).

42. This is the fundamental twist introduced by Hobbes into the old theory of the forms of government. To him, the distinction between a given form and its opposite becomes a mere matter of opinion (and, ultimately, arbitrary). "For they that are discontent with Monarchy," he states, "call it Tyranny; and they that are displeased with Aristocracy, called it Oligarchy; so also, they which find themselves grieved under a Democracy, call it Anarchy (which signifies want of Government) and yet I think no man believes, that want of Government is any new kind of Government: nor by the same reason ought they to believe that the Government is of one kind, when they like it, and another, when they mislike it" (Hobbes, *Leviathan*, chap. 19).

43. On the idea of the "grand mechanism" operating in Shakespeare's tragedies, see Jan Kott, *Shakespeare: Our Contemporary* (London: Norton, 1966).

44. Thus Lady Macbeth rebukes her husband: "Thou wouldst be great; / Art not without ambition, but without / The illness should attend it: what thou wouldst highly, / That wouldst thou holily; wouldst not play false, / And yet wouldst wrongly win (*Macbeth*, act I, scene 5). Yet, it is also true that her ignorance of moral prescriptions does not prevent the ghosts of her crimes from unconsciously emerging and haunting her, leading her to madness and, finally, to death.

45. "As the whole Subjects of our country (for the ancient and fundamental policie of our Kingdome) are diuided into three estates, so is euery estate hereof generally subject to some speciall vices; which in a maner by long habitude, are thought rather virtue then

uice among them." By way of example, he mentions the merchants: "The Merchants thinke the whole common-weale ordained for making them up; and accounting it their lawfull gaine and trade, to enrich themselues vpon the lose of all the rest of the people." James I, "Basilikon Doron," in *Political Writings: King James VI and I*, ed. Johann P. Sommerville (Cambridge: Cambridge University Press, 1994), 25, 29. As Jean-Christophe Agnew remarks, the increasing need to fix the nature of social roles runs parallel to the awareness of how fluid they had become in seventeenth-century England. Authors such as Philip Stubbes, in *Anatomy of Abuses*, expressed then their concern that it had become impossible to distinguish the social position of the subjects. See Agnew, *Worlds Apart: The Market and the Theater in Anglo-American Thought, 1550–1750* (Cambridge: Cambridge University Press, 1998), 73–74. On this topic, see also Joel Hurstfield, "The Historical and Social Background," in *A New Companion to Shakespeare Studies*, ed. Kenneth Muir and S. Schoenbaum (Cambridge: Cambridge University Press, 1971), 168–178.

46. James I, "Basilikon Doron," 26.
47. Harold Bloom, *Shakespeare: The Invention of the Human* (New York: Riverhead, 1998).
48. This view tends to place tragic conflict on the subjective side, to interpret it as revealing some personal frailty—Hamlet's fatal indecision, Macbeth's murderous ambition, and so on—thus purporting to find in Shakespearean characters a kind of psychological depth. This not only is a strange concept to the classical universe but also leads one to miss the crucial aspect of Shakespeare's worldview: uncertainty and undecidability as constitutive factors in the world. What he tells us is that the fault is in ourselves, not because of ourselves but because we are parts of a world in which dilemmas are unsolvable, where the time is out of joint. Thus, all of our decisions are inevitably wrong, and any course of action leads to a tragic end. We cannot escape from tragedy, just as we cannot escape from our worldly existence (our cage). Going back to the classical example of Hamlet: the fact that he cannot decide to kill his stepfather does not tell us merely about him or his psychological makeup. Ultimately, this aspect was not relevant for the thinking of the times and would only become central in the reading of the romantics. The crucial aspect here is that Hamlet hesitates because he knows that, to avenge his father, he must commit a new crime and thus become undistinguishable from his stepfather. And this (to become a criminal) was not seen as primarily a "subjective" problem, although it certainly has subjective repercussions, but as revealing a disorder in the constitution of the world.
49. Lucien Goldmann describes the tragic hero (the subject) as the one who lives in the world without ever accepting it, and who permanently pursues superior absolute values, which are, by definition, unattainable. "The world," Goldman writes, "is not ambiguous and contradictory in itself, for every consciousness. It is so only for man's consciousness, which lives only for the realization of strictly unattainable values . . . Although in the tragedy of negation there is no longer anything in common between God and the world, they do not cease for that reason to be parts of the same whole, the same universe, thanks to man and his mediation." Goldmann, *Le Dieu Caché: Étude sur la vision tragique dans les Pensées de Pascal et dans le théâtre de Racine* (Paris: Gallimard, 1955), 71–72.

50. On the conceptual relation between French classicism and the baroque, see René Wellek, "The Concept of Baroque in Literary Scholarship: Postscript 1962," in *Concepts of Criticism* (New Haven: Yale University Press, 1963).
51. Christopher Marlowe's translation of Ovid is another good example.
52. As René Girard remarks in *Géométries du Désir* (Paris: L'Herne, 2012), *Romeo and Juliet* is rather anomalous in this regard. The couple seems to violate the "logic" of tragic love, whereby love is inseparable from hatred. In this case, observes Girard, Shakespeare solves the problem by leaving the purity of the couple untouched and displacing the source of the conflict onto the outer world, the struggle between families.
53. See Frank Kermode, *The Sense of an Ending: Studies in the Theory of Fiction* (London: Oxford University Press, 1993).
54. See Emilio Nañez and Juan Manuel Azpitarte, introduction to *Teatro completo*, by Jean Racine (Madrid: Editora Nacional, 1982), 45.
55. The problem of expression is the issue that underlies and organizes the Hobbesian theory of political power. As Hobbes states: "To say that God hath spoken to him [a man] in the Holy Scripture is not to say God hath spoken to him immediately, but by mediation of the Prophets, or of the Apostles, or of the Church, in such a manner as he speaks to all other Christian men. To say he hath spoken to him in a Dream is no more than to say he dreamed that God spake to him" (Hobbes, *Leviathan*, chap. 32).
56. As Anthony Cascardi writes, in his analysis of Lope de Vega's *La Dorotea*, the idealization of the loved person is also destructive of her, since, from that moment, she can no longer find a place in the world as she truly exists. It is the realization of this that gives rise to "the controlling anxiety of the novel as a genre," which "is dominated by a permanent loss of faith in the existence of an 'original' context for desire rather than by the hope for its recovery." Cascardi, "The Archeology of Desire in *Don Quixote*," in *Quixotic Desire: Psychoanalytic Perspectives on Cervantes*, ed. Ruth A. El Saffar and Diana de Armas Wilson (Ithaca, NY: Cornell University Press, 1993), 43.
57. Bloom (*Shakespeare: The Invention of the Human*, 435) calls Iago the "nihilistic death-of-God theologue." According to Stephen Greenblatt, what Iago's character reveals is that transmutation (the most typical devilish ability), the improvisation of one's own identity, is the very condition for life in our secular world and, especially, for the conservation of power: "We should add that Iago includes himself in this ceaseless narrative invention. A successful improvisational career depends upon role-playing, which is in turn allied to the capacity . . . 'to see oneself in the other fellow's situation.' This capacity requires above all a sense that one is not forever fixed in a single, divinely sanctioned identity, a sense Iago expresses to Rodrigo in a parodically sententious theory of self-fashioning: 'Our bodies are gardens, to the which our wills are gardeners, so that if we will plant nettles, or sow lettuce, set hyssop, and weed up thyme; supply it with one gender of herbs, or distract it with many, either to have it sterile with idleness, or manur'd with industry, why, the power, and corrigible authority of this, lies in our wills'" (*Othello*, act I, scene 3). Greenblatt, "The Improvisation of Power," in *The Greenblatt Reader* (Oxford: Blackwell, 2005), 171.

58. This is also Don Quixote's delirium: asserting that "I am who I am . . . and I know I am capable of being not only the characters I have named, but all the Twelve Peers of France and all the Nine Worthies." Miguel de Cervantes, *The Adventures of Don Quixote*, ed. M. Cohen (Harmondsworth: Penguin, 1950), 1:5.
59. Once he is cured of his illness, he returns to his native town. But the lack of recognition of his superior mental capacity forces him to leave for Flanders, where he decides to live the purely physical life of a soldier. On this topic, see Armand Singer, "Cervantes's *Licenciado Vidriera*: Its Form and Substance," *West Virginia University Bulletin: Philological Papers* 8 (1951): 13–31; and Sybil Dünchen, "The Function of Madness in *El Licenciado Vidriera*," in Michel Nerlich and Nicholas Spadaccini, *Cervantes' "Exemplar Novels" and the Adventure of Writing* (Minneapolis: Prisma Institute, 1989), 99–123.
60. In his rules for the new art (*preceptiva nueva*), Lope himself explained the technique at work here. The parody effect is produced, as he shows, when the tragic love triangle among noble characters is replicated among popular characters. Thus, what sounds severe and tragic in the mouth of a duke or a marquess, such as talking about honor and duty, takes on a comic aspect when is repeated in the kitchen of the palace by the lowly servants.
61. The most successful scenic expression of the will for demarcation of realms, and the impossibility of it, actually comes from Cervantes's play *The Jealous Estramaduran* (*El celoso extremeño*). It is the story of a rich old man who marries a beautiful girl and, blind with jealousy, secludes her and her maids in a castle cut off from the outside world. The inhabitants of the castle can only see above to the sky—a scenic replication of the baroque architectonic ideal, which left open only a window at the top of a room; the light that entered was subsequently reflected into the interior by means of an amplified set of mirrors. Yet, the separation from the outer world is not really absolute, because the inhabitants of the palace depend on food and other needs delivered from the outside. Predictably, the room that serves to receive the tradespeople also becomes the gateway to perdition, as through it enters the young man who ends up seducing the girl. But, contrary to what we might expect, the old man, after noticing the girl's immoral behavior, does not punish her. Instead, he accepts the situation, and even lets her marry her new young partner. In any case, this acceptance of "sin," which is definitively disapproved of, is not at all atypical in the literature of the times.
62. Federico's servant, Batin, says, "If you neither wish to live or die, I'd say you are just like what they call hermaphrodite, which is to say a person who is neither man or woman, but a bit of both of them, as you yourself are split between not knowing if you are alive or dead" (Lope de Vega, *Punishment Without Revenge*, act II, 1216).
63. The duke states the same thing (Lope de Vega, *Punishment*, act III, 2657–59).
64. Margaret A. van Antwerp, quoted in Antonio Carreño, introduction to *El castigo sin venganza*, by Lope de Vega (Madrid: Cátedra, 1993), 65.
65. See Américo Castro, "Algunas observaciones acerca del concepto de honor en los siglos XVI y XVII," *Semblanzas y estudios españoles* (Barcelona: Ínsula, 1956).
66. See Carreño, introduction to *El castigo sin venganza*, 58.

67. The idea of the "externality" of the characters with respect to the play appears in *The Spanish Tragedy*, by Thomas Kyd, which Shakespeare used as a basis for the composition of *Hamlet*, and whose author is supposed to have written an ur-*Hamlet*, which is currently missing.
68. See Christoph Mencke, *Die Gegenwart der Tragödie* (Frankfurt: Suhrkamp Verlag, 2005).
69. R. D. F. Pring-Mill, introduction to *Lope de Vega: Five Plays* (New York: Hill & Wang, 1961), xxxix.
70. The price of this is that, from the moment he no longer participates in events, the sovereign no longer has a direct knowledge of them. He knows what happens only through the information provided by the mediators, who always give him different versions.
71. On the ways of representing the people in Racine, see Bernard Weinberg, *The Art of Jean Racine* (Chicago: University of Chicago Press, 1963), chap. 5.
72. As Nañez and Azpitarte say about Racine (and the same thing can be said of Lope de Vega): "Racine's ability consisted in having transferred from characters to spectators the tragic burden for election. Spectators now are the ones whose identities split before dilemmas whose terms are totally incompatible" (Nañez and Azpitarte, introduction to *Teatro completo*, 56).
73. "The spectators of the Golden Age *commedia*," says Emilie Bergmann, "perceive and interpret phenomena through the mediation of the characters, and also accept, reject, or modify those perceptions and interpretations in the course of the action as it proceeds on stage, and encompass them in the process of understanding the play. This phenomenon of paralleling and repeating offers a self-conscious perspective on the play as representation, and the gaze becomes self-conscious in the process of recognizing its double. The dual perspective prompted by the embedded works of art reminds the audience the illusory nature of the play itself, but it has a thematic function as well as a reflexive one." Bergmann, "Visual and Verbal Modes of Representation in *Peribáñez*," in *Studies in Honor of Elias Rivers*, ed. Bruno M. Damian and Ruth El Saffar (Potomac, MD: Sinpta Humanistica, 1989), 36.
74. The word *person*, remarked Hobbes, is derived from the word *persona*, which originally referred to the outward appearance or mask of a player. "So that a *person* is the same as an *actor* is, both on the stage and in common conversation, and to personate is to act or *represent* himself or another" (Hobbes, *Leviathan*, chap. 16). On the relation that Hobbes establishes between representation and politics, see José Maria Hernández, *El retrato de un dios mortal: Estudio sobre la filosofía política de Hobbes* (Barcelona: Anthropos, 2002).
75. "Pussy will always be pussy / Doggy, doggie, for eternity, amen," said Batin, the buffoonish character in *Punishment Without Revenge*, showing his incredulity regarding the duke's moral and social recovery (Lope de Vega, *Punishment*, act III, 2389).
76. This leads us back to the issue of *paradiastole*. Unlike Skinner's interpretation, *paradiastole* (the ungraspable nature of moral judgments) is, for Hobbes, not really the quintessential political problem but, on the contrary, the solution to it. It is the

break in the idea of a transcendental truth that paves the way for political order. As religious wars prove, we become able to accept the conventional norms of reason only insofar as we set aside the idea of a transcendental truth. On the dissociation between truth and obedience, in Hobbes, see Carlo Altini, *La fabrica de la soberanía: Maquiavelo, Hobbes, Spinoza y otros modernos* (Buenos Aires: El Cuenco de Plata, 2007), chap. 3.

77. In Shakespeare's *Henry V*, the chorus calls attention to the difference between the theater's power to command the imagination of the audience and the prince's power to command his subjects. As Stephen Greenblatt shows, however, as the play unfolds, those powers become merged. See Greenblatt, *Shakespearean Negotiations* (Berkeley: University of California Press, 1988), chap. 2.

78. As Jean-Christophe Agnew remarks, "He certainly never claimed to represent himself on the stage, nor did he purport to represent the playwright. Nor, finally, did he represent his 'character.' He *was* his character" (Agnew, *Worlds Apart*, 103).

79. "As central to Don Quijote's madness as the problem of distinguishing reality from illusion," states Emilie Bergmann, "is the problem of interpreting the symbolic function of artifice, not only in books, but actors in costume" (Bergmann, "Visual and Verbal Modes of Representation," 41).

80. Spinoza's oeuvre shows us how this same matrix works on the level of political philosophical thinking. In a recent article on Spinoza's concept of *conatus*, Stephen Connolly emphasizes that "the core of this definition is this: that we produce our natural right, it is the product of our labour—it is nothing other than *work*." Connelly, "Conatus, Political Being, and Spinoza," Critical Legal Thinking, March 16, 2015, http://criticallegalthinking.com/2015/03/16/conatus-political-being-and-spinoza/.

81. Maria Rosa Álvarez Sellers refers to the problem of expression in connection with linguistic manifestation. As she states, "It is forbidden to verbalize passion; recognizing means letting it escape and expand." Álvarez Sellers, "El *Castigo sin venganza*: Lope de Vega," in *Análisis y evolución de la tragedia española en el Siglo de Oro* (Kassel: Kut und Rostwitha Reichenberger, 1997), 2:473.

82. On the dialectics between innocence and guilt in state politics during the seventeenth and eighteenth centuries, see Reinhart Koselleck, *Critique and Crisis: Enlightenment and the Pathogenesis of Modern Society* (Oxford: Berg, 1988).

3. THE DISCOURSE OF EMANCIPATION AND THE EMERGENCE OF DEMOCRACY AS A PROBLEM

1. Carl Schmitt, *Political Theology: Four Chapters on the Concept of Sovereignty* (Chicago: University of Chicago Press, 2005), 5.
2. See Jacques Derrida, *The Beast and the Sovereign* (Chicago: University of Chicago Press, 2002).
3. For an analysis of this, see José L. Villacañas and Román García, "Walter Benjamin y Carl Schmitt: Soberanía y Estado de Excepción," *Revista de Filosofía* 13 (1996): 41–60.

3. THE DISCOURSE OF EMANCIPATION   201

4. Walter Benjamin, *The Origin of German Tragic Drama* (London: Verso, 2009), 70–71, 73.
5. The confusión between "indecisión" and "indecidability" is very frequent even among those authors who theorized the point. Ernesto Laclau, for example, in a conference at Berkeley, posed as an example of indecidability the case of an assembly of workers on strike that faced a dilemma because there were the same good arguments to go on with the strike and to stop it. And this was, for him, the moment when decision is necessary. However, it is the best example of what indecidability is not, the confusion of it with mere indecision. As we will see in chapter four in connection with the issue of revolutionary violence, that difference is crucial to understand the political thinking of the twentieth century and how the very horizon of the political then started dissolving.
6. The absolutization of power, she says, only served to hide the reality, in a secular context, of "some elementary lack of authority," which results in permanent instability. (See the epigraph to this chapter.)
7. As Benjamin observes, "In the drama of Calderón [the techniques of enclosure by a framework and miniaturization] correspond to the volute in the architecture of the time. It repeats itself infinitely, and reduces to immeasurability the circle which it encloses. Both these aspects of reflection are equally essential: the playful miniaturization of reality and the introduction of a reflective infinity of thought into the finite space of profane fate" (Benjamin, *Origin of German Tragic Drama*, 83).
8. As Giorgio Agamben remarks, "The sovereign is structurally *mehaignié* [wounded], in the sense that his dignity is measured against the possibility of its uselessness and inefficacy, in a correlation in which the *rex inutilis* legitimates the actual administration that he has always already cut off from himself and that, however, formally continues to belong to him." Agamben, *The Kingdom and the Glory: For a Theological Genealogy of Economy and Government* (Stanford, CA: Stanford University Press, 2011), 99. Agamben's remark is clear about the nature of the new regime of power that emerged from absolutism, but he takes it as a mere continuation of a theological concept, thereby missing the profound break produced, around the seventeenth century, in the interior of the theological universe. In any case, the crucial point is that that scission between the realms of sovereignty and government, which was the condition for the effectiveness of the mechanism for the production of the transcendence effect out of immanence, would only be achieved by introducing a fissure within the political realm, for which, as we will see, the sovereign machine would pay a very high price. The scission that permitted the absolutization of power would bring about unanticipated and dramatic consequences.
9. Baltasar Gracián, *El Criticón* (Buenos Aires: Losada, 2010), 125–126. On this topic, see José Luis Villacañas, "El Esquema Clásico en Gracián: Continuidad y variación," *Eikasia: Revista de Filosofía*, 37 (2011): 211–241.
10. Ernst Kantorowicz says that, especially in France, "the tendency was so strong to read into the individual living king features of a living *persona idealis*; it was almost to be expected that one day, sooner or later, also the phrase *Le roi ne meurt jamais* would make its appearance." Ernst Kantorowicz, *The King's Two Bodies: A Study in Medieval Political Thought* (Princeton: Princeton University Press, 1981), 409.

11. According to Guillaume de la Perrière's definition, "Government is the right disposition of things arranged so as to lead to a suitable end." La Perrière, *Le Miroir politique*, quoted in Michel Foucault, *Security, Territory, Population*, trans. Graham Burchell (New York: Palgrave Macmillan, 2007), 134.
12. See Arndt Brendecke, *Imperium und Empirie: Funktionen des Wissens in der Spanischen Kolonialherrschaft* (Köln: Böhlau 2009).
13. "If, on the one hand, it is true that man could not exist, and that only the juridical notion of the subject of right could exist when the problem of power was formulated within the theory of sovereignty; on the other hand, when population becomes the vis-à-vis of government, rather than of sovereignty, then I think we can say that man is to population what the subject of right was to the sovereign" (Foucault, *Security, Territory, Population*, 110).
14. "A constant interplay between techniques of power and their object," writes Foucault, "gradually carves out in reality, as a field of reality, population and its specific phenomena. A whole series of objects were made visible for possible forms of knowledge on the basis of the constitution of the population as the correlate of the techniques of power. In turn, because these forms of knowledge constantly carve out new objects, the population could be formed, continue, and remain as the privileged correlate of modern mechanisms of power" (Foucault, *Security, Territory, Population*, 109).
15. The term *bureaucracy* was coined by Vincent de Gournay (1712–1769). According to him, it is "a fourth or a fifth form of government," in addition to the three traditional ones (democracy, aristocracy, and monarchy) defined by the Greeks. See François Bluche, *L'Ancien Régime: Institutions et Société* (Paris: Éditions de Fallois, 1993).
16. *Del governo et amministratione di diversi regni et republiche* (1567), by the Italian F. Sansovino, is the work that initiated this genre. On this, see Michel Senellart, *Les arts de gouverner: Du regime médiéval au concept du gouvernement* (Paris: Éditions du Seuil, 1995).
17. Though, for the authors of the period, the theory of sovereignty and the art of government had completely different orientations, they did not seem to be mutually contradictory. An example of this can be seen in a book whose very title is illustrative: Andrés Mendo, *Príncipes perfectos y Ministros ajustados: Documentos politicos-morales en emblemas* (Lyon: Boissat and Remens, 1662). Mendo sought to combine the two genres of treatises, devoting one of the two parts of his book to each of them.
18. The inclusion in 1559 of Machiavelli's works in the Index of Forbidden Books by Pope Paul IV made him a kind of cursed figure in the Hispanic world. He and his followers were normally referred to, in a pejorative way, as "politicians." Yet, as different students of Hispanic intellectual history have remarked, his influence was profound and pervasive. It was expressed in an elliptical way as Tacitism. During the sixteenth and seventeenth centuries, the authority of Tacitus was invoked for the elaboration of an "art of government" founded on the concept of the reason of state, but Machiavelli's inspiration is undeniable. On the reception of Machiavelli in Spain, see B. Antón Martínez, *El tacitismo en el siglo XVII en España: El proceso de "receptio"* (Valladolid: Universidad de Valladolid, 1992); Maria Begoña Arbulu Barturen and Sandra Bagno,

eds., *La recepción de Maquiavelo y Beccaria en el ámbito hispanoamericano* (Padua: Unipress, 2005); M. F. Escalante, *Álamos de Barrientos y la doctrina de la razón de Estado en España (posibilidad y frustración)* (Barcelona, Fontamara, 1975); José A. Fernández Santamaría, *Razón de Estado y política en el pensamiento español del Barroco (1595-1640)* (Madrid: Centro de Estudios Constitucionales, 1989); José Antonio Maravall, *Teoría del Estado en España en el siglo XVII* (Madrid: Centro de Estudios Políticos y Constitucionales, 1997); José Luis Mirete, "Maquiavelo y su recepción de la teoría del Estado en España (Siglos XVI y XVII), *Anales de Derecho* 19 (2001): 139-144; and Enrique Tierno Galván, "El tacitismo en las doctrinas del siglo de oro español," in *Anales de la Universidad de Murcia, 1947-1948* (Murcia: Universidad de Murcia, 1949).

19. This leads us to the issue that separates the political thinking of the baroque from that of the Renaissance. In the history of ideas, the typical view of the early-modern, secular political tradition running from Machiavelli to Hobbes overlooks the fundamental fact that Hobbes's ways of interrogating about politics no longer had anything in common with Machiavelli's. In Hobbes's time, the main political concern was no longer about discovering the best form of government for each kind of society, according to the old theory of forms of governments. Nor was there a concern with the question of how to preserve power. The key issue now became what Otto Gierke would later call the problem of "articulation": how to reduce the plurality of singular beings into the single whole of the community. Hence the striking statement by Thomas Hobbes: "A multitude of men are made One Person, when they are by one Person Represented . . . For it is the Unity of the Represented, that maketh the Person One." Hobbes, *Leviathan* (Cambridge: Cambridge University Press, 1994), part 1, chap. 16. This means that the community takes its consistency from the field of representation. In sum, the traditional view overlooks the great discovery of the seventeenth century, the baroque: the symbolic nature of political power and the representative (illusory) character of the mediating instance. As we have seen, the correlate of this development is the emergence of an art of government, which is different tout court from the concept of reason of state (and closer to what Foucault called "biopolitics").

20. The topic appears repeatedly in *Arcano de príncipes*, but it is more crudely expressed in chapter 2, "Positive Remedies for the Growth of Population": "The Christian Powerful, more skillful in the management of state business, also relieve their dominions of the weight of overpopulation by different means. War is the most important of them." Vicente Montano, *Arcano de príncipes* (Madrid: Centro de Estudios Constitucionales, 1986), 33-37.

21. This made manifest the rising of a new class of public officers, who began to gain consciousness of their power, of performing an essential role in the kingdom. As Sánchez de Moncada stated, "Ignorance of this science is the root of all regrettable events in the kingdoms . . . , ruling is a science." Moncada, *Restauración política de España* (Madrid: Luis Sánchez, 1619), quoted in Fernández Santamaría, *Razón de Estado*, 189. It is necessary to recall that, in the early seventeenth century, the monarchy began to establish a series of conditions for obtaining a position in public administration, which included technical instruction. On the formation of a state apparatus and the growing

consciousness that public officials, see José María García Marín, *Teoria política y gobierno en la Monarquía Hispana* (Madrid: Centro de Estudios Políticos y Constitucionales, 1998), passim.

22. "To transfer transcendence to the person of the prince," wrote Senellart, "the art of governing according to moral ends becomes mysteries of the State (*arcana imperii*) . . . It seems that each of the pieces of the grand machine of the State cannot be effective unless they adjust themselves to the whole mechanism. The *power of things* replaces the human plays of power" (Senellart, *Les arts de gouverner*, 59).

23. Ponce de León, *Censura de Ponce de León sobre los* Anales e Historias *de Cayo Cornelio Tacito, para consultar si convendría imprimir su traducción en español* (1778), quoted in Fernández Santamaría, *Razón de Estado*, 169.

24. The whole expression is, "Flectere si nequeo superos, Acheronta movebo" (If I cannot move the gods of heaven, I will move those of hell) (*Eneid*, VII:312).

25. See John L. Phelan, *The People and the King: The Comunero Revolution in Colombia, 1781* (Madison: University of Wisconsin Press, 1978); and Eric Van Young, "El enigma de los reyes: Mesianismo y revuelta popular en México, 1800–1815," in *La crisis del orden colonial: Estructura agraria y rebeliones populares de la Nueva España, 1750–1821*, ed. Eric van Young (Mexico: Alianza, 1992), 399–427. In his study on the late medieval period, Carlos Barros found the expression "Viva el Rey" to be a cry of protest, but not the other part, "muera el mal gobierno." Eventually, we see the expressions "mueran los caballeros" and "mueran los clérigos" (death to the lords, death to the clergymen). See Barros, "Viva el Rey! Rey, imaginario y revuelta en la Galicia bajomedieval," http://www.h-debate.com/cbarros/spanish/viva_el_rey.htm.

26. See John H. Elliot, "Revueltas en la monarquía española," in J. H. Elliot et al., *1640: La monarquía hispánica en crisis* (Barcelona: Centre d'Estudis d'Historia Moderna Pierre Vilar/Crítica, 1992), 123–144; and Thomas Werner and Bart de Groof, eds., *Rebelión y resistencia en el mundo hispánico del siglo XVII* (Leuven: Leuven University Press, 1992).

27. Benjamin, *Origin of German Tragic Drama*, 126.

28. Some interesting studies on this are: Tamar Herzog, " 'Viva el rey, muera el mal gobierno': Sobre la división de tareas y la inversión de papeles en la administración de la justicia quiteña (siglos XVII y XVIII)," in *Dinámica del Antiguo Régimen y orden constitucional: Representación, justicia y administración en Iberoamérica (siglos XVII y XIX)*, ed. Marcos Berllingeri (Torino: Otto, 2000), 77–98; Natalia Silva Prada, *La política de una rebelión: Los indígenas frente al tumulto de 1692 en la ciudad de México* (Mexico: El Colegio de México, 2007); Wolfgang Reinhard, ed., *Las élites del poder y la construcción del Estado: Los orígenes del Estado moderno en Europa, siglos XIII a XVIII* (Madrid: FCE, 1996).

29. We find here the kind of dialectic described by Reinhart Koselleck in his 1954 doctoral dissertation (published in 1959): "Absolutism necessitated the genesis of the Enlightenment, and the Enlightenment conditioned the genesis of Revolution." Koselleck, *Critique and Crisis: Enlightenment and the Pathogenesis of Modern Society* (Oxford: Berg, 1988), 8.

30. This was the name given to a group of provinces roughly corresponding to modern-day Colombia.
31. Joaquín de Finestrad, *El vasallo instruido* (Bogota: Universidad Nacional de Colombia, 2000), 180.
32. "What disconcerting confusion will be observed in the starry sky if by some providence the stars attempted to usurp the rays of the sun, who is king among planets? This same confusion would be seen by our eyes in the kingdoms if the rays of supreme jurisdiction could be taken from the kings and appropriated by the vassals" (Finestrad, *El vasallo instruido*, 177). Thinking that they have the right to make war "is the best sign of the total destruction of the political and Christian order that consists of the subordination of subjects under their superiors, of vassals under monarchs" (179).
33. Finestrad, *El vasallo instruido*, 207.
34. Finestrad, *El vasallo instruido*, 218.
35. Finestrad, *El vasallo instruido*, 221.
36. Finestrad, *El vasallo instruido*, 308.
37. Finestrad, *El vasallo instruido*, 248.
38. See Roland Barthes, *Sur Racine* (Paris: Seuil, 1963), 55.
39. "There is no nation, regardless of how barbaric it may be," he writes, "that does not know the necessity of kings and ministers that execute and enforce the dictates of the superior authority" (Finestrad, *El vasallo instruido*, 307).
40. Finestrad, *El vasallo instruido*, 187–188.
41. Finestrad, *El vasallo instruido*, 188–189, 339.
42. The *Diccionario de la lengua* of 1732 (Madrid: Impr. Francisco del Hierro) defines *synderesis* as "the virtue and capacity of the soul regarding notice and intelligence of the moral principles that dictate a just and orderly life" (quoted in Fernández Santamaría, *Razón de Estado*, 81).
43. "Who has knowledge of the ordinary expenditures of the royal patrimony better than the king and his ministers? What knowledge of the arcane of the cabinet does a vassal have? Or of the grandiose preference our nation so honorably holds above foreign lands? Or the abundant stockpiles that must be gathered in the storehouses as preparations for war? Or of the rents that come into the royal treasury?" (Finestrad, *El vasallo instruido*, 210).
44. Finestrad, *El vasallo instruido*, 210–211.
45. Regarding the Catholic nature of the Hispanic monarchy, see José Maria Iñurritegui Rodríguez, *La gracia y la república: El lenguaje político de la teología católica y el Príncipe Cristiano de Pedro Rivadaneyra* (Madrid: UNED, 1998); and José Maria Portillo Valdés, *Revolución de nación: Orígenes de la cultura constitucional en España, 1780–1812* (Madrid: Centro de Estudios Políticos y Constitucionales, 2000). Regarding the supposed tension between the Catholic monarchy and the Enlightenment, see José Carlos Chiaramonte, *La crítica ilustrada de la realidad: Economía y sociedad en el pensamiento argentino e iberoamericano del siglo XVIII* (Buenos Aires: CEAL, 1982); and Chiaramonte, *La ilustración en el Río de la Plata: Cultura eclesiástica y cultura laica durante el Virreinato* (Buenos Aires: Puntosur, 1989).

46. Finestrad, *El vasallo instruido*, 364. The oath he refers to—not to teach the doctrine of tyrannicide, even as a hypothesis—was in fact demanded by King Charles III of Spain as a condition for receiving the title of doctor.
47. Finestrad, *El vasallo instruido*, 365.
48. "This doctrine has no place with regards to those princes who, being called to assume the crown either by God Himself or by the election of the kingdom, or by right of blood, or by just war, when seated at the throne transform the sovereign power to serve his own interests and oppress the people with ill-evoked rule. The rights of religion, of nature and of Politics, all agree in this most important of topics. Oppressions, tyrannies, and persecutions are not capable of denaturalizing the glories and justified titles of Shepherd of the People, Father of the Republic, and Lord of the Kingdom who are distinguished by the most sacred and unalterable rights. The life of the kings is the soul and the cement of the republic, and it is superior to the interests of the vassals, in such a way that it is better to suffer the violence, aggression, and servitude than leave the motherland without a leader. Regardless of how bad legitimate sovereigns can be, they can never have the title of Lord taken from them . . . The sovereign princes are appointed to the throne by God, and do not recognize any authority on earth superior to their own that can judge them but God Himself . . . Oppressed people are always inferior and do not have the right to judge the conduct of the kings" (Finestrad, *El vasallo instruido*, 367–368).
49. Finestrad, *El vasallo instruido*, 124.
50. Finestrad, *El vasallo instruido*, 127.
51. Agamben has remarked on the centrality of the subject of glory and liturgy in Christian theology insofar as it was the correlate, in the realm of the divine oikonomia, of the Holy Ghost, in the realm of the divine substance. As he says, "In the same way that Christian theology has dynamically transformed biblical monotheism by dialectically opposing within it the unity of the substance and of ontology (the theology), and the plurality of persons and practices (the oikonomia), so the *doxa theu* define the reciprocal glorification between the Father and the Son (and, more generally, of the three persons). The Trinitarian economy is constitutively an economy of the glory" (Agamben, *The Kingdom and the Glory*, 201).
52. As Paolo Prodi points out, after the Council of Trent (1545–1563) there was a crucial shift in the concepts of justice involving the evangelical practices of the church. This is most noticeable with respect to the sacrament of confession, where a dual phenomenon became clearly observable. On the one hand, the church's control of consciousness was expanded to include areas that until then had been considered private. On the other hand, and as a consequence of this control, the faithful were now encouraged to more actively participate in their own redemption by expressing their regret and guilt over the commission of sin. In this manner, Prodi states, the church decisively contributed to the establishment of the individual's own conscience as the judge of his or her actions. See Paolo Prodi, *Una storia della giustizia: Dal pluralismo dei fori al moderno dualismo tra coscienza e diritto* (Milano: Il Mulino, 2000).
53. Finestrad, *El vasallo instruido*, 147.

54. Finestrad, *El vasallo instruido*, 188.
55. Finestrad, *El vasallo instruido*, 316.
56. Francisco Martínez Marina, *Discurso sobre el origen de la monarquía y sobre la naturaleza del gobierno español* (Madrid: Centro de Estudios Constitucionales, 1988), 92–93.
57. "Revisionist" versions emphasize the continuities between the colonial regime and the national states that emerged after independence, as well as the absence of an endogenous process that prepared the way for the emergence of the latter. Thus, they interpret the break from colonial rule as a rather accidental happening resulting from a fortuitous event, such as the royal vacancy produced in 1808, after the Abdications of Bayonne. But this perspective cannot explain the fact that previous dynastic crises, such as the War of Succession (1701–1713), had not produced anything similar in the colonies. Clearly, something had changed during the intervening years that caused such an event to have the consequences it did. It is precisely these changes that are analyzed in this chapter. For a more detailed critique of these revisionist versions, see Elías J. Palti, "Beyond Revisionism: The Bicentennial of Independence, the Early Republican Experience, and Intellectual History in Latin America," *Journal of the History of Ideas* 70, no. 4 (2009): 593–614; and Palti, "¿De la *tradición* a la *modernidad*? Revisionismo e historia político-conceptual de las revoluciones de Independencia," in *Independencia y revolución: Pasado, presente y futuro*, ed. Gustavo Leyva et al. (Mexico: FCE/Universidad Autónoma Metropolitana, 2010), 174–190.
58. And this would allow an author like Victorián de Villaba to propose, in 1797, the formation in the colonies of a council. Although this council would follow a traditional principle of representation, it would radically depart from this principle from the moment that the council claimed for itself that which, until then, had been an exclusive attribute of royal sovereignty: legislative power. In this way, monarchical power was reduced to mere executive power, which would not encompass even the full territory of the state.
59. Pablo Fernández Albaladejo shows how the Spanish patriotic discourse was used by the Bourbons as an attempt to legitimize the new dynasty. The 1740s were key years in the articulation of this discourse, in the context of the conflict with England. See Fernández Albaladejo, *Materia de España: Cultura política e identidad de la España noderna* (Madrid: Marcial Pons, 2007), 197–244.
60. Gaspar Melchor de Jovellanos, "Memoria en que se rebaten las calumnias divulgadas contra los individuos de la Junta Central del Reino, y se da razón de la conducta y opiniones del autor desde que recobró la libertad," in *Escritos políticos y filosóficos* (Barcelona: Folio, 1999), 187.
61. We can observe here a fundamental difference between a conceptual history of the political and the traditional history of political ideas or the history of political philosophy. The distinction between the nation and the royal investiture was not merely the figment of the imagination of an author or authors (those whom Quentin Skinner distinguishes from the mere "reproducers of ideologies" and who would be the demiurges of semantic transformations in public discourse). It was both a conceptual transformation and an objective process, in the sense that was not the product of the mind of any particular author but a conceptual alteration produced at the very heart of political and

social practices, a shift on the level of the symbolic dimension in the regimes of exercise of political power.
62. See Gaspar Melchor de Jovellanos, "Nota a los Apéndices a la Memoria en defensa de la Junta Central" (July 22, 1810), in *Escritos políticos y filosóficos*, 210. Following this line of thought, Charles Leslie states, "Without ultimate instance there can be no government. And if it is in the people, there is no government either." Leslie, *The Best Answer That Ever Was Made*, 15, quoted in John N. Figgis, *El derecho divino de los reyes y tres ensayos adicionales* (Mexico: FCE, 1942), 298.
63. Jovellanos, "Nota a los Apéndices, 215.
64. See Charles Jago, "Habsburg Absolutism and the Cortes of Castile," *American Historical Review* 86 (1981): 307–326; and Irving A. A. Thompson, "Crown and Cortes in Castile: 1590–1665," *Parliaments, Estates and Representation* 2 (1982): 29–45.
65. See Clara García Ayluardo, ed., *Las reformas borbónicas: 1750–1808* (Mexico: FCE, 2010); and Horst Pietschmann, *Las reformas borbónicas y el sistema de intendencias en Nueva España: Un estudio político-administrativo* (Mexico: FCE, 1996).
66. "The people to whom they attributed sovereign power were themselves fictional and could most usefully remain so, a mystical body, existing as a people only in the actions of the Parliament that claimed to act for them. It would perhaps not be too much to say that representatives invented the sovereignty of the people in order to claim it for themselves." Edmund Morgan, *The Invention of the People: The Right of Popular Sovereignty in England and America* (New York: Norton, 1988), 49–50.
67. Annick Lempérière, *Entre Dieu et le Roi, la République: Mexico, XVIe–XIXe siècle* (París: Les Belles Lettres, 2004).
68. Finestrad, *El vasallo instruido*, 192. Juan Francisco Berbeo, leader of the *comuneros*, began his proclamation by declaring, "Knowing that I speak with the unanimous voice of the people . . ." (quoted in Phelan, *The People and the King*, 158). Berbeo actually signed the accords with "the representatives of the crown" as spokesmen of the people. Thus, both sides appeared to assume two different sources of legitimacy (royal and national sovereignties).
69. The *Letters to the Count of Lerena*, by León de Arroyal, is the purest expression of the Bourbons' enlightened reformism. Many consider it the first constitution written in Spain, as it contains an integral program of political reform. De Arroyal's premise was that there was no constitution in Spain and that it had to be created. León de Arroyal, *Cartas económico-políticas* (Oviedo: Instituto Feijóo, 1971).
70. The question then became somewhat more complex. The burst of the plebe (a mass of people not included within the framework of the traditional bodies of the society of the ancien régime) led the Bourbon power to appreciate anew the role of these bodies as guarantors of the social order. This also explains the reinforcing of the corporate frameworks observed in those years. In that context, although the monarchy did not abandon its ambition toward being the representation of the people, it was more willing to admit other territorial bodies as legitimate expressions of that "natural" nation. However, that new collaborative spirit was fated to be ephemeral. The growing fiscal needs of the crown, leading to the promulgation of the decree of consolidation of royal receipts (1804–1808),

marked its abrupt end. See Carlos Marichal, *La bancarrota del virreinato: Nueva España y las finanzas del Imperio colonial, 1780–1810* (Mexico: FCE, 1999); Margaret Chowning, "The Consolidation of Vales Reales in the Bishopric of Michoacán," *Hispanic American Historical Review* 69, no. 3 (1989): 451–478; and Gisela von Wobeser, *Dominación colonial: La consolidación de los vales reales, 1804–1808* (Mexico: UNAM, 2003).

71. Francisco Suárez, *Defensio fidei*, trans. José Ramón Eguillor Muniozguren (Madrid: Instituto de Estudios Politicos, 1971), book III, chap. 2, no. 6.
72. Suárez, *Defensio fidei*, book III, chap. 2, no. 6.
73. Suárez, *Defensio fidei*, book III, chap. 2, no. 6–7.
74. Juan Bautista Alberdi, *Escritos póstumos de Juan Bautista Alberdi* (Buenos Aires: Impr. Europea/Impr. A. Monkes/Impr. J.B. Alberdi, 1901), 12:113.
75. See Elías J. Palti, "Democratismo: El rechazo a la democracia en el temprano siglo XIX latinoamericano desde la perspectiva de una historia conceptual de lo *político*," in *El lenguaje de los ismos: Algunos conceptos de la modernidad en América Latina*, ed. Marta Elena Casaús Arzú (Guatemala: F&G, 2010), 37–52.
76. Mariano Moreno, "Sobre el Congreso," in *Escritos políticos y económicos* (Buenos Aires: La Cultura Argentina, 1915), 284.
77. Cornelio Saavedra, *Memoria autógrafa* (Buenos Aires: Carlos Pérez, 1969), 9–10.
78. Bernard Manin, *The Principles of Representative Government* (Cambridge: Cambridge University Press, 1997).
79. The first to present this concept was Edmund Burke, in his celebrated "Letter to the Sheriffs of Bristol" (1777). Reprinted in R. J. S. Hoffmann and P. Levack, eds., *Burke's Politics: Selected Writings and Speeches* (New York: Knopf, 1949).
80. The Latin word *repraesentare* means to make present or manifest, or to present anew, something that is absent.
81. "It is true that a man cannot be a representative—or at most is a representative 'in name only'—if he habitually does the opposite of what his constituents would do. But it is also true that a man is not a representative—or at most is a representative 'in name only'—if he himself does nothing, if his constituents act directly . . . The seemingly paradoxical meaning of representation is perpetuated in our requirement for the activity of representing: the represented must be present and not present . . . The concept of representation itself is what accounts for the truth in each of the two conflicting positions. Being represented means being made present in some sense, while not really being present literally or fully in fact. This paradoxical requirement imposed by the meaning of the concept is precisely what is mirrored in the two sides of the mandate–independence controversy" (Hanna Fenichel Pitkin, *The Concept of Representation* (Berkeley: University of California Press, 1972), 151, 153–154.
82. The questions that this raised were, first, how to identify, among all the opposing opinions present in society, the one that truly expressed the general opinion; and, second, who could decide this.
83. See Dick Howard, *The Primacy of the Political: A History of Political Thought from the Greeks to the French and American Revolutions* (New York: Columbia University Press, 2010).

84. Hegel's idea of dialectics is the best-known expression—but only one expression—of this conceptual mode of operating, of the regime of knowledge that, for Foucault, was proper to the "age of history."
85. I will not elaborate on this concept in the present book, since nineteenth-century intellectual history, and the preformationist–evolutionist view of nature and history, in particular, have been the subjects of most of my previous works. See Elías J. Palti, "The Metaphor of Life: Herder's Philosophy of History and Uneven Developments in Late-Enlightenment Natural Sciences," *History and Theory* 38, no. 3 (1999): 322–348; Palti, "The 'Return of the Subject' as a Historico-Intellectual Problem," *History and Theory* 43 (2004): 57–82; and Palti, *El tiempo de la política: El siglo XIX reconsiderado* (Buenos Aires: Siglo XXI, 2007).
86. According to Foucault, the temporalization of concepts is the distinct mark of this age in conceptual history, the "age of history." This phenomenon encompassed all fields of thinking, as can be seen in Arthur O. Lovejoy, *The Great Chain of Being: A Study of the History of an Idea* (Cambridge: Harvard University Press, 1964).
87. As Gilles Deleuze states, in his course on the work of Foucault, "So far, all along the seventeenth century, the finite was, by definition, the derived thing. Only the Infinite is original. The existence of an original finitude entails an inversion, a reversal of all the notions." Deleuze, *Curso sobre Foucault* (Buenos Aires: Cactus, 2013–2015), 2:229.
88. José de Alencar, "O principio representativo" (1868), in *Dois escritos democráticos de José de Alencar*, ed. Wanderley Guilherme dos Santos (Rio de Janeiro: UFRJ, 1991), 22. Some years later, Marco A. Avellaneda, referring to this, stated that "suffrage is in crisis everywhere." Congreso Nacional, *Diario de Sesiones del Honorable Congreso de la Nación Argentina*, session 61, November 15, 1910 (Buenos Aires: Imprenta del Congreso de la Nación, 1910).
89. José de Alencar, "O sistema representativo," in *Dois escritos democráticos*, 32.
90. Leopoldo Maupas, "Trascendencia política de la nueva ley electoral," *Revista Argentina de Ciencias Políticas* 22 (1912): 427.
91. Rodolfo Rivarola, "Crónicas y documentos," *Revista Argentina de Ciencias Políticas* 104–106 (1919): 266.
92. José Victorino Lastarria, "Elementos de derecho público constitucional teórico positivo i político" (1846), in *Obras completas*, vol. 1, *Estudios políticos y constitucionales* (Santiago: Impr. Barcelona, 1906), 42, 56.

4. THE REBIRTH OF THE TRAGIC SCENE AND THE EMERGENCE OF THE POLITICAL AS A CONCEPTUAL PROBLEM

1. The clearest example of this is Eric Hobsbawm, *The Age of Extremes: 1914–1991* (New York: Vintage, 1996).
2. Alain Badiou, *The Century* (New York: Polity Press, 2007), 58.
3. Badiou, *The Century*, 15.

4. Badiou, *The Century*, 8.
5. Badiou, *The Century*, 148.
6. Badiou, *The Century*, 132.
7. Badiou, *The Century*, 131.
8. The piece can be heard on YouTube, in a version by Alfons and Aloys Kontarsky. See https://www.youtube.com/watch?v=EmErwNo2fXo#.
9. Friedrich Kittler, *Discourse Networks 1800/1900*, trans. Michael Metteer (Stanford, CA: Stanford University Press, 1990), 106.
10. Pierre Boulez, quoted in Georgina Born, *Rationalizing Culture: IRCAM, Boulez, and the Institutionalization of the Musical Avant-Garde* (Berkeley: University of California Press, 1990), 1.
11. As Arnold Schoenberg observed, the further we move, in terms of the degree of complexity of the mathematical proportion that the harmonic sound keeps with respect to the tonic, the more dissonant it is. The dominant is closer to the tonic, since it keeps the simplest mathematical relation with the latter, and the subdominant is the result of the inversion of the dominant. The third and the sixth entail a more complex mathematical proportion, and so on, until getting the semitones of the chromatic scale. Thus, the chromatic scale merely represents the completion of the very same principle of harmony that had hitherto presided over tonal music. The penetration of the natural-acoustical basis of harmony would also explain its history. The same principle would have underlay and determined the entire progression from the baroque, to classicism, to romanticism, to impressionism, and finally to expressionism (dodecaphony), insofar as each of these periods resulted from the incorporation of further harmonics in the chromatic scale. Yet this would not be the last term in this progression. Following this logic, the next step (the result of the continuation in the incorporation of further harmonics) would be microtonalism. "It is not to our scale alone that we owe the evolution of our music," Schoenberg wrote, "and above all, this scale is not the last word, the ultimate goal of music, but rather a provisional stopping place. The overtone series, which led the ear to it, still contains many problems that will have to be faced. And if for the time being we still manage to escape those problems, it is due to little else than a compromise between the natural intervals and our inability to use them—that compromise, which we call the tempered system . . . amounts to an indefinitely extended truce. This reduction of the natural relations to manageable ones cannot permanently impede the evolution of music; and the ear will have to attack the problems, because it is so disposed. Then our scale will be transformed into a higher order, as the church modes were transformed into major and minor modes." Schoenberg, *Theory of Harmony* (Berkeley: University of California Press, 1983), 25. Thus, this rationalist bent enabled Schoenberg not only to explain past developments in musical composition but also to forecast its future evolution.
12. Leverkühn (a symbolic transposition of Shoenberg) clearly expressed this ideal behind his musical concept in Thomas Mann, *Doctor Faustus: The Life of the Composer Adrian Leverkuhn as Told by a Friend* (New York: Vintage, 1999).
13. Pierre Schaeffer, *Traité des objets musicaux: Essai interdiscipline* (Paris: Seuil, 1966), 35.

14. The best expression of a similar concept in painting is Alexander Rodchenko's *Pure Colors: Red, Yellow, Blue* (1921) (three panels in primary colors). In this way, the Russian constructivist intended to "reduce painting to its logical conclusion."
15. As Ferdinand de Saussure observed, with regard to language, if we see language from an internal perspective, as the relation among signs, it is absolutely rational, a deterministic system, but if we see language from an external perspective, as the relation between the sign and its reference, is completely arbitrary, aleatory. Kittler describes the break with the nineteenth-century concept of discourse in the following terms: "The discourse network of 1800 played the game of not being a discourse network and pretended instead to be the inwardness and voice of Man; in 1900 a type of writing assumes power that does not conform to traditional writing systems but rather radicalizes the technology of writing in general . . . Clearly, the discourse network of 1900 is a dice game with serially ordered discrete units, which in lyrics is called letters and punctuation signs, and to which writers since Mallarmé have ceded the initiative" (Kittler, *Discourse Network*, 211–213).
16. "To transfer messages from one medium to another always involves reshaping them to conform to the new standards and materials. In a discourse network that requires the awareness of the abysses which divide the one order of sense experience from the other, transposition necessarily takes the place of translation" (Kittler, *Discourse Network*, 265).
17. Kittler, *Discourse Network*, 219.
18. This also applies to the realm of art. While, for the avant-garde, only the decision of the artist turns an object into an artistic object, it does not explain *what makes a person an artist, the one who is entitled to do that*, whose mere decision suffices to transform a vulgar urinal into a work of art.
19. Theodor Adorno believed that the dismissal of tonality in contemporary music was a cry of rebellion against the constraints of forms and the liberation of man's creative potential. He also saw the avant-garde as a break with the structures of the capitalist market and the process of commoditization of art. In sum, he believed in atonalism as the source of an emancipatory potential and, therefore, as bearing definite political repercussions. See Adorno, *Philosophy of New Music* (Minneapolis: University of Minnesota Press, 2006).
20. See Elías J. Palti, "The 'Return of the Subject' as a Historico-Intellectual Problem," *History and Theory* 43 (2004): 57–82.
21. Ernst Cassirer, *Las ciencias de la cultura* (Mexico: FCE, 1982), 141.
22. Cassirer, *Las ciencias de la cultura*, 139.
23. Ernst Cassirer, *Substance and Function: Einstein's Theory of Relativity* (New York: Dover, 1923), 404.
24. Cassirer, *Las ciencias de la cultura*, 145.
25. Actually, Foucault missed this epistemic transformation produced at the end of the nineteenth century, and this led him to a number of contradictions. Friedrich Kittler noticed this and elaborated on the difference between what he calls the "discourse networks" of 1800 and 1900. See Palti, "The 'Return of the Subject'"; and Kittler, *Discourse Networks 1800/1900*.

26. Cassirer, *Substance and Function*, 414.
27. Cassirer, *Substance and Function*, 420.
28. Ernst Cassirer, *The Philosophy of Symbolic Forms*, vol. 1, *Language* (New Haven: Yale University Press, 1977), 78.
29. Cassirer, *Las ciencias de la cultura*, 152–153.
30. Gestalt theory is also illustrative of how this split operates in the field of knowledge. In the gestaltic switch, forms appear immediately to consciousness, as meaningful totalities. In order to say, "It is a duck," we do not have to recreate the duck progressively, one part after another—for example, "This is the ear," "This is the mouth," and so on—until we finally discover that it is a duck. Rather, we proceed the other way around. We must first discover that it is a duck in order to subsequently be able to discern its constituent parts. That is, in order to produce a rational knowledge of a given object, we must already know what it is that we are talking about. Conceptual thinking would entail a primitive instance of the investment of reality-senses that precede it and configure the world as a meaningful object, which operates the symbolic disclosure of it as a phenomenological field. This was also what, in the field of logic, C. S. Peirce referred to it under the name of "abduction"—the third intellectual procedure, in addition to induction and deduction, and the premise for these two. This prediscursive, preconceptual symbolic instance opens up the meaningful horizons within which concepts can eventually display themselves. It establishes the ground of evidence, which is immediately given to intentional consciousness, and eventually allows us to assert the validity (or invalidity) of a proposition.
31. Edmund Husserl, *The Crisis of European Sciences and Transcendental Phenomenology: An Introduction to Phenomenological Philosophy* (Evanston, IL: Northwestern University Press, 1970).
32. Georg Lukács, *Soul and Form* (Cambridge: MIT Press, 1974), 32.
33. For the notion of disclosure, see María Pía Lara, *The Disclosure of Politics: Struggles over the Semantics of Secularization* (New York: Columbia University Press, 2013).
34. Hans Kelsen, *The Essence and Value of Democracy* (1929) (Berkeley: University of California Press E-Books Collection, 1982–2004), 90. This work was originally a brief essay published at the *Archiv für Sozialwissenschaft und Sozialpolitik* and was subsequently expanded and published as a book in 1929. For a study on the genesis of this book, see Sara Lagi, *El pensamiento politico de Hans Kelsen (1911–1920): Los orígenes de* La esencia y el valor de la democracia (Madrid: Biblioteca Nueva, 2007).
35. See Hans Kelsen, "Causality and Imputation," *Ethics* 61 (1950): 1–11.
36. See Siegfried Marck, *Substanz und Funktionsbegriff in der Rechtsphilosophie* (Tübingen, 1925); and Carlos Miguel Herrera, *Théorie juridique et politique chez Hans Kelsen* (Paris: Kimé, 1997).
37. Kelsen, *Essence and Value of Democracy*, 86, 89.
38. On this topic, see Ralf Dahrendorf, "Max Weber and Modern Social Science," in *Max Weber and His Contemporaries*, ed. Wolfgang J. Mommsen and Jürgen Osterhammel (London: German Historical Institute/Allen & Unwin, 1987), 577 ff.

39. Hans Kelsen, *Hans Kelsen's Reply to Eric Voegelin's "A New Science of Politics": A Contribution to the Critique of Ideology* (Frankfurt: Ontos, 2004), 11.
40. This is at the basis of the set of oppositions, such as those between explanation and comprehension, *Naturwissenschaften* and *Geisteswissenschaften*, nomothetic sciences and ideographic sciences, and so on, around which the entire intellectual debate revolved during the first half of the twentieth century.
41. As Carlo Galli remarks, "Kelsen's unfounded formalism and Schmitt's unfounded decisionism, impersonal law and personal authority, certainly oppose each other, but within the very same horizon of crisis of modern mediation, that is, the attempt to keep united, with no contradictions, order and subject. Kelsen gives the priority to the latter, Schmitt to the former, but not as a subject in the sense of liberalism, or as a person in the Catholic sense, but as an authority, in the sense of a concrete instance, the formative decision that is able to found a juridical order." Galli, *Lo sguardo di Giano: Saggi su Carl Schmitt* (Bologna: Il Mulino, 2008), 61.
42. Carl Schmitt, *Political Theology: Four Chapters on the Concept of Sovereignty* (Chicago: University of Chicago Press, 2005), 5.
43. As Schmitt remarks, the nodal concept of form remains, however, ambiguous, both over- and ill-defined. "It is possible to observe three concepts of form in Max Weber's sociological theory," which, according to Schmitt, makes that theory inconsistent (Schmitt, *Political Theology*, 27).
44. Schmitt, *Political Theology*, 19–20.
45. Schmitt, *Political Theology*, 31.
46. Schmitt, *Political Theology*, 10.
47. Schmitt, *The Concept of the Political* (Chicago: University of Chicago Press, 1996), 19.
48. Schmitt, *Political Theology*, 30.
49. Schmitt, *Political Theology*, 29.
50. Kelsen, *Essence and Value of Democracy*, 84.
51. See Reinhart Koselleck, "The Historical-Political Semantics of Asymmetric Counterconcepts," in *Futures Past: On the Semantics of Historical Time*, trans. K. Tribe (Cambridge: MIT Press, 1985), 159–197.
52. Schmitt, *Concept of the Political*, 52.
53. Hans Kelsen, *Das Problem der Souveränität und die Theorie des Völkerrechts: Beitrag zu einer Reinen Rechtslhere* (Tübingen: J. C. B. Mohr, 1920), 8.
54. This is the basic contradiction in Schmitt's theory of sovereignty. The basis for its conception is the premise that the social realm lacks homogeneity, that it is, in Schmitt's words, a "pluriverse." Hence the need for a sovereign instance to provide it with unity. Yet the institution of this sovereign instance demands the people's acclamation. According to Schmitt, this is the very mechanism of its constitution. But, in such a case, the people would predate the sovereign, and the sovereign would not be necessary for its constitution. In sum, Schmitt's theory of sovereignty rejects the idea of the unity of the social realm, is contradictory with it, but, at the same time, presupposes it.
55. Jacques Derrida, *Writing and Difference* (Chicago: University of Chicago Press, 1978), 289.

56. "The modern age, after a series of historical-philosophical roundups, bets on the affirmation that it is man who 'makes' history. What that expression means can be understood only if we perceive the 'change of roles' that it produced. I have introduced and explained the concept in my *Die Legitimität der Neuzeit* (1966), but without noticing yet the whole theoretical process it implied. Since, in this fashion, it is neither discovered nor demonstrated who is the agent of history; the subject of history is merely 'named.'" Hans Blumenberg, *Wirklichkeiten in denen wir leben: Aufsätze und eine Rede* (Stuttgart: Reclam, 1999), 129.
57. See Derrida, *Speech and Phenomena, and Other Essays on Husserl's Theory of Signs* (Evanston, IL: Northwestern University Press, 1973).
58. Actually, this reformulation participates in a broader epistemic mutation that has occurred in the past twenty years, which traverses the whole of Western thinking, including natural science. In effect, a series of recent developments converged to place the notion of "event" at the center of scientific and philosophical reflection. An example of this is Ilya Prigogine's theory of dissipative structures. The notion of event forms an integral part of that theory, helping to explain the behavior of systems when away from their state of equilibrium. See Ilya Prigogine and Isabelle Stengers, *Order Out of Chaos* (New York: Bantam, 1984). The notion of event is also associated with that of metaevolution in biology (the evolution of the evolutionary processes themselves). See Humberto Maturana, *Biology of Cognition* (Urbana: University of Illinois Press, 1970); Humberto Maturana and Francisco Varela, *Autopoietic Systems* (Urbana: University of Illinois Press, 1975); and Erich Jantsch, *The Self-Organizing Universe* (Oxford: Pergamon Press, 1989). On this topic, see also Elías Palti, "Time, Modernity, and Time Irreversibility," *Philosophy and Social Criticism* 23, no. 5 (1997): 27–62.
59. See Jacques Derrida, *Khōra* (Córdoba: Alción, 1995). The first mention of this term appears at the end of *Dissemination* (1972). In *Of Grammatology* (1967), he still referred to this presignificative field in terms of "infra-structure."
60. Claude Lefort, "The Permanence of the Theological in the Political?," in *Democracy and Political Theory* (Cambridge: Polity Press, 1988), 225.
61. See Claude Lefort, "The Question of Democracy," in *Democracy and Political Theory*, 9–20.
62. See Karl Marx, "On the Jewish Question" (1843), in *The Marx-Engels Reader* (New York: Norton, 1978), 26–46.
63. Claude Lefort, "Human Rights and Politics," in *The Political Forms of Modern Society: Bureaucracy, Democracy, Totalitarianism* (Cambridge: MIT Press, 1986), 257–258.
64. This statement (that democracy can also become a form of totalitarianism) can be inferred from Lefort's theory, even though he does not say it this way (as is discussed later).
65. Lefort, "Human Rights and Politics," 260.
66. Slavoj Žižek, *The Ticklish Subject: The Absent Centre of Political Ontology* (London: Verso, 2000), 238, 251.
67. Claude Lefort, "The Logic of Totalitarianism," in *The Political Forms of Modern Society*, 279–280.

216 4. THE REBIRTH OF THE TRAGIC SCENE

68. Claude Lefort, "The Permanence of the Theological in the Political?" in *Democracy and Political Theory*, 233.
69. Claude Lefort, "Démocratie et le evénement d'un 'lieu vide,'" in *Le temps present: Écrits 1945–2005* (Paris: Belin, 2007), 468.
70. Leo Strauss, "Persecution and the Art of Writing," in *Persecution and the Art of Writing* (Chicago: University of Chicago Press, 1988).
71. Leo Strauss, *Natural Rights and History* (Chicago: University of Chicago Press, 1953).
72. Claude Lefort, "Trois notes sur Leo Strauss," *Écrire: À l' éprueve du politique* (Paris: Calmann-Lévy, 1992).
73. It is not surprising, then, that in the three decades that have passed since the end of the "short twentieth century," all of the worst atrocities have been committed in the name of democracy. Nor is it surprising that the secular tendency toward the reduction of social inequality has been drastically reversed: lacking the ghost of any alternative that might revolutionize the current order, the politics of social contention that this tendency fueled no longer makes sense.
74. Walter Benjamin, "Zur Kritik des Gewalt," in *Walter Benjamin: Gesammelte Schriften* (Frankfurt: Surkhamp, 1999), 2:179–204.
75. Lefort, "Human Rights and Politics," in *Democracy and Political Theory*, 270.
76. Jacques Rancière, *Hatred of Democracy* (London: Verso, 2006), 41.
77. Rancière, *Hatred of Democracy*, 48.
78. Rancière, *Hatred of Democracy*, 4, 52.
79. Jacques Rancière, *La Mésentente: Politique et Philosophie* (Paris: Galilée, 1995), 121.
80. See Gopal Balakrishnan, ed., *Debating Empire* (London: Verso, 2004); Paul A. Passavant and Jodi Dean, *Empire's New Clothes* (New York: Routledge, 2004); and Chantal Mouffe, *On the Political* (New York: Routledge, 2005). When it comes to explaining how the multitude could realize its supposedly emancipatory potential in a practical-political terrain, authors limit themselves to stating that, "We do not have any models to offer for this event. Only the multitude through its practical experimentation will offer the models and determine when and how the possible becomes real." Antonio Negri and Michael Hart, *Empire* (Cambridge: Harvard University Press, 2000), 411.
81. Alberto Moreiras, "A Line of Shadows: Metaphysics in Counter-Empire, *Rethinking Marxism* 13, no. 3/4 (2001): 224.
82. Mouffe, *On the Political*, 111.
83. Badiou, *The Century*, 9.
84. Perhaps the best contemporary example of this pattern is Hannah Arendt. In *On Violence* she condemns every form of violent action as contradictory with a truly political institution, which demands debate, the confrontation of ideas. As she says, the kind of brotherhood created before the danger of dying suppresses the singularity of the subject. A person thus becomes radically unable to engage himself in a critical debate. Yet, in *Between Past and Future*, she praises the French *Résistance* as the best expression of a truly political action in the sense that it gave birth to an authentic public sphere. See Arendt, *On Violence* (New York: Harcourt, Brace & World, 1970), 69; and Arendt, *Between Past and Future* (New York: Penguin, 1974), 4. Admiring the meth-

4. THE REBIRTH OF THE TRAGIC SCENE 217

ods of the French *Résistance* but not those of other groups that have undertaken violent action is certainly arbitrary, expressing a merely subjective preference. Yet it demonstrates the difficulty of any theorist exempting him- or herself from accepting some form of violent action in the constitution of the political.

85. "To examine the effects of violence it is necessary to start from its distant consequences and not from its immediate results. We should not ask whether it is more or less directly advantageous for contemporary workmen than adroit diplomacy would be, but we should inquire what will result from the introduction of violence into the relations of the proletariat with society. We are not comparing two kinds of reformism, but we are endeavouring to find out what contemporary violence is in relation to the future social revolution." Georges Sorel, *Reflections on Violence* (London: Georg Allen & Unwin, 1925), 47–48.
86. Sorel, *Reflections on Violence*, 29–30.
87. The presence of the preontological self was simply assumed as such by Sorel and Schmitt, since it was the condition for the thinking of the political. With Emmanuel Levinas, instead, it becomes a problem: how was it itself constituted? He thus starts inquiring into the nature of the admonition that constitutes it as such. He designates this admonition in terms of the impingement by an Other. For him, it is the "original traumatism" of *being impinged by an Other* that constitutes our self. See Levinas, *Otherwise Than Being, or Beyond Essence* (Pittsburgh: Duquesne University Press, 1998). However, this is the point in which the very concept of the subject becomes problematic. That admonition cannot participate in the symbolical order, because it delimits the ontological field. Yet the Other that produces it must already be, it itself, a self, otherwise it would involve us into an infinite regression. In the end, the idea of this preontological self—and, along with it, the very concept of the political—becomes radically unthinkable. On the political problems that Levinas's idea raises, see Judith Butler, *Giving an Account of Oneself* (New York: Fordham University Press, 2005).
88. Arthur Koestler, *Darkness at Noon* (Morrisville, NC: Lulu, 2010), 70.
89. Maurice Merleau-Ponty, *Humanism and Terror: An Essay on the Communist Problem* (Boston: Beacon, 1969), xxviii–xxix.
90. Merleau-Ponty, *Humanism and Terror*, xxviii, 2, 13.
91. Merleau-Ponty, *Humanism and Terror*, 1.
92. Merleau-Ponty, *Humanism and Terror*, 14–15 (his italics).
93. Merleau-Ponty, *Humanism and Terror*, 17.
94. Maurice Merleau-Ponty, *Humanisme et Terreur*, in *Oeuvres* (Paris: Gallimard, 2000), 228. This sentence is missing from the English translation.
95. Merleau-Ponty, *Humanism and Terror*, 21.
96. Merleau-Ponty, *Humanism and Terror*, 22.
97. Merleau-Ponty, *Humanism and Terror*, 36.
98. Merleau-Ponty, *Humanism and Terror*, 28.
99. Merleau-Ponty, *Humanism and Terror*, xl.
100. Merleau-Ponty, *Humanism and Terror*, 17.
101. Alain Badiou, *Peut-on penser la politique?* (Paris: Seuil, 1985), 11–12.

102. I elaborated on this further in Elías J. Palti, *Verdades y saberes del marxismo: Reacciones de una tradición política ante su "crisis"* (Buenos Aires: FCE, 2007).
103. Badiou, *Peut-on penser la politique*, 113.

CONCLUSION

1. Actually, like Merleau-Ponty in relation to the subject, Benjamin affirms the presence of a fundamental asymmetry between the two forms of violence. Mythical (conservative) violence does not have to do with values but with natural life (*das blosse Leben*), the *nuda vita*, life deprived of meaning and value. Divine violence, instead, has to do with the living (*über alles Leben*), with history, is in fact the last source of history. It sacrifices life for the sake of the living, to preserve the soul of the living (*die Seele des Lebendigen*). As in the story of the Exodus, divine violence is associated with an ideal of justice (the liberation from servitude and the reaching of the promised land). However, as Derrida shows, this distinction is soon rendered problematic by Benjamin, insofar as the content of this latter violence also reveals itself to be undecidable. "The determinant decision, the one that permits us to know or to recognize such a pure or revolutionary violence *as such*, is a decision *not accessible to man* . . . This results from the fact that divine violence, the most historic, the most revolutionary, the most decidable or the most deciding does not lend itself to any human determination, to any knowledge or decidable 'certainty' on our part." Jacques Derrida, "The Force of Law: The 'Mystical Foundation' of Authority," in *Deconstruction and the Possibility of Justice*, ed. Drucilla Cornell, Michel Rosenfeld, and David Gray Carlson (New York: Routledge, 1992), 55–56.
2. On this, see Oliver Marchart, *Postfoundational Political Thought: Political Difference in Nancy, Lefort, Badiou and Laclau* (Edinburgh: Edinburgh University Press, 2007).
3. Roberto Esposito, *Dieci pensieri sulla politica* (Bologna: Il Mulino, 2011), 31.
4. Chantal Mouffe presents a good example of the inherent impossibility of political thinking about coming to terms with antagonism. While in the preface to her book *The Return of the Political*, she states that, "The central theme that provides the unity of the book is a reflection on the political and on the ineradicable character of power and antagonism," she immediately proceeds to the reduction of antagonism to "agonism." As she states a few pages later, "Liberal democracy requires consensus on the rules of the game, but it also calls for the constitution of collective identities around clearly differentiated positions and the possibility of choosing between real alternatives. This 'agonistic pluralism' is constitutive of modern democracy and, rather than seeing it as a threat, we should realize that it represents the very condition of existence of such democracy." Mouffe, *The Return of the Political* (London: Verso, 1993), vii, 4.
5. Rauschenberg asked Willem de Kooning, a painter whom he deeply admired, for a drawing that he would then erase. According to Rauschenberg, the erasure of the drawing was an homage he paid to it.

6. As Peter Bürger eloquently remarks in his classic work, the typically avant-gardist ideal of rejoining art with life meant a reversal of the entire Western artistic tradition founded on the principle of art's autonomy. Bürger, *Theory of the Avant-Garde* (Minneapolis: University of Minnesota Press, 1989). Yet, it would never question the meaning of that life to which art is supposed to rejoin itself. He would simply take for granted the presence of it, a "life" beyond artistic representation, toward which this latter would try to converge. This is an attitude that Bürger expresses in his own work, which represents the intrinsic blind spot in his theory. For a criticism of Bürger's theory, see Hal Foster, *The Return of the Real* (Cambridge: MIT Press, 1996).
7. Michel Foucault, "La pensée du dehors," in *Dits et Écrits: 1954–1988*, vol. 1, *1954–1969* (Paris: Gallimard, 1994), 523–525.
8. Foucault, "La pensée du dehors," 523, 526.
9. Theodor Adorno, *Philosophy of New Music* (Minneapolis: University of Minnesota Press, 2006).
10. "To find oneself again beyond the song, as if one has traversed alive the death, but to reinstitute it in a second language" (Foucault, "La pensée du dehors," 532).
11. Claude Lefort, "The Permanence of the Theological in the Political?," in *Democracy and Political Theory* (Cambridge: Polity, 1988), 225.
12. Joseph Kosuth, "Art After Philosophy," in Ursula Meyer, *Conceptual Art* (New York: Dutton, 1972), 155–170; quoted in Arthur C. Danto, *After the End of Art: Contemporary Art and the Pale of History* (Princeton: Princeton University Press, 1997), 13.
13. As Michel Foucault stated, "Discursive practices are not purely and simply ways of producing discourse. They are embodied in technical processes, institutions, in patterns for general behavior." Foucault, "History of the Systems of Thought: Summary of a Course Given at the Collège de France, 1970–1971," in *Language, Counter-Memory, Practice: Selected Essays and Interviews by Michel Foucault*, ed. Donald Bouchard (Ithaca, NY: Cornell University Press, 1982), 200. This means that the changes in discursive practices are independent not only of our will but also of our conscience. We do not really know how political languages have changed in the past twenty years better than we know, for example, how the economy or society have changed in this period. In sum, just like the process of secularization, this second disenchantment of the world has nothing to do with the beliefs of the subjects (actually, even after the death of God, most people kept believing in the existence of it), since it refers to the objective alterations in the ways in which these beliefs could be publicly articulated. In sum, any approach to it has nothing to do with any history of ideas; it can only be observed from the perspective of a conceptual history of the political.

BIBLIOGRAPHY

Adorno, Theodor. *Philosophy of New Music*. Minneapolis: University of Minnesota Press, 2006.

Agamben, Giorgio. *The Kingdom and the Glory: For a Theological Genealogy of Economy and Government*. Stanford: Stanford University Press, 2011.

Agnew, Jean-Christophe. *Worlds Apart: The Market and the Theater in Anglo-American Thought, 1550–1750*. Cambridge: Cambridge University Press, 1986.

Alberdi, Juan Bautista. *Escritos póstumos de Juan Bautista Alberdi*. Buenos Aires: Impr. Europea/Impr. A. Monkes/Impr. J. B. Alberdi, 1901.

Alencar, José de. *Dois escritos democráticos de José de Alencar*. Ed. Wanderley Guilherme dos Santos. Rio de Janeiro: UFRJ, 1991.

Alighieri, Dante. *The De Monarchia by Dante Alighieri*. Trans. Aurelia Henry. Boston: Houghton, Mifflin, 1904.

Altini, Carlo. *La fabrica de la soberanía: Maquiavelo, Hobbes, Spinoza y otros modernos*. Buenos Aires: El Cuenco de Plata, 2007.

Álvarez Sellers, Maria Rosa. *Análisis y evolución de la tragedia española en el Siglo de Oro*. Kassel: Kut und Rostwitha Reichenberger, 1997.

Antón Martínez, B. *El tacitismo en el siglo XVII en España: El proceso de "receptio."* Valladolid: Universidad de Valladolid, 1992.

Aquinas, Thomas. "Gobierno de los príncipes." In *Tratado de la ley, tratado de la justicia: Gobierno de los príncipes*. Trans. Carlos Ignacio González. Mexico: Porrúa, 1975.

Arbulu Barturen, Maria Begoña, and Sandra Bagno, eds. *La recepción de Maquiavelo y Beccaria en el ámbito hispanoamericano*. Padua: Unipress, 2005.

Arendt, Hannah. *Between Past and Future: Eight Exercises in Political Thought*. New York: Penguin, 1977.

———. *On Revolution*. London: Penguin, 1987.

———. *On Violence*. New York: Harcourt, Brace & World, 1970.
Aristotle. *Politics*. Trans. Benjamin Jowett. Kittchener: Batoche, 1999.
Armitage, David, Conal Condren, and Andrew Fitzmaurice, eds. *Shakespeare and Early Modern Political Thought*. Cambridge: Cambridge University Press, 2009.
Badiou, Alain. *The Century*. New York: Polity, 2007.
———. *Peut-on penser la politique?* Paris: Seuil, 1985.
Balakrishnan, Gopal, ed. *Debating Empire*. London: Verso, 2004.
Barros, Carlos. "Viva el Rey! Rey, imaginario y revuelta en la Galicia bajomedieval." http://www.h-debate.com/cbarros/spanish/viva_el_rey.htm.
Barthes, Roland. *Sur Racine*. Paris: Seuil, 1963.
Bataille, Georges. *L'absence de myth: Ouvres completes*. Vol. 9. Paris: Gallimard, 1988.
Beiner, Ronald. *Civil Religion: A Dialogue in the History of Political Philosophy*. Cambridge: Cambridge University Press, 2011.
Benjamin, Walter. *The Origin of German Tragic Drama*. London: Verso, 2009.
———. *Walter Benjamin Gesammelte Schriften*. Frankfurt: Surkhamp, 1999.
Bergson, Henri. *L'évolution créatrice*. Paris: PUF, 1907.
Berllingeri, Marco, ed. *Dinámica del Antiguo Régimen y orden constitucional: Representación, justicia y administración en Iberoamérica (siglos XVII y XIX)*. Torino: Otto, 2000.
Bloom, Harold. *Shakespeare: The Invention of the Human*. New York: Riverhead, 1998.
Bluche, François. *L'Ancien Régime: Institutions et Société*. Paris: Fallois, 1993.
Blumenberg, Hans. *The Genesis of the Copernican World*. Trans. Robert Wallace. Cambridge: MIT Press, 1987.
———. *The Legitimacy of the Modern Age*. Trans. Robert Wallace. Cambridge: MIT Press, 1991.
———. *Wirklichkeiten in denen wir leben: Aufsätze und eine Rede*. Stuttgart: Reclam, 1999.
Born, Georgina. *Rationalizing Culture: IRCAM, Boulez, and the Institutionalization of the Musical Avant-Garde*. Berkeley: University of California Press, 1990.
Brendecke, Arndt. *Imperium und Empirie: Funktionen des Wissens in der Spanischen Kolonialherrschaft*. Köln: Böhlau, 2009.
Brett, Annabel, and James Tully, eds. *Rethinking the Foundations of Modern Political Thought*. Cambridge: Cambridge University Press, 2006.
Bürger, Peter. *Theory of the Avant-Garde*. Minneapolis: University of Minnesota Press, 1989.
Burke, Edmund. *Burke's Politics: Selected Writings and Speeches*. Ed. R. J. S. Hoffmann and P. Levack. New York: Knopf, 1949.
Butler, Judith. *Giving an Account of Oneself*. New York: Fordham University Press, 2005.
Calderón de la Barca, Pedro. *Obras completas*. Ed. Ángel Valbuena Briones. 2 vols. Tolle: Aguilar, 1969.
Camus, Albert. *Le Mythe de Sisyphe*. Paris: Gallimard, 1942.
Casaús Arzú, Marta Elena, ed. *El lenguaje de los ismos: Algunos conceptos de la modernidad en América Latina*. Guatemala City: F&G, 2010.
Cascardi, Anthony J. *The Bounds of Reason: Cervantes, Dostoevsky, Flaubert*. New York: Columbia University Press, 1986.
Cassirer, Ernst. *Las ciencias de la cultura*. Mexico: FCE, 1982.

———. *The Philosophy of Symbolic Forms*. Vol. 1, *Language*. New Haven: Yale University Press, 1977.
———. *Substance and Function: Einstein's Theory of Relativity*. New York: Dover, 1923.
Castro, Américo. *Semblanzas y estudios españoles*. Barcelona: Ínsula, 1956.
Cattin, E., L. Jaffro, and A. Petit, eds. *Figures du théologique-politique*. Paris: J. Vrin, 1999.
Cervantes Saavedra, Miguel de. *The Adventures of Don Quixote*. Ed. M. Cohen. Harmondsworth: Penguin, 1950.
———. *Novelas Ejemplares*. Madrid: Cátedra, 1992.
Chiaramonte, José Carlos. *La crítica ilustrada de la realidad: Economía y sociedad en el pensamiento argentino e iberoamericano del siglo XVIII*. Buenos Aires: CEAL, 1982.
———. *La ilustración en el Río de la Plata: Cultura eclesiástica y cultura laica durante el Virreinato*. Buenos Aires: Puntosur, 1989.
Chowning, Margaret. "The Consolidation of Vales Reales in the Bishopric of Michoacán." *Hispanic American Historical Review* 69, no. 3 (1989): 451–478.
Clavero, Bartolomé. *Antidora: Antropología Católica de la economía moderna*. Milan: Giuffrè, 1991.
Congreso Nacional. *Diario de sesiones del Honorable Congreso de la Nación Argentina*. Buenos Aires: Imprenta del Congreso de la Nación, 1910.
Connelly, Stephen. "Conatus, Political Being, and Spinoza," *Critical Legal Thinking*, March 16, 2015, http://criticallegalthinking.com/2015/03/16/conatus-political-being-and-spinoza/.
Cornell, Drucilla, Michel Rosenfeld, and David Gray Carlson, eds. *Deconstruction and the Possibility of Justice*. New York: Routledge, 1992.
Courtine, Jean-François. *Nature et empire de la loi: Études suaréziennes*. Paris: J. Vrin, 1999.
Damian, Bruno M., and Ruth El Saffar, eds. *Studies in Honor of Elias Rivers*. Potomac, MD: Sinpta Humanistica, 1989.
Danto, Arthur C. *After the End of Art: Contemporary Art and the Pale of History*. Princeton: Princeton University Press, 1997.
de Arroyal, Leòn. *Cartas económico-políticas*. Oviedo: Instituto Feijóo, 1971.
de León, Fray Luis. *De los nombres de Cristo*. Madrid: PMI, 1994.
Deleuze, Gilles. *Curso sobre Foucault*. 3 vols. Buenos Aires: Cactus, 2013–2015.
———. *En el medio de Spinoza*. Buenos Aires: Cactus, 2011.
———. *The Fold: Leibniz and the Baroque*. Minneapolis: University of Minnesota Press, 1992.
D'Entrèves, Passerin. *The Notion of the State: An Introduction to Political Theory*. Oxford: Clarendon, 1969.
de Mariana, Juan. *De la dignidad real y la educación del príncipe*. Madrid: Centro de Estudios Constitucionales, 1981.
De Molina, Tirso. *La prudencia en la mujer y El condenado por desconfiado*. Madrid: Espasa Calpe, 1968.
Derrida, Jacques. *The Beast and the Sovereign*. Chicago: University of Chicago Press, 2002.
———. *Khōra*. Córdoba: Alción, 1995.
———. *Of Grammatology*. Trans. Gayatri Chakravorty Spivak. Washington, DC: Johns Hopkins University Press, 1977.

———. *Speech and Phenomena, and Other Essays on Husserl's Theory of Signs*. Evanston, IL: Northwestern University Press, 1973.
———. *Writing and Difference*. Chicago: University of Chicago Press, 1978.
de Vega, Lope. *El castigo sin venganza*. Madrid: Cátedra, 1993.
———. *La dama boba*. Madrid: Cátedra, 1994.
———. *La Dorotea*. Madrid: Universidad de Puerto Rico, Revista de Occidente, 1955.
———. *Peribáñez y el Comendador de Ocaña: El mejor alcalde, el rey*. Barcelona: Planeta, 1990.
de Vitoria, Francisco. *La ley*. Madrid: Tecnos, 2009.
Dunn, John. *The Political Thought of John Locke: An Historical Account of the Argument of the "Two Treatises of Government."* Cambridge: Cambridge University Press, 1995.
Elliott, J. H. *Spain and Its World, 1500–1700*. 2nd ed. New Haven: Yale University Press, 1989.
Elliott, J. H., et al. *1640: La monarquía hispánica en crisis*. Barcelona: Centre d'Estudis d'Historia Moderna Pierre Vilar/Crítica, 1992.
El Saffar, Ruth A., and Diana de Armas Wilson. *Quixotic Desire: Psychoanalytic Perspectives on Cervantes*. Ithaca, NY: Cornell University Press, 1993.
Empson, William. *Seven Types of Ambiguity*. New York: Meridian, 1955.
Escalante, M. F. *Álamos de Barrientos y la doctrina de la razón de Estado en España (posibilidad y frustración)*. Barcelona: Fontamara, 1975.
Esposito, Roberto. *Categorías de lo impolítico*. Trans. Roberto Raschella. Buenos Aires: Katz, 2006.
———. *Dieci pensieri sulla política*. Bologna: Il Mulino, 2011.
Farinelli, Anturo. *La vita è sogno, parte seconda*. Torino: Fratelli Bocca, 1916.
Febvre, Lucien. *The Problem of Unbelief in the Sixteenth Century: The Religion of Rabelais*. Trans. Beatrice Gottlieb. Cambridge: Harvard University Press, 1982.
Fernández Albaladejo, Pablo. *Materia de España: Cultura política e identidad de la España noderna*. Madrid: Marcial Pons, 2007.
Fernández Santamaría, José A. *Razón de Estado y política en el pensamiento español del Barroco (1595–1640)*. Madrid: Centro de Estudios Constitucionales, 1989.
Figgis, John N. *El derecho divino de los reyes y tres ensayos adicionales*. Mexico: FCE, 1942.
Filmer, Robert. *Patriarcha and Other Writings*. Cambridge: Cambridge University Press, 1991.
Finestrad, Joaquín de. *El vasallo instruido*. Bogota: Universidad Nacional de Colombia, 2000.
Fitter, Chris. "Historicising Shakespeare's *Richard II*: Current Events, Dating, and the Sabotage of Essex," *Early Modern Literary Studies* 11, no. 2 (2005): 1–47.
Forker, Charles R. Preface to *King Richard II*, by William Shakespeare, 1–169. London: Bloomsbury, 2004.
Foster, Hal. *The Return of the Real*. Cambridge: MIT Press, 1996.
Foucault, Michel. *Dits et Écrits: 1954–1988*, vol. 1, *1954–1969*. Paris: Gallimard, 1994.
———. *Language, Counter-Memory, Practice: Selected Essays and Interviews by Michel Foucault*. Ed. Donald Bouchard. Ithaca, NY: Cornell University Press, 1982.
———. *Madness and Civilization*. New York: Random House, 1965.
———. *The Order of Things: An Archeology of the Human Sciences*. New York: Random House, 1990.

———. *Security, Territory, Population*. Trans. Graham Burchell. New York: Palgrave Macmillan, 2007.
———. *Society Must Be Defended*. Ed. Mauro Bertani and Alessandro Fontana. New York: Picador, 2003.
Freund, Julien. *L'essence du politique*. Paris: Dalloz, 2004.
Frye, Northrop. *On Shakespeare*. Markham, ON: Fitzbury & Whiteside, 1986.
Galli, Carlo. *Lo sguardo di Giano: Saggi su Carl Schmitt*. Bologna: Il Mulino, 2008.
García Ayluardo, Clara, ed. *Las reformas borbónicas: 1750–1808*. Mexico: FCE, 2010.
García Marín, José María. *Teoria política y gobierno en la Monarquía Hispana*. Madrid: Centro de Estudios Políticos y Constitucionales, 1998.
Gierke, Otto von. *Natural Law and the Theory of Society: 1500–1800*. Trans. E. Baker. Boston: Beacon, 1957.
Girard, René. *Géometries du désir*. Paris: L'Herne, 2012.
Goldberg, Jonathan. *James I and the Politics of Literature: Jonson, Shakespeare, Donne, and Other Contemporaries*. Stanford: Stanford University Press, 1999.
Goldmann, Lucien. *Le Dieu caché: Étude sur la visión tragique dans les Pensées de Pascal et dans le théâtre de Racine*. Paris: Gallimard, 1955.
Gombricht, E. H. *Art and Illusion: A Study of the Psychology of Pictorial Representation*. New York: Pantheon, 1960.
Gracián, Baltasar. *El Criticón*. Buenos Aires: Losada, 2010.
Greenblatt, Stephen. *The Greenblatt Reader*. Oxford: Blackwell, 2005.
———. *Shakespearean Negotiations*. Berkeley: University of California Press, 1988.
Halperin Donghi, Tulio. *Tradición política española e ideología revolucionaria de Mayo*. Buenos Aires: CEAL, 1965.
Hermenegildo, Alfredo. *La tragedia en el Renacimiento español*. Barcelona: Planeta, 1973.
Hernández, José Ma. *El retrato de un dios mortal: Estudio sobre la filosofía política de Hobbes*. Barcelona: Anthropos, 2002.
Herrera, Carlos Miguel. *Théorie juridique et politique chez Hans Kelsen*. Paris: Kimé, 1997.
Hilb, Claudia. *Leo Strauss: El arte de leer*. Buenos Aires: FCE, 2005.
Hintze, Otto. *Staat und Verfassung*. Gotinga: Vandenhoeck & Ruprecht, 1962.
Hirschman, Albert O. *The Passions and the Interests: Political Arguments for Capitalism Before Its Triumph*. Princeton: Princeton University Press, 1977.
Hobbes, Thomas. *Leviathan*. Cambridge: Cambridge University Press, 1994.
Hobsbawm, Eric. *The Age of Extremes: 1914–1991*. New York: Vintage, 1996.
Howard, Dick. *The Primacy of the Political: A History of Political Thought from the Greeks to the French and American Revolutions*. New York: Columbia University Press, 2010.
Hunt, John. "A Thing of Nothing: The Catastrophic Body in *Hamlet*." *Shakespeare Quarterly* 39, no. 2 (1988): 27–44.
Hunt, Maurice, ed. *Approaches to the Teaching of Shakespeare's* The Tempest *and Other Late Romances*. New York: Modern Language Association of America, 1992.
Husserl, Edmund. *The Crisis of European Sciences and Transcendental Phenomenology: An Introduction to Phenomenological Philosophy*. Evanston, IL: Northwestern University Press, 1970.

Iñurritegui Rodríguez, José Maria. *La gracia y la república: El lenguaje político de la teología católica y el* Príncipe Cristiano *de Pedro Rivadaneyra*. Madrid: UNED, 1998.

Jago, Charles. "Habsburg Absolutism and the Cortes of Castile." *American Historical Review* 86 (1981): 307–326.

Jantsch, Erich. *The Self-Organizing Universe*. Oxford: Pergamon, 1989.

Jaume, Lucien. *Le discours jacobin et la démocratie*. Paris: Fayard, 1989.

Jovellanos, Melchor Gaspar de. *Escritos políticos y filosóficos*. Barcelona: Folio, 1999.

Kantorowicz, Ernst. *The King's Two Bodies: A Study in Medieval Political Thought*. Princeton: Princeton University Press, 1981.

Kelsen, Hans. "Causality and Imputation," *Ethics* 61 (1950): 1–11.

———. *Das Problem der Souveränität und die Theorie des Völkerrechts: Beitrag zu einer Reinen Rechtslhere*. Tübingen: J. C. B. Mohr, 1920.

———. *The Essence and Value of Democracy*. Berkeley: University of California Press E-Books Collection, 1982–2004 [1929].

———. *Hans Kelsen's Reply to Eric Voegelin's "A New Science of Politics": A Contribution to the Critique of Ideology*. Frankfurt: Ontos, 2004.

Kermode, Frank. *The Sense of an Ending: Studies in the Theory of Fiction*. London: Oxford University Press, 1993.

Kittler, Friedrich A. *Discourse Networks 1800/1900*. Trans. Michael Metteer. Stanford: Stanford University Press, 1990.

Koestler, Arthur. *Darkness at Noon*. Morrisville, NC: Lulu, 2010.

Koselleck, Reinhart. *Critique and Crisis: Enlightenment and the Pathogenesis of Modern Society*. Oxford: Berg, 1988.

———. *Futures Past: On the Semantics of Historical Time*. Trans. K. Tribe. Cambridge, MA: MIT Press, 1985.

Kott, Jan. *Shakespeare: Our Contemporary*. London: Norton, 1966.

Kretzmann, Norman, Anthony Kenny, and Jean Pinborg, eds. *The Cambridge History of Later Medieval Philosophy: From the Rediscovery of Aristotle to the Disintegration of Scholasticism, 1100–1600*. Cambridge: Cambridge University Press, 1988.

Lagi, Sara. *El pensamiento politico de Hans Kelsen (1911–1920): Los orígenes de* La esencia y el valor de la democracia. Madrid: Biblioteca Nueva, 2007.

Lara, María Pía. *The Disclosure of Politics: Struggles over the Semantics of Secularization*. New York: Columbia University Press, 2013.

———, ed. *Rethinking Evil: Contemporary Perspectives*. Berkeley: University of California Press, 2001.

Lastarria, José Victorino. *Obras completas*. 2 vols. Santiago: Impr. Barcelona, 1906.

Lee, Hwa-Yong. *Political Representation in Later Middle Ages*. New York: Peter Lang, 2008.

Lefort, Claude. *Democracy and Political Theory*. Trans. D. Macey. Cambridge: Polity Press, 1988.

———. *Écrire: À l' éprueve du politique*. Paris: Calmann-Lévy, 1992.

———. *Le temps présent: Écrits 1945–2005*. Paris: Belin, 2007.

———. *The Political Forms of Modern Society: Bureaucracy, Democracy, Totalitarianism*. Cambridge: MIT Press, 1986.

Lempérière, Annick. *Entre Dieu et le Roi, la République: Mexico, XVIe—XIXe siècles.* Paris: Les Belles Lettres, 2004.
Levinas, Emmanuel. *Otherwise than Being, or Beyond Essence.* Pittsburgh, PA: Duquesne University Press, 1998.
Leyva, Gustavo, Francis Brian Connaughton, Rodrigo Díaz Cruz, Néstor García Canclini, and Carlos Illades, eds., *Independencia y revolución: Pasado, presente y futuro.* Mexico: FCE/Universidad Autónoma Metropolitana, 2010.
Locke, John. *Two Treatises of Government.* Ed. Peter Laslett. New York: Mentor, 1963.
Lovejoy, Arthur O. *Essays in the History of Ideas.* Baltimore: Johns Hopkins University Press, 1948.
———. *The Great Chain of Being: A Study of the History of an Idea.* Cambridge: Harvard University Press, 1964.
Lukács, Georg. *Soul and Form.* Trans. Anna Bostock. Cambridge: MIT Press, 1974.
Manin, Bernard. *The Principles of Representative Government.* Cambridge: Cambridge University Press, 1997.
Mann, Thomas. *Doctor Faustus: The Life of the Composer Adrian Leverkuhn as Told by a Friend.* New York: Vintage, 1999.
Maravall, José Antonio. *Culture of the Baroque: Analysis of a Historical Structure.* Trans. Terry Cochran. Minneapolis: University of Minnesota Press, 1986.
———. *Teoría del Estado en España en el siglo XVII.* Madrid: Centro de Estudios Políticos y Constitucionales, 1997.
Marchart, Oliver. *Postfoundational Political Thought: Political Difference in Nancy, Lefort, Badiou and Laclau.* Edinburgh: Edinburgh University Press, 2007.
Marck, Siegfried. *Substanz- und Funktionsbegriff in der Rechtsphilosophie.* Tübingen, 1925.
Marichal, Carlos. *La bancarrota del virreinato: Nueva España y las finanzas del Imperio colonial, 1780–1810.* Mexico: FCE, 1999.
Mariscal, George. *Contradictory Subjects: Quevedo, Cervantes, and Seventeenth-Century Spanish Culture.* Ithaca, NY: Cornell University Press, 1991.
Martel, José, ed. *Diez comedias del Siglo de Oro.* 2nd ed. Prospect Heights, IL: Waveland, 1985.
Martínez Marina, Francisco. *Discurso sobre el origen de la monarquía y sobre la naturaleza del gobierno español.* Madrid: Centro de Estudios Constitucionales, 1988.
Marx, Karl, and Friedrich Engels. *The Marx–Engels Reader.* New York: Norton, 1978.
Maturana, Humberto. *Biology of Cognition.* Urbana: University of Illinois Press, 1970.
Maturana, Humberto, and Francisco Varela. *Autopoietic Systems.* Urbana: University of Illinois Press, 1975.
Maupas, Leopoldo. "Trascendencia política de la nueva ley electoral," *Revista Argentina de Ciencias Políticas* 22 (1912): 409–428.
McIlwain, Charles H. *Constitutionalism: Ancient and Modern.* Ithaca, NY: Cornell University Press, 1958.
Melville, Herman. *Pierre; or the Ambiguities.* New York: Harper, 1995.
Mencke, Christoph. *Die Gegenwart der Tragödie.* Frankfurt: Suhrkamp, 2005.
Mendo, Andrés. *Príncipes perfectos y Ministros ajustados: Documentos politicos-morales en emblemas.* Lyon: Boissat and Remens, 1662.

Merleau-Ponty, Maurice. *Humanism and Terror: An Essay on the Communist Problem.* Boston: Beacon, 1969.
———. *Oeuvres.* Paris: Gallimard, 2000.
Meyer, Ursula. *Conceptual Art.* New York: E. P. Dutton, 1972.
Milton, John. *Paradise Lost: An Authoritative Text, Backgrounds, and Sources, Criticism.* New York: Norton, 1965.
Mirete, José Luis. "Maquiavelo y su recepción de la teoría del Estado en España (Siglos XVI y XVII)." *Anales de Derecho* 19 (2001): 139–144.
Mommsen, Wolfgang J., and Jürgen Osterhammel, eds. *Max Weber and his Contemporaries.* London: German Historical Institute/Allen & Unwin, 1987.
Montano, Vicente. *Arcano de príncipes.* Madrid: Centro de Estudios Constitucionales, 1986.
Moreiras, Alberto. "A Line of Shadows: Metaphysics in Counter-Empire." *Rethinking Marxism* 13, no. 3/4 (2001): 216–226.
Moreno, Mariano. *Escritos políticos y económicos.* Buenos Aires: La Cultura Argentina, 1915.
Morgan, Edmund. *The Invention of the People: The Right of Popular Sovereignty in England and America.* New York: Norton, 1988.
Mouffe, Chantal. *On the Political.* New York: Routledge, 2005.
———. *The Return of the Political.* London: Verso, 1993.
Muir, Kenneth, and S. Schoenbaum, eds. *A New Companion to Shakespeare Studies.* Cambridge: Cambridge University Press, 1971.
Nañez, Emilio, and Juan Manuel Azpitarte. Introduction to *Teatro completo*, by Jean Racine. Madrid: Editora Nacional, 1982, 9–165.
Negri, Antonio, and Michael Hart. *Empire.* Cambridge: Harvard University Press, 2000.
Nerlich, Michel, and Nichlas Spadaccini. *Cervantes' "Exemplar Novels" and the Adventure of Writing.* Minneapolis: Prisma Institute, 1989.
Nietzsche, Friedrich. *The Philosophy of Nietzsche.* New York: Random House, n.d.
Nussbaum, Martha C. *The Fragility of Goodness: Luck and Ethics in Greek Tragedy and Philosophy.* Cambridge: Cambridge University Press, 1989.
Pagden, Anthony, ed. *The Languages of Political Theory in Early-Modern Europe.* Cambridge: Cambridge University Press, 1990.
Palonen, Kari. *Quentin Skinner: History, Politics, Rhetoric.* Cambridge: Polity, 2003.
Palti, Elías J. "Beyond Revisionism: The Bicentennial of Independence, the Early Republican Experience, and Intellectual History in Latin America." *Journal of the History of Ideas* 70, no. 4 (2009): 593–614.
———. *El tiempo de la política: El siglo XIX reconsiderado.* Buenos Aires: Siglo XXI, 2007.
———. "The Metaphor of Life: Herder's Philosophy of History and Uneven Developments in Late-Enlightenment Natural Sciences." *History and Theory* 38, no. 3 (1999): 322–348.
———. "The 'Return of the Subject' as a Historico-Intellectual Problem." *History and Theory* 43 (2004): 57–82.
———. "Time, Modernity, and Time Irreversibility." *Philosophy and Social Criticism* 23, no. 5 (1997): 27–62.
———. *Verdades y saberes del marxismo: Reacciones de una tradición política ante su "crisis."* Buenos Aires: FCE, 2005.

Passavant, Paul A., and Jodi Dean. *Empire's New Clothes*. New York: Routledge, 2004.
Phelan, John L. *The People and the King: The Comunero Revolution in Colombia, 1781*. Madison: University of Winconsin Press, 1978.
Pietschmann, Horst. *Las reformas borbónicas y el sistema de intendencias en Nueva España: Un estudio político-administrativo*. Mexico: FCE, 1996.
Pitkin, Hanna Fenichel. *The Concept of Representation*. Berkeley: University of California Press, 1972.
Pocock, J. G. A. *The Machiavellian Moment: Florentine Political Thought and the Atlantic Republican Tradition*. Princeton: Princeton University Press, 1975.
Portillo Valdés, José Maria. *Revolución de nación: Orígenes de la cultura constitucional en España, 1780–1812*. Madrid: Centro de Estudios Políticos y Constitucionales, 2000.
Prigogine, Ilya, and Isabelle Stengers. *Order Out of Chaos*. New York: Bantam, 1984.
Pring-Mill, R. D. F. Introduction to *Lope de Vega: Five Plays*. New York: Hill & Wang, 1961.
Prodi, Paolo. *Una storia della giustizia: Dal pluralismo dei fori al moderno dualismo tra coscienza e diritto*. Milan: Il Mulino, 2000.
Pufendorf, Samuel. *On the Duty of Man and Citizen According to Natural Law*. Cambridge: Cambridge University Press, 1991.
Quijada, Mónica, and Jesús Bustamante, eds. *Élites intelectuales y modelos colectivos: Mundo ibérico (Siglos XVI–XIX)*. Madrid: CSIC, 2003.
Rabkin, Norman. *Shakespeare and the Problem of Meaning*. Chicago: University of Chicago Press, 1981.
Racine, Jean B. *Theatre complet de Jean Racine*. Paris: Flammarion, 1900.
Rancière, Jacques. *Hatred of Democracy*. London: Verso, 2006.
———. *La Mésentente: Politique et Philosophie*. Paris: Galilée, 1995.
Reinhard, Wolfgang, ed. *Las élites del poder y la construcción del Estado: Los orígenes del Estado moderno en Europa, siglos XIII a XVIII*. Madrid: FCE, 1996.
Rivarola, Rodolfo. "Crónicas y documentos." *Revista Argentina de Ciencias Políticas* 104–106 (1919): 232–286.
Rosanvallon, Pierre. *Democracy: Past and Future*. New York: Columbia University Press, 2006.
———. *El modelo politico francés: La sociedad civil contra el jacobinismo*. Buenos Aires: Siglo XXI, 2007.
———. *La démocratie inachevée: Histoire de la souveraineté du peuple en France*. París: Gallimard, 2000.
———. *Le société des égaux*. Paris: Seuil, 2011.
Rossiter, A. P. *Angels with Horns: Fifteen Lectures on Shakespeare*. New York: Theatre Art Books, 1961.
Saavedra, Cornelio. *Memoria autógrafa*. Buenos Aires: Carlos Pérez, 1969.
Saavedra Fajardo, Diego de. *Empresas políticas*. Barcelona: Planeta, 1988.
Schaeffer, Pierre. *Traité des objets musicaux: Essai interdisciplines*. Paris: Seuil, 1966.
Schmitt, Carl. *The Concept of the Political*. Chicago: University of Chicago Press, 1996.
———. *Hamlet or Hecuba: The Intrusion of the Time into the Play*. New York: Telos Press, 2009.
———. *Political Theology: Four Chapters on the Concept of Sovereignty*. Chicago: University of Chicago Press, 2005.

Schoenberg, Arnold. *Theory of Harmony*. Berkeley: University of California Press, 1983.
Seligman, Adam B. *The Idea of Civil Society*. Princeton: Princeton University Press, 1995.
Senellart, Michel. *Les arts de gouverner: Du regime médiéval au concept du gouvernement*. Paris: Seuil, 1995.
Shakespeare, William. *The Complete Works*. New York: Dorset, 1988.
Silva Prada, Natalia. *La política de una rebelión: Los indígenas frente al tumulto de 1692 en la ciudad de México*. Mexico: El Colegio de México, 2007.
Singer, Armand. "Cervantes's *Licenciado Vidriera*: Its Form and Substance." *West Virginia University Bulletin: Philological Papers* 8 (1951): 13–31.
Skinner, Quentin. *The Foundations of Modern Political Thought*. 2 vols. Cambridge: Cambridge University Press, 1988.
———. *Liberty Before Liberalism*. Cambridge: Cambridge University Press, 1998.
———. *Visions of Politics*. 3 vols. Cambridge: Cambridge University Press, 2002.
———, ed. *The Cambridge History of Renaissance Philosophy*. Cambridge: Cambridge University Press, 1988.
Smith, Molly. *The Darker World Within: Evil in the Tragedies of Shakespeare and His Successors*. Cranbury, NJ: Associated University Presses, 1991.
Sommerville, Johann P., ed. *Political Writings: King James VI and I*. Cambridge: Cambridge University Press, 1994.
Sorel, George. *Reflections on Violence*. London: Allen & Unwin, 1925.
Spinoza, Benedict de. *Theological-Political Treatise*. Trans. Michael Silverthorne and Jonathan Israel. Cambridge: Cambridge University Press, 2007.
Strauss, Leo. *Natural Right and History*. Chicago: University of Chicago Press, 1953.
———. *Persecution and the Art of Writing*. Chicago: University of Chicago Press, 1988.
Strauss, Leo, and Joseph Cropsey, eds. *History of Political Philosophy*. Chicago: University of Chicago Press, 1987.
Suárez, Francisco. *Defensa de la Fe Catolica y Apostólica contra los Errores del Anglicanismo (Defensio Fidei)*. Trans. José Ramón Eguillor Muniozguren. Madrid: Instituto de Estudios Politicos, 1971.
———. *De legibus I: De natura legis*. Madrid: CSIC, 1971.
Szondi, Peter. *Teoría del drama moderno: Tentativa sobre lo trágico*. Barcelona: Destino, 1994.
Talbert, Ernest William. *The Problem of Order: Elizabethan Political Commonplaces and an Example of Shakespeare's Art*. Chapel Hill: University of North Carolina Press, 1962.
Thomas, Werner, and Bart de Groof, eds. *Rebelión y resistencia en el mundo hispánico del siglo XVII*. Leuven: Leuven University Press, 1992.
Thompson, Irving A. A. "Crown and Cortes in Castile: 1590–1665." *Parliaments, Estates and Representation* 2 (1982): 29–45.
Tierno Galván, Enrique. "El tacitismo en las doctrinas del siglo de oro español." In *Anales de la Universidad de Murcia, 1947–1948*. Murcia: Universidad de Murcia, 1949.
Todorov, Tzvetan. *The Conquest of America*. New York: Harper & Row, 1984.
Ullmann, Walter. *Escritos sobre teoría política medieval*. Buenos Aires: Eudeba, 2003.
———. *Individual and Society in the Middle Ages*. Baltimore, MD: Johns Hopkins University Press, 1966.

Van Young, Eric, ed. *La crisis del orden colonial: Estructura agraria y rebeliones populares de la Nueva España, 1750–1821*. Mexico: Alianza, 1992.
Villacañas, José Luis. "El Esquema Clásico en Gracián: Continuidad y variación." *Eikasia: Revista de Filosofía* 37 (2011): 211–241.
———. *Tragedia y teodicea de la historia: El destino de los ideales en Lessing y Schiller*. Madrid: Visor, 1993.
Villacañas, José L., and Román García. "Walter Benjamin y Carl Schmitt: Soberanía y Estado de Excepción." *Revista de Filosofía* 13 (1996): 41–60.
von Wobeser, Gisela. *Dominación colonial: La consolidación de los vales reales, 1804–1808*. Mexico: UNAM, 2003.
Weiger, John G. *In the Margins of Cervantes*. Lebanon, NH: University Press of New England, 1988.
Weinberg, Bernard. *The Art of Jean Racine*. Chicago: University of Chicago Press, 1963.
Wellek, René. *Concepts of Criticism*. New Haven: Yale University Press, 1963.
Wilks, Michael. *The Problem of Sovereignty in Later Middle Ages*. Cambridge: Cambridge University Press, 1963.
Žižek, Slavoj. *The Ticklish Subject: The Absent Centre of Political Ontology*. London: Verso, 2000.

INDEX

Abbé Siéyès, 100
Adorno, Theodor, 125, 177, 212n19
Agamben, Giorgio, v, xviii, 1, 19, 91, 184n10, 201n8, 206n51
Alberdi, Juan Bautista, 98, 209n74
Alencar, José de, 105, 106, 210n88
Alighieri, Dante, 8–10, 20, 186n32
Arendt, Hanna, 66, 68, 216n84
Aristotle, 4–9, 22, 23, 96, 97, 185nn13, 22, 25, 191n4, 194n33

Bach, Johann Sebastian, 118
Badiou, Alain, xii, xviii, 110–14, 120, 140, 153, 155, 163, 164, 166, 179
Barthes, Roland, 78
Bates, David William, x, 181n2
Benjamin, Walter, 14, 44, 45, 67, 70, 75, 149, 170, 194n38, 195nn38–39, 201n7, 218n1
Bergson, Henri, 122, 123, 130, 156, 157
Blanchot, Maurice, 177, 178
Blumenberg, Hans, 141, 188n42, 215n56
Bodin, Jean, 28, 44
Boulez, Pierre, 114, 116, 118, 121
Bukharin, Nicolai, 157

Calderón de la Barca, Pedro, 37, 38, 201n7
Cassirer, Ernst, 126, 127, 128
Cervantes, Miguel de, 57, 197n56, 198nn58, 61
Creuzer, Georg Friedrich, 44

De Kooning, Willem, 175, 176, 218n5
de León, Fray Luis, 74
Deleuze, Gilles, 16, 30, 44, 146, 184n12, 210n87
Derrida, Jacques, xii, 124, 141, 142, 145, 173, 177, 215n59, 218n1
De Vries, Hugo, 125
Duchamp, Marcel, 121

Einstein, Albert, 128
El Greco, ix, 11, 12, 14, 15, 18, 20, 31, 58, 62, 65, 68, 69, 70, 73, 91, 168, 174, 175, 188n45
Empson, William, 33
Espósito, Roberto, xviii, 171

Faraday, Michael, 126
Febvre, Lucien, 2, 3, 184nn7, 8, 9
Finestrad, Joaquín de, 76–89, 94, 205nn32, 39, 42, 206nn46, 48, 208n68

Foucault, Michel, xix, 48, 53, 72, 104, 127, 177, 178, 188*nn*46, 47, 48, 192*n*16, 202*nn*13, 14, 203*n*19, 210*nn*84, 86, 87, 212*n*25, 219*n*13

Galli, Carlo, xviii, 214*n*41
Gálvez, José de, 93
Goldmann, Lucien, 31, 190*n*65, 191*n*8, 192*n*8, 196*n*49
Gombricht, E. H., 39
Gracián, Baltasar, 14, 15, 71, 187*n*41

Hardt, Michael, 148, 153, 154, 155, 216*n*80
Hegel, G. W. F, 210*n*84
Heidegger, Martin, 142
Henry, Pierre, 118
Hobbes, Thomas, 15, 28, 32–35, 48, 63, 67, 192*n*11, 195*n*42, 197*n*55, 199*nn*74, 76, 203*n*19
Hobsbawm, Eric, 140, 179
Howard, Dick, 103, 108, 181*n*3
Hunt, John, 42, 191*n*4, 194*n*32
Husserl, Edmund, 129, 135, 183*n*6

Jago, Charles, 92
James I, 20, 21, 22, 24, 49, 50, 189*nn*51, 59, 190*n*61, 191*n*5, 193*n*24, 194*n*31, 195*n*39, 196*n*45
Jovellanos, Melchor Gaspar de, 89, 90, 207*n*60

Kant, Immanuel, 44, 45, 128
Kantorowicz, Ernst, 14, 33, 50, 55, 71, 187*n*37, 201*n*10
Kelsen, Hans, xii, 131, 133–39, 144, 214*n*41
Kierkegaard, Soren, 124, 130
Kittler, Friedrich, 116, 123, 212*nn*15, 16, 212*n*25
Koestler, Arthur, 157, 158, 162
Koselleck, Reinhart, xviii, 2, 4, 11, 53, 75, 125, 168, 179, 183*n*6, 191*n*7, 204*n*29
Kosuth, Joseph, 179

Laclau, Ernesto, xviii, 201*n*5
Lastarria, José Victorino, 107

Lefort, Claude, xii, xiii, xvii, 110, 142–49, 153, 163, 164, 172, 173, 178, 179, 182*n*4, 215*n*64
Lempérière, Annick, 94
Levinas, Emmanuel, 157, 217*n*87
Locke, John, 28, 34, 35, 162, 163, 165, 192*n*12
Lope de Vega, ix, 57, 58, 61–64, 84, 197*n*56, 198*n*62, 199*nn*72, 75, 200*n*81
Lukács, Georg, 45, 130, 137, 191*n*8, 194*n*38

Machiavelli, Niccolò, 73, 74, 183*n*4, 202*n*18, 203*n*19
Malevich, Kazimir, 173, 174, 175, 177
Malraux, André, 112, 165
Manin, Bernard, 100
Maravall, José Antonio, 92, 192*n*17, 203*n*18
Marsilius of Padua, 1, 182*n*2
Martínez Marina, Francisco, 89
Marx, Karl, xii, 111, 144, 152, 153, 159, 160, 161, 164
Maupas, Leopoldo, 106
Maxwell, James, 126
Melville, Herman, 167
Merleau-Ponty, Maurice, 157–64, 218*n*1
Messiaen, Olivier, 114, 116
Montano, Vicente, 73, 74, 75, 203*n*20
Moreiras, Alberto, xv, 154
Moreno, Mariano, 99
Morgan, Edmund, 93, 208*n*66
Mouffe, Chantal, 154, 216*n*80, 218*n*4

Negri, Antonio, 148, 153, 154, 155, 216*n*80
Nietzsche, Friedrich, 36, 64, 165, 192*n*14

Peterson, Eric, 19
Phillip II, 10
Plato, 4, 142, 177

Rabelais, François, 2, 184*nn*7, 9
Racine, Jean, 51–56, 78, 190*n*65, 192*n*8, 196*n*49, 199*n*72
Rancière, Jacques, xviii, 150–54
Rauschenberg, Robert, 175, 176, 178, 218*n*5
Rousseau, Jean Jacques, 30, 101, 133

INDEX 235

Saavedra, Cornelio, 99
Schaeffer, Pierre, 118
Schmitt, Carl, x, xii, xvii, xviii, 67, 131, 136, 137–41, 157, 161, 169, 171, 181n2, 195n39, 214nn41, 43, 54, 217n87
Schoenberg, Arnold, 118, 120, 121, 211n11
Shakespeare, William, x, 14, 33, 39, 47, 49, 50, 51, 88, 191nn2, 3, 4, 192n18, 193nn24, 27, 194nn30, 31, 32, 195nn39, 41, 43, 196nn45, 48, 197n52, 199n67, 200n77
Skinner, Quentin, 1, 32, 48, 182nn3, 4, 183n4, 184n11, 199n76, 207n61
Smith, Molly, 43, 194n32
Sorel, Georges, 156, 157, 165, 217nn85, 87
Stalin, Joseph, 157
Stirner, Max, 144

Stockhausen, Karlheinz, 121
Strauss, Leo, 147, 148
Suárez, Francisco, 19–26, 28–30, 55, 89, 96, 97, 185n37, 187n35, 189n55, 190n61

Thomas Aquinas, 4–9, 22, 82, 185nn21, 23, 24, 186nn26, 27
Thomson, Irving, 92

Velázquez, Diego, 13, 188nn46, 47
Voegelin, Eric, 134

Weber, Max, 134, 160, 214n43
Webern, Anton, 114
Weyl, Hermann, 126

Žižek, Slavoj, xviii, 146, 149

GPSR Authorized Representative: Easy Access System Europe, Mustamäe tee 50, 10621 Tallinn, Estonia, gpsr.requests@easproject.com